YO-EHC-775

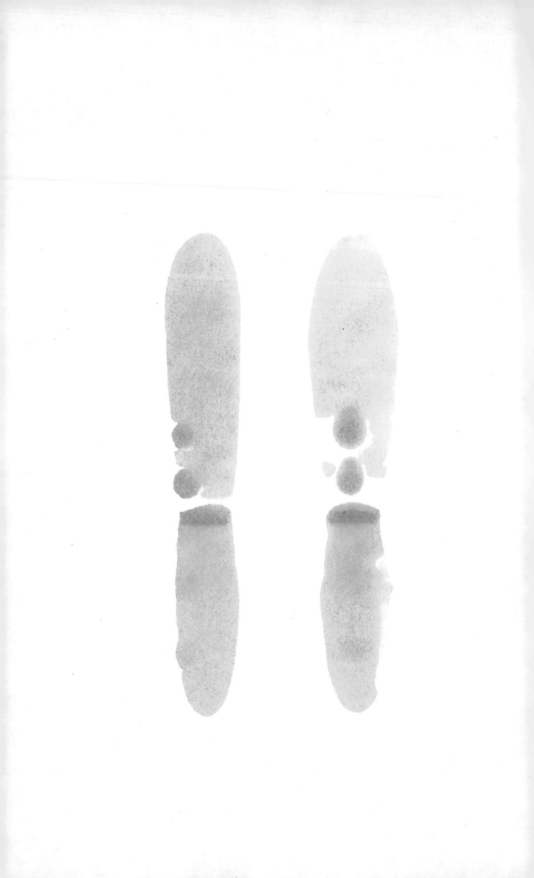

VOLUME 496   MARCH 1988

THE ANNALS

of The American Academy *of* Political
and Social Science

RICHARD D. LAMBERT, *Editor*
ALAN W. HESTON, *Associate Editor*

STATE CONSTITUTIONS IN A FEDERAL SYSTEM

Special Editor of this Volume

JOHN KINCAID

*U.S. Advisory Commission on
Intergovernmental Relations
Washington, D.C.*

Ⓢ SAGE PUBLICATIONS *NEWBURY PARK BEVERLY HILLS LONDON NEW DELHI*

THE ANNALS

© 1988 *by* The American Academy *of* Political *and* Social Science

ERICA GINSBURG, *Assistant Editor*

Editorial Office: 3937 Chestnut Street, Philadelphia, Pennsylvania 19104.

For information about membership* (individuals only) and subscriptions (institutions), address:

SAGE PUBLICATIONS, INC.

2111 West Hillcrest Drive   275 South Beverly Drive
Newbury Park, CA 91320   Beverly Hills, CA 90212

From India and South Asia,   *From the UK, Europe, the Middle*
write to: *East and Africa, write to:*

SAGE PUBLICATIONS INDIA Pvt. Ltd.   SAGE PUBLICATIONS LTD
P.O. Box 4215   28 Banner Street
New Delhi 110 048   London EC1Y 8QE
INDIA   ENGLAND

SAGE Production Editors: JANET BROWN and ASTRID VIRDING
* Please note that members of The Academy receive THE ANNALS with their membership.

Library of Congress Catalog Card Number 86-063023
International Standard Serial Number ISSN 0002-7162
International Standard Book Number ISBN 0-8039-3011-9 (Vol. 496, 1988 paper)
International Standard Book Number ISBN 0-8039-3010-0 (Vol. 496, 1988 cloth)
Manufactured in the United States of America. First printing, March 1988.

The articles appearing in THE ANNALS are indexed in *Book Review Index; Public Affairs Information Service Bulletin; Social Sciences Index; Monthly Periodical Index; Current Contents; Behavioral, Social Management Sciences;* and *Combined Retrospective Index Sets.* They are also abstracted and indexed in *ABC Pol Sci, Historical Abstracts, Human Resources Abstracts, Social Sciences Citation Index, United States Political Science Documents, Social Work Research & Abstracts, Peace Research Reviews, Sage Urban Studies Abstracts, International Political Science Abstracts, America: History and Life,* and/or *Family Resources Database.*

Information about membership rates, institutional subscriptions, and back issue prices may be found on the facing page.

Advertising. Current rates and specifications may be obtained by writing to THE ANNALS Advertising and Promotion Manager at the Newbury Park office (address above).

Claims. Claims for undelivered copies must be made no later than three months following month of publication. The publisher will supply missing copies when losses have been sustained in transit and when the reserve stock will permit.

Change of Address. Six weeks' advance notice must be given when notifying change of address to insure proper identification. Please specify name of journal. Send change of address to: THE ANNALS, c/o Sage Publications, Inc., 2111 West Hillcrest Drive, Newbury Park, CA 91320.

The American Academy of Political and Social Science

3937 Chestnut Street   Philadelphia, Pennsylvania 19104

Origin and Purpose. The Academy was organized December 14, 1889, to promote the progress of political and social science, especially through publications and meetings. The Academy does not take sides in controverted questions, but seeks to gather and present reliable information to assist the public in forming an intelligent and accurate judgment.

Meetings. The Academy holds an annual meeting in the spring extending over two days.

Publications. THE ANNALS is the bimonthly publication of The Academy. Each issue contains articles on some prominent social or political problem, written at the invitation of the editors. Also, monographs are published from time to time, numbers of which are distributed to pertinent professional organizations. These volumes constitute important reference works on the topics with which they deal, and they are extensively cited by authorities throughout the United States and abroad. The papers presented at the meetings of The Academy are included in THE ANNALS.

Membership. Each member of The Academy receives THE ANNALS and may attend the meetings of The Academy. Membership is open only to individuals. Annual dues: $28.00 for the regular paperbound edition (clothbound, $42.00). Add $9.00 per year for membership outside the U.S.A. Members may also purchase single issues of THE ANNALS for $6.95 each (clothbound, $10.00).

Subscriptions. THE ANNALS (ISSN 0002-7162) is published six times annually—in January, March, May, July, September, and November. Institutions may subscribe to THE ANNALS at the annual rate: $60.00 (clothbound, $78.00). Add $9.00 per year for subscriptions outside the U.S.A. Institutional rates for single issues: $10.00 each (clothbound, $15.00).

Second class postage paid at Philadelphia, Pennsylvania, and at additional mailing offices.

Single issues of THE ANNALS may be obtained by individuals who are not members of The Academy for $7.95 each (clothbound, $15.00). Single issues of THE ANNALS have proven to be excellent supplementary texts for classroom use. Direct inquiries regarding adoptions to THE ANNALS c/o Sage Publications (address below).

All correspondence concerning membership in The Academy, dues renewals, inquiries about membership status, and/or purchase of single issues of THE ANNALS should be sent to THE ANNALS c/o Sage Publications, Inc., 2111 West Hillcrest Drive, Newbury Park, CA 91320. *Please note that orders under $25 must be prepaid.* Sage affiliates in London and India will assist institutional subscribers abroad with regard to orders, claims, and inquiries for both subscriptions and single issues.

THE NINETIETH ANNUAL MEETING OF THE AMERICAN ACADEMY OF POLITICAL AND SOCIAL SCIENCE

APRIL 29 and 30, 1988
THE BARCLAY HOTEL
PHILADELPHIA, PENNSYLVANIA

The annual meeting of the The Academy is attended by many distinguished scholars, statesmen, authors, and professionals in diverse fields, including representatives of many embassies, academic institutions, and cultural, civic, and scientific organizations.

This 90th Annual Meeting will be addressed at each session by prominent scholars and officials and will be devoted to the topic of

WHITHER THE AMERICAN EMPIRE: EXPANSION OR CONTRACTION?

Members of the Academy are cordially invited to attend and will receive full information. Information on Academy membership can be found in each volume of THE ANNALS.

- Proceedings of the 90th Annual Meeting will be published in the November 1988 volume of THE ANNALS.

- All members and attendees who have published a book may participate in the exhibits at the hotel. Contact Harve C. Horowitz & Associates, 10369 Currycomb Court, Columbia, MD 21044, tel. (301) 997-0763.

**FOR DETAILS ABOUT THE ANNUAL MEETING WRITE TO
THE AMERICAN ACADEMY OF POLITICAL AND SOCIAL SCIENCE
BUSINESS OFFICE • 3937 CHESTNUT STREET
PHILADELPHIA, PENNSYLVANIA 19104**

CONTENTS

BOOK DEPARTMENT CONTENTS

SOCIOLOGY

ECONOMICS

PREFACE

Most of the articles in this volume are revised versions of papers presented at an international conference, "State Constitutional Law in the Third Century of American Federalism." The conference, held in Philadelphia in March 1987, was sponsored by the Center for the Study of Federalism, Temple University, Philadelphia, Pennsylvania, in cooperation with the American Bar Association, the Philadelphia Bar Association, and the U.S. Advisory Commission on Intergovernmental Relations.

Members of the Conference Advisory Board were its chairperson, Robert N.C. Nix, Jr., chief justice of the Supreme Court of Pennsylvania; Shirley S. Abrahamson, associate justice of the Supreme Court of Wisconsin; James L. Dennis, associate justice of the Supreme Court of Louisiana; Robert B. Hawkins, Jr., chairperson of the U.S. Advisory Commission on Intergovernmental Relations; Edward H. Hennessey, chief justice of the Supreme Judicial Court of Massachusetts; Seymour Kurland, Esq., chancellor of the Philadelphia Bar Association; Hans A. Linde, associate justice of the Supreme Court of Oregon; James T. McDermott, associate justice of the Supreme Court of Pennsylvania; and Stewart G. Pollock, associate justice of the Supreme Court of New Jersey.

Members of the Conference Planning Committee were Ellis Katz, Temple University; Ronald K.L. Collins, University of Puget Sound; Daniel J. Elazar, Temple University; A.E. Dick Howard, University of Virginia; John Kincaid, North Texas State University; Robert Peck, American Bar Association; Kenneth Shear, Philadelphia Bar Association; G. Alan Tarr, Rutgers University; Mary Cornelia Porter, Roosevelt University; and Robert F. Williams, Rutgers University.

Special thanks are due to the National Endowment for the Humanities, which provided a grant in support of the conference. The views expressed by the authors of the articles in this volume do not necessarily represent the views of the Endowment or the views of the sponsoring organizations.

The articles endeavor to present, analyze, and debate recent developments in state constitutional law, developments that have been largely unnoticed by the media and the public. Compared to developments in the constitutional law of the United States, developments in state constitutional law, particularly through the decisions of state supreme courts, receive little attention outside of a relatively small but growing circle of students and practitioners of state constitutional law. Indeed, given the dominance of federal constitutional law in contemporary American legal thought, state constitutional law is not formally taught in most law schools. Yet the nation's 50 state constitutions are the primary domestic governing documents in American life, and despite decades of expansion of federal constitutional law, state constitutional law is not in retreat but is being reasserted in increasingly numerous and diverse ways.

During the past decade, there has emerged a new judicial federalism, which has involved, among other things, a greater reliance upon state constitutions by state courts as independent and adequate grounds for state action. Perhaps the most publicized aspect of this new judicial federalism has been the willingness of many state supreme courts to extend broader rights to individuals under state declarations of rights than those rights granted individuals by U.S. Supreme Court interpretations of the U.S. Bill of Rights. Several articles in this volume examine individual rights under state constitutional law; however, because there is a sizable literature on certain aspects of state constitutional rights protection, we have sought in this volume to examine in addition other historical and substantive issues of state constitutional law that are less well developed in the courts and in the literature.

Together, the articles provide a fairly broad picture of an array of important and interesting issues being debated and decided under the terms of constitutional documents once thought by many observers to be, in most important respects, dead letters in the American federal system. Given that the United States Constitution was preceded by 18 state constitutions, this volume is an appropriate complement to the attention being given to the United States Constitution during the bicentennial commemoration of its writing and ratification.

JOHN KINCAID

ANNALS, *AAPSS*, **496**, March 1988

State Constitutions in the
Federal System

By JOHN KINCAID

ABSTRACT: State constitutionalism has undergone a certain revitalization in recent decades due to the efforts of state electorates and officials to reform and modernize state government, the willingness of many state high courts to redevelop state constitutional law as an independent body of law, and the expansion of federal constitutional law requiring adjustments in state constitutional law. State constitutions remain important as instruments of local self-government even though the field of state constitutional choice has been circumscribed by federal constitutional law. A basic distinguishing characteristic of state constitutions is their reliance on direct popular consent and control. This characteristic is a matter of conflict in state constitutional change because it produces long and detailed constitutions subject to easy popular amendment. Despite reform efforts to streamline state constitutions and limit majoritarian influences, most state electorates continue to prefer more consent and control of government under state constitutions than are available under the U.S. Constitution.

John Kincaid is acting executive director and director of research of the U.S. Advisory Commission on Intergovernmental Relations, Washington, D.C. He is on leave as associate professor of political science at North Texas State University, Denton, where he also served as director of the Classic Learning Core of the College of Arts and Sciences. He is an editor of Publius: The Journal of Federalism.

COMMEMORATION of the bicentennial of the Constitution of the United States of America marks an accomplishment unequaled in world history. Never have so many human beings of such diverse origins as the Americans occupied so vast a land for so long a time under a constitutional regime that has been fundamentally republican, respectably democratic, ordinarily peaceful, dynamically stable, comparatively prosperous, and reasonably humane. It is not without cause, therefore, that the U.S. Constitution enjoys a measure of veneration that approaches the sacred for many Americans.

The success of the American constitutional experiment is due in no small part to the fact that the Constitution of the United States is not the only constitution in the United States. There are 50 other constitutions. Although the term "American Constitution" is often used synonymously with "Constitution of the United States," the operational American constitution consists of the federal Constitution and the 50 state constitutions. Together, these 51 documents comprise a complex system of constitutional rule for a republic of republics.

Compared to most national constitutions, the Constitution of the United States is, as Alexis de Tocqueville observed, incomplete.[1] It cannot be understood or activated without reference to the state constitutions. The state documents define and implement many provisions of the U.S. Constitution and structure the potentially vast domestic powers reserved to the states and to the people by the U.S. Constitution. In 1787, the framers of the federal Constitution could build upon the state constitutions as the basic foundation of a republican polity because those governing documents were already in place.

Nevertheless, the expansion of federal constitutional law in this century has tended to eclipse not only the contemporary role of state constitutions in American government but also their historical role. During this bicentennial era, for example, it is not unusual for editorial writers to refer to the U.S. Constitution as the oldest written constitution in the world. This is not quite accurate. The Massachusetts Constitution of 1780 is the oldest written constitution still in effect in the modern world.[2] Of course, some observers might argue that the Massachusetts Constitution has been amended so many times— 116—that its original form is no longer recognizable; however, other observers argue that the U.S. Constitution has been interpreted so many times and in so many ways that it, too, is no longer recognizable in its original form.

Herein lies a basic difference between the U.S. Constitution and the state constitutions. Federal constitutional law is changed primarily by acts of interpretation by the U.S. Supreme Court, the Congress, and the presidency. State constitutional law is changed primarily by amendment, a procedure that usually involves voter participation. State constitutions are occasionally rewritten in whole or in part. Since 1775, the states as a group have written and ratified 146

1. Alexis de Tocqueville, *Democracy in America*, ed. J. P. Mayer, trans. G. Lawrence (Garden City, NY: Doubleday Anchor, 1969), p. 157. Donald S. Lutz has written extensively on this idea. See, for example, Lutz, "The Purposes of American State Constitutions," *Publius: The Journal of Federalism*, 12:27 (Winter 1982).

2. See also Ronald M. Peters, Jr., *The Massachusetts Constitution of 1780: A Social Compact* (Amherst: University of Massachusetts Press, 1978); Paul C. Reardon, "The Massachusetts Constitution Marks a Milestone," *Publius: The Journal of Federalism*, 12:45 (Winter 1982).

constitutions. Louisiana holds the record for the largest number of constitutions: 11. Only 20 states are governed by their original constitutions.[3]

At the same time, state constitutions are themselves part of what can be regarded as a larger network of constitutional relationships in America. If one looks at the American "compound republic," to use James Madison's term,[4] from an Aristotelian perspective on what actually constitutes a polity, one sees that this compound republic is fundamentally constitutional or, more properly, covenantal—beginning with the Mayflower Covenant of 1620, the charters of the original colonies, and town covenants of the early frontier era. Most human relationships in the United States are founded upon and governed by covenants and their derivatives: compacts, contracts, charters, and constitutions. Marriages, businesses, voluntary associations, religious congregations, municipal corporations, residential community associations, and other joint enterprises are ordinarily covenantal in that they are constituted by agreements, usually written, that are ratified by mutual consent of the relevant parties.[5] The word "federal" itself is derived from the Latin word "foedus," meaning "covenant." Thus, in this larger respect, the Constitution of the United States is the tip of an immense constitutional iceberg.

THE IMPORTANCE OF
STATE CONSTITUTIONS

State constitutions occupy a curious position in American life. They are important, but then again, they seem to be not so important.

On the one hand, state constitutional law is not formally taught in most law schools, and there is no casebook of state constitutional law comparable to the many casebooks available on federal constitutional law. For most Americans today, "constitutional law" is understood to be federal constitutional law. Moreover, if the average American knows little about the contents of the U.S. Constitution, he or she is likely to know even less about the contents of his or her state constitution.

On the other hand, the realm of state constitutional law is a beehive of activity. State constitutions are objects of perennial change and reform. Together, the present constitutions of the 50 states have been amended more than 5300 times. No constitution lacks amendments. In 1984-85 alone, 238 proposed amendments were submitted to voters in 45 states.[6] This penchant for amending state constitutions has been called "amendomania,"[7] a disability commonly attributed to Californians, who have amended their constitution 450 times, but characteristic of Southerners as well. Since 1776, Americans have also held 232 state constitutional conventions. Not surprisingly, the high point for constitu-

3. The number is 19 if one treats Rhode Island's colonial charters as having served as the state's first constitution from 1776 to 1842.

4. *Federalist* Numbers 51 and 62.

5. See also Donald S. Lutz, "From Covenant to Constitution in American Political Thought," *Publius: The Journal of Federalism*, 10:101 (Fall 1980); John Kincaid and Daniel J. Elazar, eds., *The Covenant Connection: Federal Theology and the Origins of Modern Politics* (Durham, NC: Carolina Academic Press, 1988).

6. Albert L. Sturm and Janice C. May, "State Constitutions and Constitutional Revision: 1984-85," in *The Book of the States, 1986-87* (Lexington, KY: Council of State Governments, 1986), 26:4.

7. See, for example, Note, "California's Constitutional Amendomania," *Stanford Law Review*, 1:279 (1949); Donald E. Wilkes, "First Things Last: Amendomania and State Bills of Rights," *Mississippi Law Journal*, 54:223 (1984).

tional conventions occurred during the Civil War and Reconstruction eras.

Significantly, however, 36 conventions have been held since World War II. Fourteen states are governed by constitutions adopted since 1944. Most other states have amended their constitutions so as to facilitate the modernization of state governance and adapt state institutions and policies to postwar conditions, including new legal conditions brought about by the activism of the U.S. Supreme Court.

By itself, activity is not a measure of importance; however, it is difficult to imagine state electorates engaging in such constitutional activity if they did not believe that state constitutional law was important. Changing gubernatorial terms from two years to four years, altering methods of judicial selection, unifying courts, fixing debt and expenditure limits, providing for public education, extending constitutional home rule to local governments, enacting an Equal Rights Amendment, formulating a privacy right, and perhaps even providing a right for farmers to sell produce door-to-door can all have significant consequences for the lives and fortunes of the people of a state. The provisions of a state constitution applicable to capital punishment can mean the difference between life and death for some individuals.

The relevance of state constitutions can be highlighted comparatively. For example, the U.S. Constitution contains no debt limits or balanced-budget requirement, while 25 state constitutions limit full faith and credit debt, and 34 state constitutions have balanced-budget requirements that indirectly control debt. During the years 1960-85, state debt grew from $19 billion to $212 billion; the federal government's debt increased from

$286 billion to $1.8 trillion. State debt equaled 4-5 percent of the nation's gross national product (GNP) from 1960 to 1985. The federal government's debt declined from 56 percent of the GNP in 1960 to 33 percent in 1980 but then climbed to 46 percent of the GNP by 1985. State debt remained about equal to annual state tax revenues from 1960 to 1985. The debt of the federal government, however, was about two and a half times greater than its annual tax revenues during the years 1960-80 and then had escalated to four times its annual tax revenues by 1985. At the same time, federal aid to state and local governments, as a percentage of state and local revenues, has been declining since 1978. Thus, even though state constitutional debt limits and balanced-budget requirements do not work as well as some citizens would like, they do seem to make a difference.[8]

Historically, the state constitutions may well have made the U.S. Constitution possible. Endeavoring to establish the first new nation of the modern era and the first continental-sized republic in history, the framers of the U.S. Constitution faced a formidable task, one that any reasonable observer, reflecting upon the history of republics, could have properly regarded as impossible. The framers would surely have failed if they had had to formulate a complete national constitution settling all matters of fundamental law for 13 diverse states. Aside from slavery, many other divisive issues—such as the establishment of religion—would have prohibited union if the framers had not been able to defer

8. See also U.S. Advisory Commission on Intergovernmental Relations, *Fiscal Discipline in the Federal System* (Washington, DC: U.S. Advisory Commission on Intergovernmental Relations, 1987).

many of the most important issues of the day to state constitutional law.

In this respect, state constitutions perform an important function. They help to diffuse conflict in the federal system and to prevent conflict from building into a fire storm at the center of the political system. In this capacity, state constitutional law helped to preserve the federal union during its fledgling years. Indeed, because of the expansion of federal constitutional law since the 1930s, there is a tendency to forget that state constitutional law was the basic covering law of the land for about the first 150 years of the Republic's history.

Having the experience of state constitution making under their belts, the framers of the U.S. Constitution were well equipped for their novel enterprise. In turn, the framers could draw positive and negative lessons from the states' experiences with constitutions. Concepts and provisions of state constitutions found their way into the U.S. Constitution, and the Bill of Rights was quickly added to the federal Constitution after a significant number of Americans, accustomed to some affirmation of natural rights in a constitution, were alarmed by the absence of such an affirmation in the proposed federal document.

Nor did the early state constitutions go unnoticed elsewhere. The Virginia Declaration of Rights of 1776, the Pennsylvania Constitution of 1776, and the Massachusetts Constitution of 1780, for example, attracted attention abroad. Unfortunately, perhaps, the Pennsylvania Constitution of 1776 was acclaimed by French radicals and served as a model for the Jacobin constitution of 1793. Pennsylvanians themselves had adopted a new constitution by 1790.

Self-governance

The Pennsylvania experience of 1790, regarded by some observers as a setback for democracy, was nevertheless a victory for a fundamental federal and republican principle: the right of self-government. It is here that state constitutions have made, and can continue to make, a significant contribution to democracy. State constitution making allows a broad range of citizens to engage in constitutional design and experimentation and to gain some competence in constitutional governance.

In this, citizens of the states are accorded considerable freedom to make genuine constitutional choices about how to govern themselves. Although the expansion of federal constitutional law has circumscribed this freedom, state constitution making still involves important choices about such basic matters as human rights, structures of government, the scope of governing power, the behavior of state authorities, taxing and spending, budgeting, local government, voting and election rules, land and water use, intrastate commerce, and a host of public services, including education, welfare, mental health care, housing, and roads and highways.

In this respect, the overwhelming attention given to federal constitutional law is a loss for the federal republic because it deprives state constitutional law of the insights of theory and inquiry characteristic of federal constitutional law scholarship. Overemphasis on federal constitutional law inhibits state experimentation, inclines citizens to wait for federal action to resolve certain issues, and blinds citizens to the double security offered by two constitutional systems as when, for instance, citizens fail to assert rights guaranteed by their state constitution but not by the U.S. Constitution.[9]

State constitution making allows different communities of citizens to formulate different solutions to problems affecting the nation and to resolve problems peculiar to their state. The role of state constitutional law in experimentation should not be overlooked either. Damage resulting from unwise experiments can be contained within one or a few states; successful experiments can be emulated by other states and even by the federal government. The state role in policy experimentation may become more important as the federal government confronts fiscal and political limits of its own and as the nation confronts such matters as international economic competition, technological innovation, and the revolution in family life, including, for example, surrogate motherhood, test-tube babies, adoption, and care of the elderly.

Justice and quality of life

State constitution making also allows citizens to institutionalize conceptions of justice and quality of life, especially where constitutional amendments can be initiated by voters. This aspect of state constitution making often involves matters of rights and revenue. The constitutional structuring of budgetary priorities, levels of taxation, tax and expenditure limits, local revenue discretion, and the degree of progressiveness or regressiveness in the state revenue system both reflect and shape justice and the quality of life. State declarations of rights and other provisions for rights are

especially indicative of the different conceptions of justice and quality of life that exist among Americans on such matters as capital punishment, victims' rights, privacy, gender discrimination, alcoholic beverage control, environmental protection, property, and individual dignity.

The Montana Constitution, for example, includes environmental rights, a right of privacy, the right to know, rights of participation, and rights pertaining to "individual dignity." The Louisiana Constitution adds a right to "humane treatment." The Montana Constitution also prohibits discrimination on grounds of "race, color, sex, culture, social origin or condition or political and religious ideas." The Oregon Constitution guarantees citizens a right to "pure water"; the Rhode Island and Pennsylvania constitutions guarantee a right to fish; the Tennessee Constitution guarantees its citizens an inherent right to sail on the Mississippi River; the Virginia Constitution protects oyster beds; the New York Constitution protects bingo and lotto games; the Texas Constitution protects homesteads against certain debt seizures; and the California Constitution provides for a "right to safe schools."[10]

Historically, most states have not had a good record of protecting rights, as rights are commonly understood today, but the state record is improving. Prior to the nationalization of the federal Bill of Rights by the U.S. Supreme Court, however, the federal government did not have a much better record of rights protection. In some respects, the federal record was worse than that of many states, as in the federal government's

9. See also Vincent Ostrom, *The Political Theory of a Compound Republic*, 2d ed. (Lincoln: University of Nebraska Press, 1987).

10. See Ronald K.L. Collins, "Bills and Declarations of Rights Digest," *American Bench* (1985), p. 2483.

treatment of Indians and in federal court nullification of state efforts to protect individual rights against corporate power in the late nineteenth century. Nevertheless, during the 150-some years of state constitutional law prevalence, the United States remained comparatively free and democratic, with the conspicuous exception of race relations.

Although some observers argue that "amendomania" has led voters in recent years to restrict rights, as when voters in California and Massachusetts restored capital punishment to constitutional status after their supreme courts had struck it down, on balance, state declarations of rights remain, as a group, broader and more liberal than the federal Bill of Rights.[11] Furthermore, some of the newer state constitutional rights, such as environmental and individual-dignity rights, pose formidable problems of enforcement. How, for example, does a state enforce a right to pure water or safe schools? Litigating pure-water rights could be a judicial nightmare. Whether or not such rights can be strictly enforced, they do serve a symbolic function in political society and can serve as guidelines for policymakers.

In the final analysis, state constitutions remain important because the states continue to be important polities in the federal system. The states remain important, in part, because their constitutions continue to structure the broad range of activities and responsibilities of state government, including the administration of myriad federal policies and programs.

11. See the discussion of ballot propositions in Janice C. May, "Constitutional Amendment and Revision Revisited," *Publius: The Journal of Federalism*, 17:153 (Winter 1987).

THE CHARACTER OF STATE CONSTITUTIONS

The 50 state constitutions are remarkably similar with respect to certain basics, such as the separation of powers; legislative bicameralism, except in Nebraska; four-year gubernatorial terms, except in Rhode Island and Vermont; four-year terms for senators and two-year terms for representatives, in most states; and voter participation in selecting or retaining state court judges, in most states. These similarities reflect the effects of three things: (1) a general consensus about certain fundamentals of political theory, such as the separation of powers; (2) the sharing and borrowing of constitutional ideas among states; and (3) constitutional reform movements that have periodically swept the states. Within regions of the nation, there is often greater similarity among constitutions. Otherwise, the details of constitutional design vary substantially across the nation.

A common criticism of state constitutions is that they are too long. On average, state constitutions are about three times as long as the U.S. Constitution. The Alabama Constitution is the longest at 174,000 words. The Vermont Constitution, the shortest at 6600 words, is the only constitution shorter than the federal document. The greater length of state constitutions is due in part to the need to structure and limit the powers of governments that inherently possess all governmental powers not delegated to the U.S. government. The U.S. Constitution is one of limited, delegated powers. In addition, state constitutions must attend to such matters as local government and public health, safety, and welfare, which are not directly covered by the U.S. Constitution.

The length of state constitutions is

also due to the desire of state electorates to load them with detail. As many critics have argued, state constitutions ordinarily contain "a great deal of matter which is in no distinctive sense constitutional law, but general law . . . fit to be dealt with in ordinary statutes."[12] This criticism is difficult to evaluate because there is no sure standard for distinguishing constitutional from legislative matters. James Bryce judged state constitutions against European preferences for brief documents. American reformers have judged state constitutions against the shorter federal document. Neither the European nor the federal constitutional standards are necessarily appropriate, however, for the democratic populist orientations of state constitutions.

Initially, state constitutions were not excessively long; they became longer during the nineteenth century. As the nation's primary constitutions, the state documents had to be revised so as to adapt state governments and citizen rights to the tremendous social and economic changes of the nineteenth century. The shift from a rural, agricultural to an urban, industrial society is one of the most wrenching, violent, and revolutionary transitions that developing societies experience in the modern era. In the United States, this transition was accomplished largely through processes of state constitutional change fraught with considerable political conflict but comparatively little bloodletting.

Also, because state constitutions were documents subject to fairly easy popular change, citizens, as Lord Bryce noted, often found constitutional revision to be "a simpler and quicker method than waiting for legislative action."[13] In those

12. James Bryce, *The American Commonwealth* (New York: Macmillan, 1907), 1:443.
13. Ibid., pp. 443-44.

days, citizens could not always count on legislative action because many legislatures were dominated by corrupt political machines and/or corporations. In addition, legislatures were usually controlled by Protestants unfriendly to Roman Catholics. Clashes of culture and religion arising from massive immigration stimulated further constitutional change as various groups sought to institutionalize their values and protect their interests in state constitutions.

The details added to state constitutions corresponded, therefore, to social change: (1) limits on legislative power, especially taxing and spending; (2) the regulation of corporations, particularly banks and railroads; (3) public economic rights, especially those of farmers and industrial laborers; (4) local government, because of the rise of big cities; (5) cultural issues, such as gambling, alcoholic beverages, and church-state relations; (6) electoral rules and voter registration; and (7) race relations, primarily in the South.

Some critics argue that frequent and detailed change trivializes state constitutions. Such change, however, can also be regarded as a measure of the importance that the citizens attribute to state constitutions. Furthermore, during the nineteenth century, state constitutions were the last resort for citizens desiring to maintain democratic self-government. The federal government was not an agent for reform and economic regulation, and the U.S. Supreme Court was not available to adjudicate the grievances of farmers, laborers, Roman Catholics, Jews, and others.

More fundamentally, though, state constitutional change is a consequence of the chief distinguishing characteristic of state constitutionalism: a reliance on direct popular consent. Unlike the U.S.

Constitution, which relies upon indirect popular consent and complex majoritarianism, state constitutions are instruments of majoritarian democracy. Since the drafting of the first state constitutions in 1776, state constitution makers have evidenced a strong desire to base government very directly upon public consent and to ensure the ability of citizens to control government.[14] This is one reason why state supreme courts have not developed state constitutional law in the same manner as the U.S. Supreme Court has developed federal constitutional law. In the early years, consent and control were institutionalized primarily by constitutional requirements for frequent elections and rotation of elected officials. As these mechanisms proved to be less effective during the nineteenth century, citizens sought to reinstitutionalize consent and control by adding detail to state constitutions.

Herein lies a basic conflict in state constitutional development since the late nineteenth century. Many constitutional reformers have what can be regarded as a Federalist orientation toward state constitutionalism, an orientation that emphasizes short documents, parsimonious bills of rights, streamlined government, longer terms of office, fewer elected officials, greater discretion for public officials, and principles of modern public administration and management. This Federalist orientation is more than a different emphasis; it is a different political theory of constitutional government from that which has prevailed in state constitutional history. In place of democratic majoritarianism, Federalist reformers have sought to establish a

kind of democratic managerialism.[15]

Although reform principles have influenced the character of state constitutional change in this century, the latter-day Antifederalism of voters continues to keep most state constitutions more detailed and more closely tied to popular consent and control than the U.S. Constitution. One indicator of this Antifederalism is that even among the 14 state constitutions adopted since 1944, the average length is slightly more than 20,000 words, which is more than twice the length of the U.S. Constitution. The average number of amendments is 26, the same number as the 200-year-old federal document.

Another indicator is that voters have been reluctant to relinquish a right to have a voice in selecting or retaining state judges. Because voters rarely unseat a judge, some reformers have argued that it would be better to appoint state judges in a manner similar to that of federal judges. Most state electorates, however, prefer to preserve their right of voice and to hold it in reserve, so to speak, for judges who stray too far too frequently from majority sentiment, as in the unseating of Chief Justice Rose Bird and two colleagues from the California Supreme Court in 1986.

Events such as the downfall of Justice Bird activate a primal Federalist fear: majority tyranny. In the tradition of federal constitutional law, there is a profound ambivalence about majority rule. Two basic principles of rights protection in this tradition are that individual rights should be shielded or even immune from majority invasion and that judges should be protected from

14. Donald S. Lutz, *Popular Consent and Popular Control: Whig Political Theory in the Early State Constitutions* (Baton Rouge: Louisiana State University Press, 1980).

15. Daniel J. Elazar, "The Principles and Traditions Underlying State Constitutions," *Publius: The Journal of Federalism*, 12:11 (Winter 1982).

electoral retribution so as to be accountable to the Constitution, not to the prevailing majority of the day. In the tradition of state constitutionalism, however, popular consent has been regarded as the fundamental right of self-government. Citizens should be free to determine the nature and extent of their own rights, not have them determined for them by judges. In this respect, the state constitutional tradition is more democratic than its federal counterpart and more willing to assume that citizens are sufficiently competent and responsible to govern themselves.

Another factor behind the desire for popular control is the daily presence and comprehensiveness of state government compared to the originally limited jurisdiction of the federal government. State governments have primary, frontline responsibility for protecting the rights of greatest concern to citizens: life, liberty, and property. It is state government that deals with murderers, muggers, rapists, prostitutes, careless physicians, barking dogs, traffic lights, divorces, occupational licensing, civil suits, and so on. More than 95 percent of the nation's litigation occurs in state courts. States and their local governments also provide or regulate nearly all of the daily services essential to a safe and decent life.

Consequently, state electorates evidence a strong desire to maintain a constitutional right of consent and control, even if voters do not exercise that right frequently or in large numbers. So long as state government remains within the generally broad and porous boundaries of public opinion, voters are fairly quiescent. Indeed, loading the state constitution with detail reduces the need to be constantly watchful. If state action does go seriously awry, or if voters feel unsafe, they want to be able to throw the rascals out, vote for hanging judges, or amend the constitution.

A REVITALIZATION OF
STATE CONSTITUTIONS?

Although conflict between the Federalist and Antifederalist views of state constitutionalism is likely to endure for some time, the conflict has been mitigated by the expansion of federal power and, thereby, extension of the Federalist principles that underlie the U.S. Constitution. Federal constitutional law is now the primary guarantor of individual rights. The U.S. Supreme Court has established national standards that apply to state action. The Court has also shielded a large number of rights from majority invasion. More generally, the federal government has established standards and requirements in virtually every policy field, including highway speed limits, that once belonged largely or exclusively to state government.

At first blush, the expansion of federal power would seem to make state constitutional law nearly obsolete, just as the states themselves were thought by some reformers to have become obsolete in the twentieth century.[16] Yet one of the most significant developments in American federalism since World War II has been the modernization and strengthening of state governments.[17] One result is that the distribution of power in the federal system is no longer viewed as a zero-sum game. Just as state power can

16. Harold J. Laski, "The Obsolescence of Federalism," *New Republic*, 98:367 (May 1939).
17. See, for example, U.S. Advisory Commission on Intergovernmental Relations, *The Question of State Government Capability* (Washington, DC: U.S. Advisory Commission on Intergovernmental Relations, 1985).

expand along with federal power, so can state constitutional law become more vigorous along with federal constitutional law. State constitutional law continues to have many roles to play in the federal system.

State modernization, for example, has been accomplished largely through constitutional reform, both state—as in, for example, the establishment of four-year gubernatorial terms—and federal— for example, as in reapportionment. Modernization has been necessary in part to improve the carrying capacity of states, namely, their ability to meet contemporary demands and to administer federal grants and implement federal policies. State law must also fill in the many gaps and ambiguities of federal law and policy. State constitutional law can pioneer new approaches to old problems and innovative approaches to new issues untouched by federal law. State constitutional law can, to some extent, counteract deficiencies in federal law and policy, such as federal fiscal irresponsibility.

The establishment of national standards by federal law does not necessarily preclude states from exceeding those standards, whether it be in the field of environmental protection, nuclear regulation, or civil rights. One of the most interesting developments in state constitutional law has been the willingness of many state supreme courts to grant greater rights protection to individuals under state constitutions than the U.S. Supreme Court has been willing to grant under the U.S. Constitution. Nearly 400 such rights-extending decisions have been handed down by state high courts since 1970. Contrary to what might be expected, these decisions have not been confined to states where judges are immune from electoral retribution. California, Oregon, and Washington, for example, have been very active in state constitutional rights litigation.[18] Such developments may once again offer citizens the double security of two vigorous constitutional systems.

Finally, state constitutions remain as instruments for local self-government— a matter that appears to be of growing concern to many citizens as they survey the behavior of the national government, and a matter that appears to be a growing possibility as the nation settles such basic issues as civil rights and environmental protection, issues that once rallied advocates of states' rights against progress. The federal government is not likely to retreat into its nineteenth-century cubbyhole, but the modernization of state governments, the diversification of most state economies, the increased sophistication of state electorates, the presence of a more tolerant pluralism within most states, the increased diffusion of ideas among the states themselves, and the emergence of new problems and issues that require state action all point to the possibility of a new vitality and sophistication for state constitutionalism.

18. Ronald K.L. Collins, Peter J. Galie, and John Kincaid, "State High Courts, State Constitutions, and Individual Rights Litigation since 1980: A Judicial Survey," *Publius: The Journal of Federalism*, 16:141 (Summer 1986).

ANNALS, *AAPSS*, **496**, March 1988

The United States Constitution as an Incomplete Text

By DONALD S. LUTZ

ABSTRACT: Viewing the Constitution of the United States of America as a political text leads to the application of techniques of textual analysis when reading it. Textual analysis shows the Constitution to be incomplete, both as a constitution and as a founding instrument of the federal union. A complete text of a constitution for the United States requires inclusion of the state constitutions, and a complete text of a founding instrument for the United States requires inclusion of the Declaration of Independence. Any meaning to be derived from the U.S. Constitution, including the intentions of the Founders, requires taking into account the purpose for which the Constitution is being read, what constitutes a complete text for that purpose, and the context in which the document was written.

Donald S. Lutz is professor of political science at the University of Houston, where he teaches political theory, specializing in American political theory and American constitutionalism. He has written six books, the most recent being The Origins of American Constitutionalism, *and has published several dozen articles and monographs.*

AMERICANS are the heirs of a constitutional tradition that was mature by the time the national Constitution was framed in 1787. The national document was preceded by 18 constitutions adopted by the states, as well as by the Articles of Confederation, the first national constitution. The 3 states of Rhode Island, Connecticut, and Massachusetts used as their first state constitutions colonial charters that had been written during the previous century and that described systems of politics that had been developed by the colonists. The other 10 states also wrote constitutions that essentially enshrined the institutions they had also developed when colonies. With the Declaration of Independence, the Americans did not so much reject the British constitution as affirm their own constitutional tradition. Derived in part from English constitutional theory and practice, American constitutionalism was distinct from the English tradition in which it was partly rooted.[1]

Although Britain had a constitution before the colonists, it was not written in a single document as American constitutions are. Putting the essentials of a political system in a single document reflects a high level of commitment to citizen participation. Americans felt perfectly comfortable with the idea that they, as a people, could do the following things on their own authority: form themselves into a new community; create or replace a government whenever they wish; select and replace all those holding important positions of political power; determine which values bind them as a community and thus which values should

guide those in government when making decisions for the community; and replace political institutions that operate at variance with these values. The British constitution, resting upon the common law, a long history of institutional evolution from feudalism, and to a significant degree on aristocratic institutions, could not yet begin to generate the same commitment to popular sovereignty that Americans by 1776 took for granted.

We could also point to a functional separation of powers, a bicameralism resting upon a completely different basis from that in Britain, the use of different constituencies for electing different government officials, different terms of office for different branches, an independent judiciary, an elaborate and formalized system of checks, and a formalized method for amending American constitutions—all of these features distinguished American from British constitutionalism.

The most critical difference, however, was the institution of federalism. The state constitutions were the culmination of a process that had evolved, prior to 1776, most of the political institutions and practices we have just identified as peculiarly American. One does not have to resolve the controversy of whether the Declaration of Independence created 13 independent states or a unified nation with 13 states in order to recognize that the existence of those states was a brute fact of central importance. Confederation was tried and found to be inadequate, so Americans evolved a system they now term federalism to create an effective national government in the context of that brute fact.

The use of federalism as a central organizing principle for America's second national constitution had a peculiar effect on its contents. The states are

1. See Donald S. Lutz, *Popular Consent and Popular Control: Whig Political Theory in the Early State Constitutions* (Baton Rouge: Louisiana State University Press, 1980).

mentioned explicitly or by direct implication 50 times in 42 separate sections of the U.S. Constitution. Anyone attempting to do a close textual analysis of the document is driven time and again to the state constitutions to determine what is meant or implied by the national Constitution. This has the effect of raising an obvious question: what was the intention of the Founders in forcing us to consult the state documents?

One of the most important passages involving the states describes an amendment procedure. The concept of formal amendment can arise only after the invention of a written constitution to be amended. The idea of an amendment procedure is not only innovative; it also conveys an important message to a reader of the Constitution—that the document is not yet finished. Alexander Hamilton states, at the very beginning of *Federalist* Number 1, that the American political system is an experiment in government directed by a free people using reflection and choice as opposed to accident and force. Thomas Jefferson said that each generation must add its page to America's unfolding story and that the ability of each generation to do so is part of the story's historical significance. At the very least, it was expected that the formal institutions of decision making would require some adjustment in the future, for it is in the nature of an experiment that one learns from the mistakes that appear during its operation. There was probably another use for amendments foreseen by the drafters, however—completing a definition of citizenship.

Article IV, section 2, of the Constitution establishes that every American is simultaneously a citizen of the United States and of the state wherein he or she resides, a situation known as dual citizenship. Dual citizenship requires two court systems, national and state, one to take care of each citizenship. Here a close textual analysis reveals an interesting version of "the dog that didn't bark." The U.S. Constitution contains no definition of citizenship.

The American national document does not tell how to distinguish a citizen from a noncitizen. On the one hand, we might infer that because the ability to vote is an essential aspect of citizenship, and because those who can vote for the lower house in their respective states can vote in federal elections, we are driven once again to the state constitutions to determine what is meant in the national Constitution. On the other hand, while this analysis of voting nicely illustrates the close connection between national and state constitutions, it still leaves open the question of why the United States needs two court systems if what appears to be a dual citizenship amounts to a single one defined by the states. There is the further problem that the states are far from agreeing on a definition of citizenship.

In 1787, most states had a property requirement for voting and for holding office. This property requirement varied widely in the percentage of the population it enfranchised. Some states completely excluded blacks from citizenship; others included them. In some states, religious tests were applied to those wishing to hold office; in others, not. In short, while a given state might have a reasonably clear definition of citizenship, the variety of definitions among the states precluded there being a common national definition.

If there are seams in the United States Constitution where the fabric does not quite fit together, they are often a reflection of this problem of citizenship. Without mentioning slavery directly, there are passages that attempt to find a *modus vivendi*, such as the three-fifths compromise and the prohibition on the importation of slaves after 1808. It is reasonable to conclude that citizenship was one of the things left for future generations to work out, and the amendment process was one obvious way to do so.

TOWARD A DEFINITION OF A COMPLETE TEXT

We have laid out some of the reasons why the U.S. Constitution may be viewed as an incomplete text. In order to provide a more complete analysis of the Constitution as an incomplete text, we must move to a more general discussion of texts. This will allow us to say something about what a complete text should include, who ought to be included among the Founders, and how we might fruitfully address the vexing question of the Founders' intentions.

When we analyze texts, we are interested in the meaning attached to words and sentences and in the logical structure formed by their order. Even if our investigation is limited to a grammatical analysis, the logic of the relationships between words, sentences, and punctuation depends upon the meaning we are trying to render.

Whenever we study a text, we have a purpose for doing so.[2] At the very least,

we are asking what the specific words, ordered as they are, denote. Denotation is meaning at the simplest level, as opposed to connotation, which is meaning in a broader sense of significance. Even determining denotation is potentially complex. Most words denote several things. By studying the context in which words are used, however, as well as the structure of the argument, we can go a long way toward solving the problem of denotation. Yet even at the simple level of denotation, we must ask whether we are seeking the meaning for the author's contemporary audience, the author's intended meaning, or the meaning the words have for us today.

Meaning is not limited to denotation but depends also on broader contexts. This broader sense of significance has two components: significance in terms of how the total linguistic structure fits together, and significance in terms of how the total argument or structure is evaluated. For example, the denotative meaning of John Locke's phrase "an appeal to Heaven" may be quite different from its meaning within the entire argument where it appears to become an ironic statement. Furthermore, how the reader responds to this phrase is part of its meaning.

Put most baldly, the meaning of a text appears to be a function of the words as written, the author's intention, and the reader's appropriation. Each of these three entities plays a role in establishing the meaning of the text at both the denotative and the connotative levels. Unraveling the relationship between these three entities—the author, his or

2. The position being developed in this section is my own, but I am indebted to the work of others for guiding my thinking on the subject. See, for example, Wayne C. Booth, *A Rhetoric of Irony* (Chicago: University of Chicago Press, 1975); E. D. Hirsch, Jr., *The Aims of Interpretation* (Chicago: University of Chicago Press, 1976); Wolfgang Iser, *The Act of Reading* (Baltimore, MD: Johns Hopkins University Press, 1978); Frank Kermode, *The Genesis of Secrecy* (Cambridge, MA: Harvard University Press, 1979); Paul Ricoeur, *Interpretation Theory: Discourse and the Surplus of Meaning* (Fort Worth: Texas Christian University Press, 1976); Walter J. Slatoff, *With Respect to Readers* (Ithaca, NY: Cornell University Press, 1970).

her written words, and the reader—is essential if we are to understand what constitutes a text and thus a complete text.

The purpose we bring to a text carries with it certain implicit questions, which the reader hopes to have answered by reading the text. For example, a reader may have as his or her purpose the determination of an author's intended meaning for a particular concept; or a reader may be seeking further insight into a concept regardless of the author's position on the matter; or a reader may be seeking an understanding of the context surrounding the writing. The reader's role in defining a complete text, then, is considerable. The reader's purpose leads him or her to pick as a text this piece of writing rather than another. This purpose thus leads the reader to make a provisional closure of what constitutes a complete text. Then it leads to questions that help determine whether a piece of writing is an adequate text. Finally, whatever meaning is extracted from the text is partly a function of the questions generated by the reader's purpose.

Where does the author fit in? Presumably he or she is the key person for defining a text and its meaning. The author had a purpose for writing the text. Part of the author's intention as author is that the meaning be understood by the reader. We can speak, then, of an ideal text. Such a text is one in which the author's intended meaning is always the way the words are read by any reader. There is perfect singularity and congruence at both the denotative and the connotative levels of meaning between the author and every reader. The piece of writing is a faultless transmitter, and the author is the dominant part of the trio of author, writing, and reader. The author not only dominates meaning; he or she dominates the contexts in which the text can be read, the purpose for which it must be read, the questions that are to be asked by the reader, and thus what constitutes a complete text.

Even though such a perfect text could never exist, many readers probably approach a text assuming this model. The text is a given, and uncovering the author's intention is the only reason for studying the text. One indication that such a model is being used in textual analysis is that the analyst, or reader, treats the author with obvious and continual reverence. Our point is not to reject the perfect text model. Rather it is to

—illustrate that this is only one way to approach a text;
—uncover the assumptions in such an approach;
—argue that even if it is attempted, the perfect text can only be approximated; and
—alert us to the dangers of assuming a model of textual analysis that may not always be useful, appropriate, or even possible when analyzing a constitution.

It is frequently assumed that a constitution is an ideal text. Failure to recognize the problem of textual incompleteness often leads readers to analyze one part of a constitution in isolation from the rest of the document. Analysts may also fail to consider other sources or contexts relevant to determining the Founders' intended meaning and may assign a singular meaning to words, phrases, or sentences that are irredeemably equivocal. The use of such an approach to texts is sometimes termed legalism. Instead, it should be called something like abstract pedantry.

For example, in article I, section 8, paragraph 1, of the U.S. Constitution, the text speaks of the "common welfare." Reading this phrase in isolation from its context has led some modern readers to conclude that the Founders intended the national government to involve itself in what we now call welfare programs. In fact, the phrase "common welfare" was, at the time the Constitution was written, a linguistic alternative for "common good," a notion that certainly leaves open the possibility of welfare programs but does not imply that such programs are constitutionally mandated.

Words and phrases, already equivocal from the nature of language, become highly equivocal in the absence of a context that is our best means for overcoming equivocation. Consideration of a word out of its complete context may lead to the imposition of a singular meaning by a court. Because the choice of one abstract definition over the many available in a purely logical exercise does not preclude another definition from being used later by another court, the meaning of a word, phrase, or sentence can vary a good deal over time without the discipline imposed by consideration of the complete text.

Too much of this reasoning and some judge can in truth say that a constitution is simply what a judge says it is, and the model of an ideal text can be transformed into a model where the author and his or her intentions have been dropped altogether. It is then a natural step to search for any word upon which a predetermined meaning can be hung, regardless of the structure, intentions, wordings, and theory contained in an entire document—an activity that can be condoned only by those who no longer believe in constitutional government.

At the same time, there is the danger of going too far the other way. Out of misguided reverence for the Founders, one can assume a perfect, complete text where there is none. Although the framers of a constitution usually seek to use words that narrow the meaning toward singularity for any potential reader, there are times when framers equivocate in order to get around a point upon which there is no consensus. Determining when a constitution has been left equivocal on purpose is part of textual analysis. This equivocalness in turn leaves open the possibility of a constitution's being intentionally incomplete, just as it will sometimes be unintentionally incomplete because of a lack of foresight. At such times we are invited to make a completion.

While any given reader may have a single purpose, over any set of possible readers, the odds that all will have the same purpose approach zero. The text mediates between the author and the reader, carrying a singular meaning from the author's point of view but simultaneously having to stand the scrutiny of a potential set of readers with a set of purposes quite beyond the ability of the writer to predict. Unable to predict the possible purposes to be brought to the text in the future, the author cannot create closure for the text by responding ahead of time to these potential questions.

A further problem, already alluded to, is that we can know the author's intended meaning only with probability. This is a function both of the inevitable equivocation inherent in language and of the uncertain context in which the author wrote. Anyone whose purpose is the determination of an author's meaning must carefully examine the use of words as well as the linguistic-social-political-historical context. At the very least, the careful study of the words in a text must involve the meanings in use when the text was written.

All of this assumes that the author's logical presentation of his or her argument is sufficiently careful that it cannot be construed in too many ways. We do not wish to imply, though, that no timeless meaning can be extracted from a text, or that meaning is simply a function of the historical circumstances. Some texts do contain timeless truths, but this must be established empirically by many readers, over time, finding the same meaning and accepting its truth. Only the continued return of readers to the same text over a long period of time with approximately the same reading and same affirmation of its truth will confirm timelessness.

Once again we are led to conclude that what we call a text is a confluence of three things: an author or authors, a piece of writing, and a reader or readers. The reader defines a text for his or her purpose and thus, by implication, what will constitute a complete text. The author attempts to do the same thing. The author's text and the reader's text do not have to be the same unless the questions asked by each are the same and unless the purpose of the reader is to uncover the probable intended meaning of the author.

It is possible now to examine the United States Constitution as a founding text and avoid the dangers resulting from hidden assumptions. There is no doubt that the document constitutes a text, but whether it is a complete text will depend on the question brought to it. To supplement the conclusions in the first part of the discussion concerning the Constitu-

tion as an incomplete text, we will now turn to supporting those conclusions by showing what would be a complete text for the American Founding.

TOWARD A COMPLETE TEXT FOR THE AMERICAN FOUNDING

Americans had by 1776 evolved a form of foundation document they called a compact, which included as a second part something they called a constitution. The constitution described the basic institutions for collective decision making, distributed power among these institutions, and established the basic procedures for their operation. The first part of this compact often included a long preamble that created a people and laid out the basic political principles shared by that people. Often, but not always, there was also a bill of rights that articulated in greater detail basic political principles, shared values, and common goals. The bill of rights was an implied limit on governmental power, not in a legalistic sense but more often in an admonitory sense through the use of words like "should" and "ought" rather than "shall" and "will." With only a few exceptions, the first state constitutions were in fact compacts as just described.

The Declaration of Independence contained all the elements that belong to the first part of a compact; the Articles of Confederation contained the elements ascribed to a constitution. Together the Declaration and Articles composed America's first national compact. When the Articles were replaced by the Constitution of 1787, the Declaration of Independence was not repudiated but remained as the first part to our second national compact.

Those who wrote the early state constitutions tended to keep the two parts of the compact distinct so that the first portion was not included in the constitution; instead, it was an introduction to it. The bill of rights did not have constitutional status. Insistence by the Antifederalists that a bill of rights be added to the U.S. Constitution resulted in a new form of document, one with perhaps unforeseen consequences. Because the Bill of Rights was added as a series of amendments to the Constitution, these rights were by implication part of it and thus had constitutional status. One indication of the changed status of the bill of rights was that now it, too, contained the words "shall" and "will," just like the rest of the Constitution, rather than the traditional admonitory language of "ought" and "should." The second national compact thus had two bills of rights: one that was admonitory and symbolic—the Declaration—and the other with legal status as part of the Constitution. We do not usually consider the Declaration of Independence in this light, but if one reads it as a series of negative statements about what Britain had done to contravene American rights, values, and shared commitments, one can assemble a very interesting list.

Some of the charges against the king laid out the American commitment to a deliberative process embodied in a legislature of their own choosing. This legislature was supposed to seek the common good, something that the king had threatened, thwarted, or neglected. Several charges laid out the American commitment to freedom of movement, especially as it related to westward expansion. The Americans asserted their preference for an independent judiciary, the rights of peaceful assembly, petition, and trial by jury, as well as their dislike of the quartering of troops in peacetime and standing armies. There was even a statement of American attachment to frugality, frugality often being mentioned in early state constitutions as being a "fundamental political principle." The positive values, principles, and commitments that stand as the basis for the Declaration's charges against the king constitute a comprehensive statement of what we find in the first part, the preambles and bills of rights, of the state compacts. Although the list is much longer and has more rights than the U.S. Bill of Rights, all but a very few things found in the Bill of Rights are also found in the Declaration. Notwithstanding the different perspective injected by the Federalists in the Constitution of 1787, there is remarkable continuity beginning with the Declaration and running through the state constitutions, the Articles of Confederation, and the Constitution.

If we ask what the foundation text is for the American political system, the answer would appear to be the Declaration of Independence, the state constitutions, and the Articles of Confederation. The replacement of the Articles by the new Constitution did not eliminate the others as part of the foundation text. Obviously, the Declaration did not have constitutional status, so that if we ask what the complete text of the Constitution comprises, it is not to be included as part of the answer. On the other hand, as was demonstrated earlier, the answer to this question must include the state constitutions. The U.S. Constitution is part of the American national compact and is thus incomplete as a founding document without the Declaration. At the same time, considered just as a constitution, it is incomplete without the state constitutions.

Those who wrote the foundation text

must therefore be the "Founders," a term now more problematic than is usually realized. The problem can be illustrated in two ways. First, who actually wrote the United States Constitution? It was the result of committee work and of frequent reconsiderations introduced by many people. A simple solution is to say that those who signed the document were its authors, but we know from James Madison's notes that some of the people who refused to sign were far more active in the debate leading to its design than some of the signers. Even among those who signed there was a considerable disparity in quantity and quality of contribution. Still, no one person or small coalition dominated the Constitutional Convention. Even Madison, often considered the father of the Constitution, did not play a dominating role. Using Madison's notes to the convention, Forrest McDonald concludes, "Overall, of seventy-one specific proposals that Madison moved, seconded, or spoke unequivocally in regard to, he was on the losing side forty times." The constitution that Madison preferred was at considerable variance with the constitution he defended in *The Federalist*.[3]

A second point is that just as some of those present at the Constitutional Convention are not normally considered among the Founders, so too there are many considered Founders who were not present at the convention. For example, the eighth edition of a book originally written by Edward S. Corwin begins by discussing not the Constitution, but the Declaration of Independence.[4] Link-

ing the two documents is typical of treatments elsewhere in the literature. Most Americans view the Declaration as an essential part of the Founding. Thus Thomas Jefferson, John Adams, and the 54 others who signed the Declaration qualify as Founders.

From the evidence presented here, it is reasonable to conclude that those who wrote the first state constitutions and the Articles of Confederation must also be included among the Founders. If we now ask the question, What was the intention of the Founders? the answer is both problematic and potentially misleading. We must consider the intentions of many more people than those in attendance in Philadelphia in the summer of 1787. Nor can we identify a single person or small group and examine their private or public writings to determine the Founders' intentions. If Madison's notes to the convention are reliable, Madison himself is exemplary only in that he, like many others, defended a founding in which he managed to achieve only a part of what he wanted but worked hard anyway to defend the work of many. Whether his writing was typical for Federalists is questionable.[5]

The question, What was the intention of the Founders? may at times be used to ask a slightly different question, What was the intention of those who wrote the Constitution of 1787? This is a relevant but narrower question than the former. Part of any answer given to this narrower question must now include the statement, The writers of the Constitution intended for us to read the state constitutions as

3. Forrest McDonald, *Novus Ordo Seclorum: The Intellectual Origins of the Constitution* (Lawrence: University Press of Kansas, 1985), pp. 208-9.
4. J. W. Peltason, *Corwin and Peltason's*

Understanding the Constitution (New York: Holt, Rinehart & Winston, 1979).
5. See Herbert J. Storing, "The 'Other' Federalist Papers: A Preliminary Sketch," *Political Science Reviewer*, 6:215-47 (Fall 1976).

well. Without the state constitutions, the national Constitution, as originally written, was an incomplete text.

CONCLUSION

It is reasonable to conclude that the Founders viewed American government as an experiment directed by a free people attempting to use reflection and choice rather than accident or force. The Constitution is incomplete, therefore, because it was looked upon as an experiment that needed careful control and some means for future adjustment. The provision of an amendment process is one clear manifestation of this perspective. Putting significant power in the hands of state government is another. It was left for future generations to judge the progress of the experiment, make adjustments, and add their own considered innovations to the Constitution.

The Constitution is incomplete because a significant number of questions we can bring to it are not answerable using the one document alone. The general question of what the Founders intended, depending upon the specific topic, almost always takes us beyond the national Constitution for resolution. The prominence of the states in 42 separate sections of the Constitution is one reason. Another is that the term "Founders," given the relationship of the Constitution to the state constitutions, Declaration of

Independence, and Articles of Confederation, must include far more than those who attended the Philadelphia convention in 1787.

Beyond questions about the Founders' intentions, it is in the nature of textual analysis that even without the relationship of the Constitution to these other documents, there will be significant questions that cannot be resolved without expanding the text. One does not need to believe in historical relativism to note that old problems take on new forms. For example, it is now possible for authorities to listen to our every word without tapping a phone line. Technology has advanced to a point where the issue of privacy needs further constitutional development, but nothing in the U.S. Constitution deals explicitly with privacy. If ever there was a potential constitutional issue that pleaded for state action, this is one.

Viewing the Constitution as a political text and examining it in light of the principles of textual analysis, we are led to prospects and conclusions somewhat at variance with standard constitutional analysis. At the same time, we are led back to a more traditional perspective on the Constitution that, ironically, opens up the possibility of a deeper involvement by contemporary Americans in constitutional development, development that could more actively involve the states.

ANNALS, *AAPSS*, **496**, March 1988

State Constitutions in Historical Perspective

By LAWRENCE M. FRIEDMAN

ABSTRACT: Scholars have tended to neglect the history of state constitutions, though these are interesting in themselves and also shed light on federal developments. State constitutions have tended, on the whole, to be less durable and to contain more superlegislation than the U.S. Constitution. Early state constitutions provided for a weak executive. In the nineteenth century, states began to restrict legislatures as well. Recent state constitution making has tended to be technocratic, less overtly political than in the nineteenth century, although the use of initiative and referendum processes is a somewhat contradictory trend. Judicial review in state courts developed along lines generally parallel to those in federal courts. Judicial review flowered after the Civil War; in this period, many innovative doctrines first arose in state courts. The center of innovation shifted to the federal courts in the twentieth century. Judicial review continued and grew in state courts, however, and the recent expansion of the doctrine of independent state grounds may increase the power and significance of state courts.

Lawrence M. Friedman is the Marion Rice Kirkwood Professor of Law at Stanford University. He is the author of a number of books, including A History of American Law *(2nd edition, 1985),* The Legal System: A Social Science Perspective *(1975), and* Total Justice *(1985). His published work deals mainly with American legal history and with the relationship between law and society. He is past president of the Law and Society Association and is a member of the American Academy of Arts and Sciences.*

A striking feature of American law and government is the constitutional system. As it evolved, it developed two salient and closely linked features. The first is the reliance on written constitutions. The United States Constitution is a major American presence, but every state has its own constitution, and the constitutional history of each state is unique, revealing, and important. The idea of a charter, fundamental law, or constitution is a deeply ingrained cultural trait; one might almost say "habit." Clubs, miners' groups, the Confederate States of America, and the Mormons in the State of Deseret all drafted constitutions.

The second feature is the American brand of judicial review, which lodges tremendous power in the various high-court judges. This, of course, is connected to the trait just mentioned; without written constitutions, it would be harder if not impossible for courts to wield the power that they do. Furthermore, it is a judicial power that is general. The United States Supreme Court has power of judicial review, notoriously so; but so does the Supreme Court of Rhode Island. And the Rhode Island court has two strings to its bow: if federal constitutional law does not suit it, it can always rely on its state constitution.

In the light of this fact, it is surprising how little attention scholars give to state constitutions; they are treated as mere stepsisters. This neglect is particularly striking in law schools. Federal constitutional law is a staple of the curriculum; state constitutional law is taught almost nowhere. Legal education emphasizes whatever is national and general and looks down on the local and particular.

The state constitutions do not deserve this neglect. They are, to begin with, significant in their own right. The California Constitution is the highest law on many issues for a domain of over 25 million people. Moreover, during most of American history, economic and social development—not to mention conflict and dispute—centered on the states. Washington, D.C., was not a world capital, but a muddy village; not the nerve center of the nation but more like a dinosaur's tiny mind, a clump of nerves in a vast, decentralized body.

The history of state constitutions is also full of little surprises. These surprises often shed light, if only obliquely, on federal constitutional law and American history. Article 9, section 4, of the Washington Constitution of 1889, for example, declares that public schools "shall be forever free from sectarian control or influence"; article 1, section 11, of the same constitution forbids spending public money on any "religious worship, exercise or institution" or for the "support of any religious establishment."

Under this and similar provisions in other states, questions were raised about Bible reading in the schools. In Washington, in 1918, the supreme court struck down a plan to give high school credit for Bible study.[1] Other states upheld Bible readings and similar arrangements. Yet as far as the world of constitutional scholarship is concerned, school prayer and Bible reading appeared as issues quite suddenly, in *Engel* v. *Vitale* and

1. A student could earn one credit each for Old Testament and New Testament proficiency. The instruction was to be given "in the home or by the religious organizations with which the students are affiliated." *State ex rel. Dearle* v. *Frazier*, 102 Wash. 369, 173 Pac. 35 (1918); see also *State ex rel. Clithero* v. *Showalter*, 159 Wash. 519, 293 Pac. 1000 (1930).

Abington School District v. *Schempp*, in the early 1960s.[2]

Equally important, historically, is the opposite kind of evidence. There are no cases on freedom of speech in the United States Supreme Court before the time of World War I. Was the issue not salient at all, or was it not salient only at the federal level? As it turns out, state cases were also rare; only a handful were reported for the whole nineteenth century. Thus the question of why freedom of speech became an issue in the twentieth century can be posed more sharply than if the only evidence was evidence of federal decisions.

WHAT IS A CONSTITUTION?

The historical study of state constitutions also forces us to ask, What is a constitution? This may seem an obvious, even foolish question, but it needs to be asked. Our viewpoint, by now, is totally fixed on the U.S. Constitution, a venerable document spoken of with awe, as a kind of sacred relic, enshrined in glass, and surrounded by little tokens of devotion.[3]

Is this veneration more than skin deep? Note that the state constitutions, whatever else they are, lack this quality. They are not sacred texts; they are not enshrined in glass, literally or figuratively. They are, to begin with, much more impermanent. By 1985, the states had produced about 150 state constitutions, according to the *Book of the States*.[4] Louisiana took some sort of

2. 370 U.S. 421 (1962); 374 U.S. 203 (1963).

3. On constitution worship, see Michael Kammen, *A Machine That Would Go of Itself* (New York: Knopf, 1986).

4. *The Book of the States, 1986-87*, vol. 26 (Lexington, KY: Council of State Governments, 1986).

prize with 11; Georgia had had 10; South Carolina, 7; Alabama, Florida, and Virginia, 6 each. Only 18 states had made do with a single constitution. Only 6 of the constitutions in force now were drafted before 1850. Existing documents had been amended nearly 5000 times. Massachusetts has the oldest constitution (1780) though it too has been much amended—116 times.

The appetite to scrap whole constitutions and adopt newly minted ones began early—Pennsylvania's constitution of 1776 was replaced in 1790—and reached some sort of pinnacle between 1876 and 1900. The process has abated somewhat in the twentieth century. The urge seems to come in spasms; between 1964 and 1982, there were new constitutions or total revisions in Michigan, Connecticut, Florida, Pennsylvania, Illinois, Virginia, North Carolina, Montana, and Louisiana, and Georgia had two in this period. At the moment, all appears to be quiet, at least as far as root-and-branch change is concerned. The amending process, however, gallops on. California is a notable example. There is a certain degree of constancy underneath, and the California Constitution celebrated its centennial a few years back. There are, however, so many amendments and additions, and so often, that the constitution is actually in a kind of constant flux.

If state constitutions are not sacred texts, then what are they? This is not an easy question to answer. State constitutions do much the same thing that the U.S. Constitution does and have given rise to some of the same institutions. There is judicial review in the states, just as there is in the federal courts. Indeed, it could be argued that state constitutional law and constitutional practice are essentially like the federal version.

Yet state constitutionalism is not a civil religion, as federal constitutionalism is said to be. On the other hand, it produces some of the same results. The phrase "civil religion" implies a certain degree of passion. Most people, however, are quite ignorant about the constitutional system, and there is little evidence that they revere it, though they no doubt believe that constitutional arrangements, whatever they are, should not be tampered with. They cling to the existing form of government out of habit and satisfaction.

Basically, state constitutions contain the same sorts of matter as the federal Constitution, only in somewhat different proportions. First, they describe and establish the frame or scheme of government—legislative, executive, and judicial branches and their powers; modes of voting; and so on. Second, they set out fundamental civil rights of the citizens, which are supposed to be beyond the reach of temporary majorities. Third—and here they deviate the most from the federal model—they contain a vast, miscellaneous storehouse of provisions, which we might call superlegislation. These provisions do not have a constitutional flavor at all; they are no different in quality or type from ordinary laws; and yet, for some political reason, they have been upgraded from the statute books to constitutional status.

The U.S. Constitution is relatively though not entirely free of superlegislation. The first part of article IX put the slave trade off limits to congressional legislation until 1808, and many people would classify the Eighteenth Amendment, concerning prohibition, as a classic example of superlegislation and a bad example at that. State constitutions, on the other hand, are often riddled with the stuff; historically, it has

been an important source of constitutional instability.

Ordinarily, behind each instance of superlegislation there lurks some concrete story, some concrete factional dispute or clash between interest groups. Without close study of the political history of the states, it is hard to know why Wyoming, for example, in its 1890 constitution, prohibited the legislature from prescribing school textbooks, or why Arkansas put a law concerning married women's property into its constitutions of 1868 and 1874.[5]

But these are mild examples, which at least laid down general rules. Article 11, section 30, of the Tennessee Constitution of 1796 fixed the governor's salary at $750. Article 11, section 229, of the Mississippi Constitution of 1890 established a Yazoo-Mississippi Delta Levee District and authorized the governor to "appoint a stockholder in the Louisville, New Orleans and Texas Railway Company as an additional commissioner." My personal favorite is article 16 of the Minnesota Constitution, proposed by the legislature in 1919[6] and in force in 1920. This created a "trunk highway system" to be maintained by the state "forever." It set out 70 specific highway routes—for example, Route Number 65, "beginning at a point on Route No. 8 at Bagley and thence extending ... to a point on Route No. 32 southerly of Red Lake Falls."

Provisions about the frame of government, powers of the governor, the suffrage, and so on are not merely technical. They establish or maintain distributions of power. Thus Southern constitutions in the late nineteenth century reeked of white supremacy. Louisiana pioneered

5. Wyo. Const. art. VII, § 11; Ark. Const. art. XII, § 6 (1868); Ark. Const. art. IX, § 7 (1874).
6. Laws Minn. 1919, chap. 530.

the infamous grandfather clause to keep blacks from voting;[7] other states, too, supplemented private terror with public law.

Of course, issues of power and social structure were central to the federal debates in 1787 as well. In the U.S. Constitution, the open texture and the bland neutrality of style tend to obscure the point. In any event, whether by design or evolution, the federal Constitution has become a much more flexible instrument—a vessel, a container, whose contents change with the passing of time. The state constitutions, blunter and more explicit, have been rather brittle. The U.S. Constitution survived the Civil War; state constitutions, in the South, did not.

STAGES IN STATE
CONSTITUTIONAL
DEVELOPMENT

The states embarked on the constitution-making process earlier than the federal government. Some of the early constitutions are uncommonly interesting. They exerted considerable influence on the drafting of the federal Constitution and, very notably, on the Bill of Rights.[8]

After 1787, the main lines of influence went the other way. States often used other states as models, but the shape of the federal Constitution and some of its language were influential. States sometimes copied material blindly. It is hard to imagine, for example, that Iowa in 1857 really needed a clause on quartering

soldiers in private homes in time of peace.[9]

In the early constitutions, the executive branch tended to be weak; governors wielded relatively little power. Some constitutions prescribed rotation in office. The Maryland governor was to be elected by the legislature, but only for a one-year term. He could be reelected, but no more than three years in succession. Fears of a strong executive reflected vivid colonial memories. The states did not want state officials to be courtiers or careerists; the ideal was the virtuous amateur, who would put aside his plow for a time to serve the people.

Power taken from the executive passed to the legislatures. Later, disillusionment set in. One reason was corruption; scandals rocked legislatures from time to time, and there was also rank inefficiency. By the middle of the nineteenth century, constitutions devoted considerable attention to this problem. The tendency was to put limits on legislatures, in hopes of curing or curbing their vices. The Maryland Constitution of 1851 forbade the legislature from appropriating money for internal improvements or from contracting debts of more than $100,000. Quite commonly, there were rules against specific kinds of special or local laws—legislative divorces, for example.

Other provisions aimed at preventing certain mischief in drafting and passing laws. This was the point of one common clause that, in its Indiana version of 1851, read as follows: "Every act shall embrace but one subject . . . which subject shall be expressed in the title." No such clause appears in the U.S. Constitution, though it was popular enough by the 1860s to be inserted into the short-lived Confederate Constitution.

7. La. Const. art. CXCVII, § 5.

8. For an overview of the subject, see Willi Paul Adams, *The First American Constitutions: Republican Ideology and the Making of the State Constitutions in the Revolutionary Era* (Chapel Hill: University of North Carolina Press, 1980).

9. Iowa Const. art. I, § 15.

Whether such a clause is actually useful in the legislative process is unknown, but the clause was a gleeful and constant inspiration to litigants who wanted to attack a statute. Just as no one knows what "equal protection" or "due process" means, no one knows, or can know, whether a complex law only "embrace[s]" one "subject" or whether the title gives adequate notice of that subject.

Of course, the real issue in these cases was never stylistic; it was some specific economic and political struggle. These clauses are still useful for tactical or strategic purposes. In the 1980s, California, by initiative, adopted a victim's bill of rights, a law-and-order measure. An attack on the measure in court leaned heavily on the one-subject-title provision of the California Constitution. The measure was upheld—by a bare majority.[10]

Who was corrupting legislatures in the nineteenth century? Big corporations, banks, and railroads; or so people thought. Thus, in the 1870s and after, legislatures placed restrictions on corporate power or constitutionalized labor legislation. The Illinois Constitution of 1870 provided for regulation of grain elevators and warehouses; the Pennsylvania Constitution of 1873 attacked the problem of taxation of railroads. Colorado, in 1876, and Idaho, in 1889, tried to outlaw the labor of children in "underground mines." States adopted provisions outlawing convict labor. At the very end of the century, some constitutions began to sound themes of conservation of resources.

As we noted, the process of making and remaking state constitutions has not ended; about a quarter of the states

have adopted new constitutions since 1945. The pace has slackened, however, and the question remains, Why do some states tamper so little with their constitutions, and others so much?

Of course, as mentioned, an unreplaced constitution is not the same as an unamended constitution. Just over half the states have initiative or referendum provisions or both. Essentially this was a twentieth-century development, usually associated with the Progressive movement. Progressivism has come and gone, but the initiative and referendum still flourish. The passion for amending state constitutions has shown no signs of abating. In some states—and California is a prime example—the initiative and referendum are very widely used; some would say abused. In a sense, then, there is not much point in redoing the constitution of California; it changes year by year, election by election.

Although it is not easy to make generalizations, there do seem to be systematic differences between constitution making in the nineteenth century and constitution making today. In the nineteenth century, constitutions were intensely political, in the most literal sense. They not only set out the frame of government; they also expressed the basic power structure of the state: they were pro-railroad or anti-railroad; they favored the northern part of the state or the southern part, this party or that party, this faction or that. Thus, when the wheel of politics turned, the constitution itself had to go, to be replaced by an instrument embodying the aims and policies of the victors.

In the twentieth century, this does not seem to be so much the case. Perhaps changes in factional power in this century focus more on seizure and control of the bureaucracy. At any rate, minor political

10. *Brosnahan* v. *Brown*, 32 Cal.3d 236, 186 Cal. R. 30, 651 P.2d 274 (1982).

revolutions, when they occur, do not seem to require a brand-new constitution. Recent constitutions do reflect political realignment, but they are primarily technicians' constitutions. Perhaps the paradigm case is the New Jersey Constitution of 1947. One major goal was to reform New Jersey's creaky and archaic court system. The guiding impulse was not a change in substantive law or in the balance of power; the impulse was strictly technocratic.

The two trends just mentioned are, to be sure, contradictory. The technocratic approach to state constitution making is inconsistent with the initiative and referendum process, which practically guarantees a bloated, conflated constitution. The direct popular vote shoehorns all sorts of provisions into constitutional texts. Experts are not happy with the initiative. In theory it is all nicely democratic; yet the voters are manipulated and befuddled by a combination of misleading billboards, rock videos, and texts that would baffle a Philadelphia lawyer. Still, the process marches on.

JUDICIAL REVIEW

The most dramatic aspect of American constitutionalism is, of course, judicial review. The U.S. Constitution is the supreme law of the land, but, as Charles Evans Hughes put it, the Constitution is what the judges say it is. This dictum is hard to deny, though some do deny it. Hence to talk about state constitutions means to talk about state high courts and the way they use, interpret, or manipulate the state constitutions.

I will not address the vexed question of the origins of judicial review. The evidence is in hopeless conflict. The state constitutions do, in fact, shed some light on the question. In the Pennsylvania

Constitution of 1776, for example, there was a curious provision for a Council of Censors, a kind of watchdog over constitutional behavior. New York's first constitution set up a Council of Revision, made up of the governor, the chancellor, and the supreme court judges. The council had the job of reviewing the validity of bills passed by the legislature.

These provisions point in two directions. The Pennsylvania arrangement was certainly not itself judicial review. Nonetheless, it gropes toward a solution to a perceived problem. Checks and balances were in the air, so to speak, and judicial review was the ultimate solution. Whether it was literally intended or not, it came to be accepted as the best way to control the other two branches.

In the states, judicial review followed, more or less, the same general course of development that it followed in the U.S. Supreme Court. Review was rather rare before the Civil War.[11] The great flowering of judicial review took place between 1870 and 1900. In fact, in this period, state courts were probably bolder and more inventive than the federal courts. Many of the famous or infamous doctrines familiar to law students—substantive due process, the liberty-of-contract doctrine, and so on—were invented and tried out first in the states.[12]

This makes state constitutional history, in the late nineteenth and early twentieth centuries, extraordinarily rich

11. Margaret V. Nelson, *A Study of Judicial Review in Virginia, 1789-1928* (New York: Columbia University Press, 1947), p. 54, found only 35 cases in Virginia before the Civil War; only four challenged statutes failed the test.

12. See, for example, *In re Jacobs*, 98 N.Y. 98 (1885); *Godcharles* v. *Wigeman*, 113 Pa. St. 431 (1886); see, in general, Arnold M. Paul, *Conservative Crisis and the Rule of Law: Attitudes of Bar and Bench, 1887-1895* (Ithaca, NY: Cornell University Press, 1960).

and significant, though it is not an easy history to sum up. There were great differences in activism between one state court and another. It is also easy to exaggerate the destructive force of judicial review. Most state statutes passed their constitutional tests, if they were reviewed at all. It is the infamous cases that are widely known. Exactly what was the impact of judicial review on state legislation? There is no way to answer this question systematically, but surely the impact was less than is ordinarily surmised.[13]

The use of judicial review has continued, of course, in the twentieth century.[14] State supreme courts continue to decide many cases on classic issues of state constitutional law and also in proportions that have remained more or less stable since the 1870s.[15] In addition, state courts have been increasingly active in new fields of constitutional law, especially the rights of criminal defendants. In the years 1965-70, according to a study by Robert Kagan and associates, almost half of all criminal cases before state supreme courts posed constitutional issues—a dramatic increase.[16]

To be sure, over the last century or so, there have been changes in the power of state high courts to create national constitutional doctrine. It is doubtful that any major new ideas in constitutional law, since the 1950s, have originated in

state courts or have been first devised as a reading of some state constitution. The deafening silence that has enveloped the field works against that. More significantly, the incorporation doctrine has led to a kind of nationalization of judicial review. As the Fourteenth Amendment gulped down bigger and bigger chunks of the Bill of Rights, the "freedom"—if that is the word—of state courts to interpret their own texts shrank. The center of attention passed to federal courts, which could impose a national standard on the states. State jurisprudence became, necessarily, much more of a wallflower.

Thus the power and scope of state judicial review suffered somewhat, relative to review in federal courts, and the state courts sank into a kind of obscurity. But this did not necessarily mean an absolute decrease in power and scope. Many striking examples of judicial lawmaking come from the state courts—outside the constitutional sphere, to be sure. The total transformation of tort law owes almost nothing to the federal courts.

In constitutional law, the federal influence is, of course, much greater than state influence. Even so, the sheer quantity of state judicial review has increased in recent years. The courts still decide a substantial number of cases under clauses that have no counterpart in the U.S. Constitution. State cases are an extremely miscellaneous lot. Many deal with the validity of tax or regulatory laws. Substantive due process never really died in the states. Many cases arise under clauses dealing with the legislative process or with the jurisdiction and tenure of judges.[17] This suggests that state courts, quietly, have been playing a

13. See Lawrence M. Friedman, "Freedom of Contract and Occupational Licensing, 1890-1910: A Legal and Social Study," *California Law Review*, 53:487 (May 1965).
14. New York's courts, for example, between 1906 and 1938 upheld 451 statutes and struck down 136. Franklin A. Smith, *Judicial Review of Legislation in New York, 1906-1938* (New York: Columbia University Press, 1952), p. 223.
15. Robert Kagan et al., "The Business of State Supreme Courts, 1870-1970," *Stanford Law Review*, 30:121, 150 (Nov. 1977).
16. Ibid., p. 147.
17. Ibid., p. 150.

powerful political role. They insert themselves into economic issues on which the U.S. Supreme Court has given up almost entirely. The whole area is obscure and badly needs research.

Moreover, in recent years, state courts have been increasingly showing their muscle. This is not surprising. Structural reasons may account for some of this development. Over the course of the last century or so, high courts in more and more states have gained total control over their dockets. High courts are free to choose important cases, which in turn perhaps encourages more activism than would otherwise be the case. The powerful work of the U.S. Supreme Court may also have an impact: Supreme Court cases generate controversy, make headlines, and serve as models.

One vehicle for state court activism is the doctrine of independent state grounds. This doctrine, moreover, permits something close to outright defiance of federal doctrine. In the U.S. Supreme Court, the germ of this doctrine can be traced back to language in a case of 1874.[18] The doctrine has received a tremendous burst of energy in the last decades, and there is a growing literature on the subject.

Some of the most interesting cases arise under state bills of rights. To be sure, state courts cannot interpret their own cruel-and-unusual-punishment clause, for example, to permit torture. The federal standard overrides theirs, even if they claim to be merely interpreting their own constitution. But they are allowed to give clauses a more expansive reading than the federal courts. The issue was posed in the well-known *Pruneyard*

case.[19] Under U.S. Supreme Court doctrine, a privately owned shopping center did not have to permit every Tom, Dick, and Jane to make speeches or distribute leaflets. But in *Pruneyard*, California read its constitution as granting broader rights of free speech. No problem, said the U.S. Supreme Court; California was entitled to "adopt . . . individual liberties more expansive than those conferred by the Federal Constitution."

A number of states have leaped eagerly into the breach.[20] Massachusetts is an egregious example. Here the state supreme court has declared the death penalty unconstitutional, as a violation of article 26 of the state's declaration of rights, which for all practical purposes is identical with the language of the Eighth Amendment of the federal Constitution.[21] Thus the Massachusetts high court goes its own way, ignoring rulings of the U.S. Supreme Court.[22]

In the Alaskan case of *Shagloak* v. *State*[23] the defendant, Davis Shagloak,

18. *Murdock* v. *Memphis*, 87 U.S. 590, 636 (1874). See also Carolyn Jourdan, "Tennessee Judicial Activism: Renaissance of Federalism," *Tennessee Law Review*, 49:135 (Fall 1981).

19. *Pruneyard Shopping Center* v. *Robins*, 447 U.S. 74 (1980).

20. For an overview, see Peter J. Galie, "The Other Supreme Courts: Judicial Activism among State Supreme Courts," *Syracuse Law Review*, 33:371 (Summer 1982).

21. See *District Att'y of Suffolk* v. *Watson*, 381 Mass. 648, 411 N.E.2d 1274 (1980); *Commonwealth* v. *O'Neal*, 369 Mass. 242, 339 N.E.2d 676 (1975); Opinion of the Justices, 372 Mass. 912, 364 N.E.2d 1984 (1977).

22. *Gregg* v. *Georgia*, 428 U.S. 153 (1976), and its offspring and companions have of course upheld the death penalty. In Massachusetts, after the *Watson* case, article 26 was amended to read that "no provision of the Constitution. . . . shall be construed as prohibiting the imposition of the punishment of death." But proponents of the death penalty underestimated the talents of the Massachusetts court; see *Commonwealth* v. *Colon-Cruz*, 393 Mass. 150, 470 N.E.2d 116 (1984), striking down the next attempt at a capital-punishment statute.

23. 597 P.2d 142 (Alaska 1979).

was a man with an incurable itch to burglarize. The legal issue was this: if a criminal defendant wins a new trial and loses again, can the judge at the second trial give him a stiffer sentence than he received at the first trial? Yes, according to the United States Supreme Court; no, according to the Alaska Supreme Court, under its own due process clause.

In constitutional law, textual interpretation is often or perhaps usually disingenuous; these cases may be a bit more disingenuous than usual. And there are those who think these cases pose a problem for the federal system. One job of the courts is to establish the limits and meaning of such basic rights as freedom of speech. Values may be in conflict; the court is after the right line, or the best line, between rights of the individual and the collectivity. The U.S. Supreme Court, in *Pruneyard*, allowed California to grant more free speech, which it presumed to be some sort of absolute good, so that there can never be too much of it. In fact, however, what it allowed was a different rule about free speech—the

drawing of a different line. There will be no uniform standard.

There are, of course, policy arguments on both sides of this question. Probably it makes sense to argue the issue point by point and area by area; what works for leaflets in a shopping mall may not work for the rights of people arrested for burglary. For our purposes, it is worth noting that the doctrine of independent state grounds fosters a revival of interest in state constitutional law and underscores the importance of the subject. The years of scholarly neglect may come to an end.

We are also reminded that state constitutions, even when they use the same words as the federal Constitution, are not the same beasts, either as compared to each other or as compared to the U.S. Constitution. State constitutions, too, are not simply documents, that is, words, pieces of paper. They have lives of their own. They are part of a complex process, a history, a context, a tradition. They should be studied from that standpoint. For that matter, so should the U.S. Constitution.

ANNALS, *AAPSS*, **496**, March 1988

Evolving State Legislative and Executive Power in the Founding Decade

By ROBERT F. WILLIAMS

ABSTRACT: The crucial questions surrounding the first state constitutions concerned suffrage, officeholding requirements, legislative structure, and the relationship of legislative to executive power. These questions were debated vigorously, and a vision of the proper structure of government based on unicameralism, a weak executive, and no checks and balances was advocated in nearly all the states by radical democrats. Their most conspicuous victory was in Pennsylvania in 1776, where a unicameral legislature was established and powers were separated but no checks were provided for legislative encroachments upon the other branches' responsibilities. Constitutional framers in other states rejected Pennsylvania's example, delayed their constitutional drafting processes, and succeeded in adopting a more balanced government with checks, such as upper houses and gubernatorial vetoes. Still, legislative supremacy prevailed under all the new state constitutions, making possible the legislative policies of the founding decade on debtor-creditor relations, paper money, and taxation that were of such great concern to the framers of the United States Constitution.

Robert F. Williams is associate professor of law at Rutgers University, Camden. He earned a J.D. from the University of Florida in 1969, an LL.M. at New York University in 1971, and an LL.M. at Columbia University in 1980. He teaches state constitutional law at Rutgers and is the editor of Materials of State Constitutional Law *(to be published in 1988 by the Advisory Commission on Intergovernmental Relations).*

NOTE: Support for this article was provided by an American Council of Learned Societies/Ford Fellowship.

D URING the decade after the American colonies achieved independence, the cardinal question in discussions over the proper constitutional structure of the new state governments concerned the nature and powers of the legislative and executive branches and their relationship to each other.[1] By the time the Constitutional Convention met in the summer of 1787, the 13 independent states had debated, framed, adopted, rejected, modified, and continued to debate at least twenty state constitutions in the period since 1775.

The founding decade of 1776-87 witnessed the internal political struggle over "who should rule at home" as well as the larger Revolutionary struggle for "home rule."[2] The principal controversies over the first state constitutions had little to do with rights. What was primarily at stake was how the new state governments would be structured and what groups in society would have the dominant role in making policy under the new governments.

1. For summaries of this decade of state constitution making, see Jackson Turner Main, *The Sovereign States, 1775-1783* (New York: Franklin Watts, 1973), pp. 143-95; Willi Paul Adams, *The First American Constitutions: Republican Ideology and the Making of the State Constitutions in the Revolutionary Era* (Chapel Hill: University of North Carolina Press, 1980), pp. 63-93; Donald S. Lutz, *Popular Consent and Popular Control: Whig Political Theory in the Early State Constitutions* (Baton Rouge: Louisiana State University Press, 1980); Gordon Wood, *The Creation of the American Republic, 1776-1787* (Chapel Hill: University of North Carolina Press, 1969), pp. 125-255; Elisha P. Douglass, *Rebels and Democrats: The Struggle for Equal Political Rights and Majority Rule during the American Revolution* (Chapel Hill: University of North Carolina Press, 1955).

2. Carl Lotus Becker, *The History of Political Parties in the Province of New York, 1760-1776* (Madison: University of Wisconsin Press, 1909), p. 22.

It is now apparent that there was much greater diversity of opinion and interest reflected in the state constitution-making processes during the founding decade than was earlier thought. The ultimate outcomes of the constitutional battles in the states were also much closer and more contingent than has been commonly recognized. In this sense, the general consensus in favor of "republican" government was "a consensus that promoted discord rather than harmony."[3]

Obviously, the stakes surrounding the question of who was to rule at home were very high. Independence, coupled with drastic change in the political system of the past, was feared by those who had held power under the colonial regimes. To those who sought power, independence without real change in the political system was not worth the effort. This tension would form the basis for the struggles over the framing and implementation of the state constitutions between 1776 and 1787.

The need for separation of powers was a priority in the minds of the framers of the new state constitutions because of the nature of the colonial dispute over England's arbitrary exercise of power and because of abuses arising from dual officeholding in the colonies. These early constitution drafters were therefore led to include statements of the principle of separation of powers within the texts of the constitutions. Because many of the first state constitutions contained what seemed to be explicit statements concerning separation

3. Robert E. Shalhope, "Toward a Republican Synthesis: The Emergence of an Understanding of Republicanism in American Historiography," *William and Mary Quarterly*, 3d ser. 29:72 (Jan. 1972).

of powers,[4] it is easy to assume that concerns about the proper balance of power and relationships among the branches had been worked out by 1776. Nothing could be further from the truth.[5] Also, merely stating the principle of separation of powers did nothing to establish any firm mechanisms of checks to prevent, or at least remedy, encroachments of one branch into the proper domain of the others. Struggles over government structure and power occurred throughout the founding decade. The evolution of state constitutions during this period reflects a transition from early recognition of separation of powers to a later emphasis on checks and balances.

Historians and political scientists have identified two major waves of state constitution making during the founding decade.[6] The key point in the first wave

was the Pennsylvania Constitution of 1776; the Massachusetts Constitution of 1780 was the central feature of the second wave.

THE FIRST WAVE

The first wave of state constitutions generally includes those adopted during the first year after independence. These were drafted quickly at the beginning of the Revolution, usually by legislative bodies, and did not differ much from the colonial charters except with respect to weakened executive power and the inclusion of declarations of rights. Little consideration was given to structural mechanisms to check the dominant legislatures, although South Carolina's 1776 constitution contained an absolute gubernatorial veto—only in effect until 1778—and most of the constitutions created upper houses. Pennsylvania's 1776 constitution does not fit this description in a number of respects, but it represents the culmination of the first wave and the direct stimulus for the second wave.

Pennsylvania's radical 1776 constitution was drafted by a separate convention elected for that purpose and followed Thomas Paine's recommendation in *Common Sense* that "simple" governments be established.[7] Under the frame of government, legislative power was placed in a unicameral assembly—often attributed to Benjamin Franklin's influence[8]—with virtually no structural checks, such as a veto power for the weak, albeit elected, plural executive, headed by a "president" chosen by the assembly.

---

4. See, for example, Mass. Const. (1780), declaration of rights, § 30: "The legislative department shall never exercise the executive and judicial powers, or either of them; the executive shall never exercise the legislative and judicial powers, or either of them; the judicial shall never exercise the legislative and executive powers, or either of them." Quoted in William Clarence Webster, "Comparative Study of the State Constitutions of the American Revolution," *The Annals* of the American Academy of Political and Social Science, 9:389 (Jan. 1897). For an in-depth discussion of the implications of this provision, see Ronald M. Peters, Jr., *The Massachusetts Constitution of 1780: A Social Compact* (Amherst: University of Massachusetts Press, 1978), pp. 163-76.

5. Webster, "Comparative Study," p. 403. See also Edward S. Corwin, "The Progress of Constitutional Theory between the Declaration of Independence and the Meeting of the Philadelphia Convention," *American Historical Review*, 30:514 (Apr. 1925). Corwin notes that separation of powers in early state constitutions "was verbal merely."

6. Wood, *Creation of the American Republic*, p. 435; Lutz, *Popular Consent and Popular Control*, pp. 44-45.

7. *The Complete Writings of Thomas Paine*, ed. Philip S. Foner (New York: Citadel Press, 1969), 1:4-46.

8. Rosalind A. Branning, *Pennsylvania Constitutional Development* (Pittsburgh, PA: University of Pittsburgh Press, 1960), p. 14.

Similarly, members of the supreme court could be removed by the legislature for "misbehavior." The constitution contained provisions aimed at making the assembly an open, deliberative body, accountable to the voters. Bills had to be enacted by two successive legislative sessions before becoming law. Legislators served one-year terms and could serve no more than four out of seven years. Such legislative accountability provisions were virtually unknown in other state constitutions and generally would not appear until well into the nineteenth century. These provisions relating to the otherwise dominant legislative branch could be seen as a form of popular check on legislative authority.

The Pennsylvania Constitution established the principle of apportionment by "the number of taxable inhabitants," with regular reapportionment. Property requirements for voting were eliminated, and the much broader requirement that a voter pay taxes was substituted in its place.[9] Finally, a Council of Censors was to be elected by the people every seven years to review legislative actions for conformity "to the principles of the constitution" and to propose amendments to the constitution.

From the moment it was implemented, controversy raged over whether the constitution should be changed. This controversy dominated most elections in Pennsylvania until a new constitution was substituted 14 years later, in 1790, as part of the overall movement leading to the federal Constitution.[10] This split

9. Paine supported an even broader franchise. See Eric Foner, *Tom Paine and Revolutionary America* (New York: Oxford University Press, 1976), pp. 142-43.

10. See generally Richard Alan Ryerson, "Republican Theory and Partisan Reality in Revolutionary Pennsylvania: Toward a New View of the Constitutionist Party," in *Sovereign States in*

in Pennsylvania, between what came to be known as the Constitutionalist and Republican "parties,"[11] reflected in a general sense the controversies that would surround the new constitutions in other states and carry over into legislative politics in the lawmaking branches created by the new constitutions.

Almost immediately after *Common Sense* was published, John Adams published his *Thoughts on Government* as, among other things, a response to Paine.[12] Adams set forth an alternative, more traditional vision of how the new state governments should be constituted. He proposed a model based on "balanced government," or separation of powers backed by checks, to which bicameralism and executive power were central. He also advocated property requirements for officeholding and voting.

The contending visions in the state constitution making of the founding decade were, therefore, generally delineated as early as 1776. The opposing visions of the proper structure of state government were embraced by contending factions in each of the states, where, with some variations, the visions collided throughout the decade of 1776-87. As

an Age of Uncertainty, ed. Ronald Hoffman and Peter J. Albert (Charlottesville: University Press of Virginia, 1981), p. 95; Robert L. Brunhouse, *The Counter-Revolution in Pennsylvania 1776-1790* (Harrisburg: Pennsylvania Historical Commission, 1942), p. 17.

11. Robert Kelley, *The Cultural Pattern in American Politics: The First Century* (New York: Knopf, 1979), pp. 79-80; Ryerson, "Republican Theory"; J. Paul Selsam, *The Pennsylvania Constitution of 1776: A Study in Revolutionary Democracy* (Philadelphia: University of Pennsylvania Press, 1936), pp. 173-74; Brunhouse, *Counter-Revolution.*

12. George A. Peek, Jr., ed., *The Political Writings of John Adams* (Indianapolis: Bobbs-Merrill, 1954), pp. 83-92.

Edward Countryman has noted, "The dominant and ultimately triumphant [view] was toward constitutional stability. The other, weaker but still noteworthy, was toward some form of popular council democracy."[13]

After what happened in Pennsylvania, which was watched with great interest and concern in other colonies,[14] traditional leaders in a number of colonies adopted a strategy of delay. In North Carolina, for example, this delay was a defensive response to a radical faction in the Provincial Congress and has been described as a defeat for the "democratic faction."[15]

The November 1776 Orange and Mecklenburg County, North Carolina, instructions to their Provincial Congress delegates reflected the same notions of a simple, popular government as those espoused by Paine and the Pennsylvania Constitutionalists.[16] The outcome in North Carolina, however, was a compromise, including, for example, a bicameral legislature but with a wider franchise.

THE SECOND WAVE

The state constitutions of the second wave were adopted in a more deliberate fashion, often by specially elected conventions, and reflected a direct concern with mechanisms to check actions by the dominant legislative branches. The second wave was much longer than the first, lasting from 1777 through 1784, when New Hampshire finally revised its 1776 constitution.

The New York experience leading to its 1777 constitution marked the beginning of the second wave of state constitution making during the founding decade. The committee drafting the New York Constitution stretched out the process for eight months.[17] The convention avoided an earlier suffrage proposal for all white male taxpaying freeholders[18] but did agree to annual assembly elections, improved apportionment, and the gradual elimination of voice voting—a crucial change in a tenant state like New York. On the other hand, the constitution provided for a senate and for an executive veto, exercised by the governor, chief justice, and chancellor acting as the Council of Revision. The victory achieved by the radicals in Pennsylvania was transformed into, at best, a compromise in New York.[19] The experience of

13. Edward Countryman, "Some Problems of Power in New York 1777-1782," in *Sovereign States in an Age of Uncertainty*, ed. Hoffman and Albert, pp. 158-59. See also n. 31 in this article and accompanying text.

14. Selsam, *Pennsylvania Constitution of 1776*, p. 215. A North Carolina delegate to the Continental Congress wrote that "the Pennsylvania Constitution has made more tories than the whole treasury of Britain." Elisha Douglass, "Thomas Burke, Disillusioned Democrat," *North Carolina Historical Review*, 26:159, n. 34 (1949).

15. Douglass, *Rebels and Democrats*, pp. 121, 129. See also ibid., p. 123. Delay helped conservatives.

16. Philip B. Kurland and Ralph Lerner, eds., *The Founders' Constitution* (Chicago: University of Chicago Press, 1987), 1:56-58. See also M.J.C. Vile, *Constitutionalism and the Separation of Powers* (New York: Oxford University Press, Clarendon, 1967), p. 141.

17. Alfred F. Young, *The Democratic Republicans of New York: The Origins 1763-1797* (Chapel Hill: University of North Carolina Press, 1967), p. 18; Bernard Mason, *The Road to Independence: The Revolutionary Movement in New York 1773-1777* (Lexington: University of Kentucky Press, 1966), pp. 219-20.

18. Staughton Lynd, *Class Conflict, Slavery and the United States Constitution* (Indianapolis: Bobbs-Merrill, 1967), p. 38; Young, *Democratic Republicans*, pp. 18-19.

19. Young, *Democratic Republicans*, pp. 20-21. Bernard Mason concluded that the 1777 New York Constitution was a compromise but weighted on the conservative side. Mason, *Road to Independence*, p. 243.

Massachusetts with constitution making from 1776 to 1780, however, represents the best example of the second wave. In contrast to most of the other states, the processes leading to the well-known Massachusetts Constitution of 1780 are very well documented.[20]

The pressure for a legitimate state constitution to replace the modified colonial charter led to the unsuccessful legislatively proposed constitution of 1778[21] and, ultimately, to the famous Massachusetts Constitution of 1780, the oldest American constitution and a document bearing the personal mark of John Adams. The Massachusetts Frame of Government created a bicameral legislature consisting of a senate and house of representatives, "each of which shall have a negative on the other." The governor was given the veto power, subject to being overridden by a two-thirds vote in the legislature. Property requirements were imposed for voting and officeholding. Judges served during good behavior, and advisory opinions could be requested from the Supreme Judicial Court by either branch of the legislature, as well as by the governor and council.

Thus, in the period from 1776 to 1780, the clash of ideas in state constitutional conventions resulted in the development of opposing visions of government structure and power. After an initial, resounding victory in Pennsylvania in 1776, the radical vision slowly lost ground until, in 1780, it was completely rejected in Massachusetts and in the later state constitutions.

LEGISLATIVE DOMINANCE

The primary focus of the radical democrats was on the legislative branch. Issues relating to broader suffrage, fairer apportionment, annual elections, elimination of property requirements for officeholding, unicameralism, and elimination of executive interference with legislative policy were raised in virtually all of the states. Although some of the early state constitutions contained express recognition of the doctrine of separation of powers, most "tended to exalt legislative power at the expense of the executive and the judiciary."[22] This increased legislative dominance came primarily at the expense of the executive— identified with the British crown[23]— against which the colonial assemblies had struggled but never succeeded in achieving anything but shared power.

In 1787, James Madison told the federal Constitutional Convention that state legislatures had become "omnipotent" because "experience had proved a tendency in our governments to throw all power into the Legislative vortex."[24]

20. See, for example, Oscar Handlin and Mary Handlin, *Popular Sources of Political Authority: Documents on the Massachusetts Constitution of 1780* (Cambridge, MA: Harvard University Press, 1966); Robert J. Taylor, *Massachusetts, Colony to Commonwealth: Documents on the Formation of Its Constitution, 1775-1780* (Chapel Hill: University of North Carolina Press, 1961).

21. This document is found in Handlin and Handlin, *Popular Sources of Political Authority*, p. 190. This constitution and its rejection is discussed in Stephen E. Patterson, *Political Parties in Revolutionary Massachusetts* (Madison: University of Wisconsin Press, 1973), pp. 171-96.

22. William M. Wiecek, *The Guarantee Clause of the U.S. Constitution* (Ithaca, NY: Cornell University Press, 1972), p. 21.

23. For a summary of the powers of the colonial executive, see Main, *Sovereign States*, pp. 99-103. On the transitions in executive power under the first state constitutions, see Charles Thach, Jr., *The Creation of the Presidency, 1775-1789* (Baltimore, MD: Johns Hopkins Paperback, 1969), p. 27.

24. Max Farrand, ed., *The Records of the*

Even though only three states created unicameral legislatures, the radical democrats' constitutional platform in the other states advocated unicameralism as a central feature. They knew that a unicameral legislature was susceptible to vices, but they sought, according to Jesse Lemisch, to "check it from below—with more democracy—rather than from above, with less."[25] Lemisch was referring primarily to the continued use of extra-legal conventions and congresses—the people "out of doors"—and binding instructions for representatives, but the legislative accountability provisions in Pennsylvania's 1776 constitution could also be seen as examples of such checks from below.

The two basic factions that developed in each of the states during the battles over the state constitution, and that contended over the franchise, legislative structure, and executive powers, carried over into the legislative politics of the founding decade. In virtually all of the states, two "parties," described by Jackson Turner Main as the "Localists" and the "Cosmopolitans," clashed again and again over the key legislative issues of the founding decade.[26] These issues included the treatment and punishment of loyalists, price regulation, issuance of paper money, payment of the public debt, taxation policy, debtor-creditor relations, public spending, and a range

of social and cultural issues.[27]

In the majority of states, even though bicameral legislatures were created, the lower houses were clearly the more important. Not only did the membership in the lower houses expand to include "new men" through reapportionment and lower suffrage and officeholding requirements, but at the same time these bodies took on new powers formerly exercised by the colonial magistracy. Those persons who had been accustomed to controlling the colonial governments, at least within their scope of authority,[28] were extremely uncomfortable sharing with, or even losing power to, new, inexperienced, lower-class representatives. For example, "Francis Kinloch found it 'dreadful' to be mixed up with 'butchers, bakers [and] blacksmiths,' and Henry Laurens denounced inexperienced and unqualified representatives: They thought business could be 'completed with no more words than are necessary in the bargain and sale of a cow.' "[29]

There were also serious criticisms of the legislative product of the newly powerful legislatures. It was the new state legislatures' substantive record, both on its merits and in terms of the sheer volume of laws and amendments,

27. Ibid., pp. 44-79. See also Forrest McDonald, *Novus Ordo Seclorum: The Intellectual Origins of the Constitution* (Lawrence: University of Kansas Press, 1985), pp. 143-79.

28. Merrill Jensen makes the important point that in colonial times the elites actually relied on British authority to overrule unwelcome colonial decisions. Merrill Jensen, *The American Revolution within America* (New York: New York University Press, 1974), pp. 107-8.

29. Jerome J. Nadelhaft, "'The Snarls of Invidious Animals': The Democratization of Revolutionary South Carolina," in *Sovereign States in an Age of Uncertainty*, ed. Hoffman and Albert, p. 65. See also Lynd, *Class Conflict*, pp. 109-32, describing entry of "new men" into New York politics during the founding decade.

Federal Convention of 1787 (New Haven, CT: Yale University Press, 1966), 2:35.

25. Jesse Lemisch, "The American Revolution Seen from the Bottom Up," in *Towards a New Past: Dissenting Essays in American History*, ed. Barton J. Bernstein (New York: Pantheon Books, 1968), pp. 14-15.

26. Jackson Turner Main, *Political Parties before the Constitution* (Chapel Hill: University of North Carolina Press, 1973), p. 24.

that drew the most sustained criticism from traditional leaders and ultimately served as a powerful stimulus for the federal Constitutional Convention in 1787.

In those states with bicameral legislatures, the upper houses, or senates, had been intended to serve as a buffer or check on the popular lower houses. The upper houses in the Revolutionary state constitutions were the direct descendants of the colonial governors' councils,[30] which performed both executive and legislative functions. The members of the pre-Revolutionary councils, however, owed their positions to the British crown. Independence brought a dramatic change to these governmental bodies. The senators no longer owed their seats to the crown. After the Revolution, the senators were responsible to the expanded electorate.

Donald Lutz described the general picture: "The overall result was that senates were somewhat more conservative than lower houses and protected property more carefully; but they failed to provide a consistent check on lower houses, as had been intended."[31] The senators began to respond to the electorate in basically the same way as members of the lower house were responding.

GUBERNATORIAL POWER

The governorship underwent a profound transformation from an instrument of British policy during the colonial period, exercising prerogative powers, including an absolute veto of legislative

acts, to a legislatively appointed officer almost totally beholden to the newly dominant state legislatures. After struggling so long against powerful governors, it would have been impossible for the newly independent states to adopt a strong governorship. This was true even though at the time of independence there was great need for the exercise of decisive power, particularly in the context of the war.[32] A number of states initially did not even use the title "governor," preferring instead "president."

Although, as a general matter, the early state constitutions reflected a weak, legislatively dominated governor, this was not a result that was approved unanimously. Pennsylvania, in its radical 1776 constitution, provided for no executive veto. By contrast, South Carolina, in its conservative 1776 constitution, provided its president with an absolute veto over legislation. But the presidential veto in South Carolina became a target for reformers[33] and was eliminated in the 1778 revised constitution adopted by the legislature. John Rutledge had served as president under the 1776 South Carolina Constitution. He tried unsuccessfully to exercise that constitution's absolute veto to block the 1778 instrument that eliminated that very power. Rutledge also opposed the change in electing the upper house, the Legislative Council, from the assembly to the electorate.

Despite the relative weakness of most Revolutionary executives, which led James Madison to characterize the

30. Jackson Turner Main, *The Upper House in Revolutionary America 1763-1788* (Madison: University of Wisconsin Press, 1967).

31. Lutz, *Popular Consent and Popular Control*, p. 92. See also Wood, *Creation of the American Republic*, pp. 503-4.

32. Margaret Burham MacMillan, *The War Governors in the American Revolution* (New York: Columbia University Press, 1943), p. 14.

33. Nadelhaft, "'Snarls of Invidious Animals,'" p. 69; Richard Walsh, *Charleston's Sons of Liberty: A Study of the Artisans 1763-1789* (Columbia: University of South Carolina Press, 1959), pp. 81-82.

branch as "the grave of all useful talents,"[34] a number of distinguished leaders in addition to Rutledge served in the post. Among them were Patrick Henry, Thomas Jefferson, and Benjamin Harrison in Virginia; John Hancock in Massachusetts; John Dickinson in both Pennsylvania and Delaware; William Livingston in New Jersey; and Joseph Reed in Pennsylvania. Partly as a result of the stature of these governors, and partly because they exercised a wide range of statutorily granted powers beyond those formally reflected in the state constitutions, the governors, it has now been recognized, were more important, and stable, during the founding decade than it was once thought. Governors generally opposed the legislatures' popularly inspired measures to delay taxes and permit payment of debts and taxes in other than hard money. They used the medium of their annual messages to the legislature to set the agenda of public issues. For example, Edward Countryman describes the importance of the governor's constitutionally mandated message to the legislature in New York: "Clinton took that charge seriously, recommending policy after policy in his messages to the legislature. The editor of those messages finds that some 170 laws were passed and 40 other actions taken during the Confederation period in response to the governor's suggestions."[35]

New York provided for the first popularly elected governor,[36] beginning a trend toward a republican executive, elected by, and responsible to, the electorate. Also, New York began a trend toward stronger executive power. The New York Council of Revision went on to veto 58 legislative enactments prior to the federal Constitutional Convention.[37]

The question of whether a state constitution should include a gubernatorial veto became a crucial one in the processes leading to the Massachusetts Constitution of 1780. An early committee report on the rejected 1778 constitution proposed a veto power, but it did not appear in the final version rejected by the people of the towns.[38] John Adams's draft of the 1780 constitution provided for an absolute gubernatorial veto. The constitutional convention, after initially rejecting the veto on a close vote,[39] ultimately modified Adams's proposal to permit a legislative override of gubernatorial vetoes, a change that Adams later said was made "to my sorrow."[40]

34. Irving Bryant, *James Madison: The Virginia Revolutionist* (Indianapolis: Bobbs-Merrill, 1941), 1:316, quoted in Emory G. Evans, "Executive Leadership in Virginia 1776-1781: Henry, Jefferson and Nelson," in *Sovereign States in an Age of Uncertainty*, ed. Hoffman and Albert, p. 186.

35. Edward Countryman, *A People in Revolution: The American Revolution and Political Society in New York, 1760-1790* (Baltimore, MD: Johns Hopkins University Press, 1981), p. 210.

36. Main, *Sovereign States*, p. 174. Main concludes, however, that the New York governor was not a "democratic creation." Ibid., pp. 174-75. See also Wood, *Creation of the American Republic*, p. 448. Pennsylvania's 1776 constitution provided for an elected executive, but it was a weak plural Executive Council.

37. Thach, *Creation of the Presidency*, p. 39. The veto messages are contained in *Messages from the Governors*, ed. Charles Z. Lincoln (Albany, NY: J. B. Lyon, 1909), vol. 2.

38. Main, *Sovereign States*, p. 178; Thach, *Creation of the Presidency*, p. 49.

39. The vote in the convention was 44-32 to reject the veto. Two days later, the compromise proposal carried on a vote of 44-24. Oscar Handlin and Mary F. Handlin, *Commonwealth: A Study of the Role of Government in the American Economy: Massachusetts, 1774-1861*, rev. ed. (Cambridge, MA: Harvard University Press, Belknap Press, 1969), p. 25, nn. 73, 77.

40. Douglass, *Rebels and Democrats*, p. 197.

CONCLUSION

The clearly established pattern during the founding decade was a gradual transition from the early legislative dominance, or "omnipotence," toward an increased role for the executive and judicial branches.[41] The new executive and judicial powers operated as a check on recognized legislative power rather than a sharing of legislative power. It is in this sense that the concern evolved from a focus on separation of powers, which responded to grievances against the crown before the Revolution, toward practical mechanisms of checks and balances, in response to the experiences with legislatively dominated republican governments from 1776 to 1787.

In 1776 and the years immediately following, virtually all of the newly independent constitution makers' trust was placed in the legislative branch, albeit usually with two houses. As Gordon Wood has observed, at this time "a tyranny by the people was theoretically inconceivable."[42] The legislative branch had been identified with the people themselves and was viewed as a safeguard against executive abuses rather than a possible source of abuses itself. Under these circumstances, the 1776 brand of legislative supremacy, although not supported unanimously, was not surprising. Effective checks on this legislative power were not viewed, by many, as necessary. Executive and judicial power was recognized as important and distinct from legislative power but not as serving as a check on exercises of legislative power

that might encroach either on individuals' rights or upon the prerogatives of the other two branches. The 1776 Pennsylvania Constitution is the purest example of this early American constitutional thinking recognizing separation of powers but not checks and balances.[43]

This philosophy soon began to change, however, as experience under the new legislative supremacy began to be felt. More traditional leaders in the states began to frame arguments against the simple republicanism of the first wave and to argue that, for example, increased executive veto power was not inconsistent with popular sovereignty but, rather, was a necessary mechanism to control legislative power. Further, these conservatives were able to begin to separate government from the people or society and to demonstrate the need for protections from abuses by the government. In this way, even within revolutionary republican rhetoric, with its absence of reliance on hierarchical social structure that had justified "balanced government," the case could be made for checks on the misuse of power by government officials.[44] As early as 1777, in the New York Constitution, there is evidence of a distrust of the legislative branches' willingness to stay within the confines of the legislative power and to honor the limits of the state declaration of rights. The transition begun in New York was, in effect, completed with the approval of the 1780 Massachusetts Constitution. In Gordon Wood's words, "The Americans' inveterate suspicion and jealousy of political power, once

41. Wood, *Creation of the American Republic*, p. 452. The rise of judicial power during the founding decade is beyond the scope of this article. See generally ibid., pp. 453-63; Vile, *Constitutionalism*, pp. 157-58.

42. Wood, *Creation of the American Republic*, p. 62.

43. Vile, *Constitutionalism*, pp. 134-43.

44. Peter S. Onuf, "State Politics and Ideological Transformation: Gordon S. Wood's Republican Revolution," *William and Mary Quarterly*, 3d ser. 44:614 (July 1987).

concentrated almost exclusively on the Crown and its agents, was transferred to the various state legislatures."[45]

This transition in constitutional philosophy, design, and structure, however, was not purely a question of ideology.[46] In the eyes of the participants, there were immediate, practical consequences to the outcome of the debate over who should rule at home. Legislative supremacy proved to be extremely unpopular with the more traditional leaders in the states. They worked very hard to overcome the "omnipotence" of the state legislative branch, the "vortex" into which virtually all political authority was initially thrown and, later, dragged. These traditional leaders finally succeeded in surrounding the legislative branch with various checks and balances.

45. Wood, *Creation of the American Republic,* p. 409.

46. For Gordon Wood's most recent discussion of the interrelationship of ideology and human behavior, see Gordon S. Wood, "Ideology and the Origins of Liberal America," *William and Mary Quarterly,* 3d ser. 44:628-34 (July 1987). See also Jay M. Feinman, "The Role of Ideas in Legal History," *Michigan Law Review,* 78:722 (Mar. 1980).

ANNALS, *AAPSS*, **496**, March 1988

The Emerging Agenda in
State Constitutional Rights Law

By STANLEY MOSK

ABSTRACT: Since the late 1960s, more and more state high courts have placed greater reliance on their own state constitutions in extending rights protections to individuals. Because many state bills of rights are more expansive than the federal Bill of Rights, state courts have often extended rights protections beyond those granted by the U.S. Supreme Court under its interpretation of the U.S. Constitution. As a result, one can speak of an emerging agenda of rights protection in state constitutional law. Among the important items on this agenda are privacy rights, education as a fundamental right, aid to religious schools, *Miranda* warnings, searches and seizures, self-incrimination, discriminatory peremptory challenges, obscenity, and freedom of speech, including free speech in shopping centers. Such state court activity suggests a revitalization of federalism, at least within the judicial sphere.

Stanley Mosk is the senior justice of the Supreme Court of California. He has served on that court since 1964. Prior to that he was attorney general of California for six years and earlier was a trial judge in Los Angeles. He is a graduate of the University of Chicago and has honorary doctorate degrees from six law schools.

I T may appear to be species of heresy to mention alternatives to the U.S. Constitution when Americans have so recently celebrated the bicentennial of that remarkable document. My only response is that human liberty is so fundamental that we must explore every avenue for its preservation. As Justice Robert H. Jackson wrote in 1952, "We can afford no liberties with liberty itself."[1]

There are times the U.S. Constitution does not meet all the convolutions of a problem. Under those circumstances, it may be expedient to look up to international instruments or down to state constitutions. Our attention will be devoted to the latter, but we should note that there have been times, and there will be more, when courts will rely on international documents that have the force of treaties for authority to protect individual rights. These include the Universal Declaration of Human Rights and subsequent international instruments prohibiting, among other vices, torture. These acts were employed as authority by the Second Circuit in a trailblazing 1980 opinion written by Chief Judge Irving Kaufman.[2] There are a growing number of cases in which at least reference is made to, if there is not reliance on, international human rights declarations.

In recent years, however, greater reliance has been placed on individual rights protections found in state constitutions. So much activity has occurred in this field that we can speak of an emerging agenda. By definition, any agenda is a compilation of items; consequently, there will be no opportunity

here to delve into any aspect in length. The intention is to provide an overview of salient, emerging issues.

PRIVACY

Consider, for openers, the right of privacy. In courts throughout the land, that somewhat elusive concept is being urged and generally accepted. It must be placed high on any agenda.

It is significant that in many respects the Universal Declaration of Human Rights and the American state constitutions protect individuals in a similar manner and more expansively than does the U.S. Constitution. For example, although the U.S. Supreme Court has on occasion found privacy to be among so-called penumbral rights, there is no specific guarantee of privacy in the federal Bill of Rights. On the other hand, in the Universal Declaration, article 12, there is this broad language: "No one shall be subject to arbitrary interference with his privacy, family, home or correspondence, nor to attacks upon his honour and reputation." Article I, section 1, of the California Constitution declares that among the inalienable rights are "pursuing and obtaining safety, happiness, and privacy." This kind of protection of privacy can be found in a number of other state constitutions.

Consider, for example, that a police officer or a public prosecutor may walk into a bank and, with no authority of process, demand to examine the bank records of a named individual or corporation. There is no constitutional violation here, said the U.S. Supreme Court in *United States* v. *Miller*.[3] Some state courts, however, have argued that a person's canceled checks, loan applications, and other banking transactions

1. *United States* v. *Spector*, 343 U.S. 169, 180 (1952).
2. *Filartiga* v. *Pena-Irala*, 630 F.2d 876 (1980).

3. 425 U.S. 435 (1976).

are a minibiography, that one reasonably expects one's bank records to be used only for internal bank processes, and that, therefore, an examination of them violates the state constitutional right of privacy, unless the records are obtained by a warrant or subpoena.[4] Does one reasonably expect privacy in credit card records or unlisted telephone numbers? Tune in later.

EDUCATION

To most of us, learning and knowledge are our most prized possessions. Yet the U.S. Supreme Court has never recognized education to be a fundamental right. Indeed, in *San Antonio Independent School District* v. *Rodriguez*,[5] the Court specifically held that education is not a fundamental right. The Court has never retreated from that position. In 1986, it reached a similar conclusion in *Papasan* v. *Allain*.[6] The Court has come no closer than *Plyer* v. *Doe*,[7] in which it applied a higher scrutiny standard to a statute that denied basic education to alien, undocumented school-age children; yet even under that standard, it reiterated that education is not a fundamental right under the U.S. Constitution.

Contrast that result with the growing number of states that have recognized the inherent value of public education. California, in its celebrated *Serrano* v. *Priest* case,[8] openly broke away from the U.S. Supreme Court's reticence and firmly declared that "the distinctive and priceless function of education in our society warrants, indeed compels, our treating it as a fundamental interest." Relying on state authority, particularly requirements of compulsory school attendance, the *Serrano* court quoted the credo of Horace Mann:

I believe in the existence of a great, immortal, immutable principle of natural law, or natural ethics—a principle, antecedent to all human institutions, and incapable of being abrogated by any ordinance of man . . . which proves the *absolute right* to an education of every human being that comes into the world, and which, of course, proves the correlative duty of every government to see that the means of that education are provided for all.[9]

High courts in Connecticut, Michigan, Wyoming, Arizona, Mississippi, Washington, Wisconsin, and West Virginia have reached the same fundamental conclusion.

Aid to religious schools

The revival of religious fervor in the United States—and throughout the world—and the aggressiveness of the fundamentalist movement indicate future church-state conflict. In this area, U.S. Supreme Court cases have not been a model of clarity.

In *Everson* v. *Board of Education* (1947),[10] the Court upheld a New Jersey statute that authorized reimbursement of parents for fares paid by them to transport their children to public or nonprofit private schools, including religious schools, by carrier. In a 5-4 decision, the majority held that the legislation did no more than provide a general program to assist parents, regard-

4. *Burrows* v. *Superior Court*, 529 P.2d 590 (Cal. 1974).
5. 411 U.S. 1 (1973).
6. 92 L. Ed. 2d 209 (1986).
7. 457 U.S. 202 (1982).
8. 487 P.2d 1241 (Cal. 1971).

9. Quoted in *Readings in American Education*, ed. William H. Lucio (Chicago: Scott, Foresman, 1963), p. 336, italics in original.
10. 330 U.S. 1 (1947).

less of their religion, to get their children to school safely and expeditiously.

The first case dealing with the constitutionality of providing textbooks for use in religious schools was *Board of Education* v. *Allen* (1968).[11] Under consideration was a New York law that authorized public school authorities to lend textbooks free of charge to all students in certain grades, including students in private schools. The Court invoked what has come to be called the child-benefit theory. It held that the financial benefit provided by the program was to the children and their parents rather than to the parochial schools and that no funds or books were furnished to the schools. Moreover, the Court held that books, unlike buses, are critical to the teaching process, that religious schools pursue both religious instruction and secular education, and that the record did not support the proposition that textbooks on nonreligious subjects were used by the parochial schools to teach religion. Still later, the Supreme Court declared that a law that confers an indirect, remote, and incidental benefit on religious institutions is not for that reason alone unconstitutional.[12]

Trying to reconcile those cases with others, such as *Meek* v. *Pittenger, Wolman* v. *Walter, Levitt* v. *Committee for Public Education, Lemon* v. *Kurtzman, Walz* v. *Tax Commission*, and *Norwood* v. *Harrison*,[13] is an exercise in futility. In *California Teachers Association* v. *Riles*,[14] the California Supreme Court bluntly declared, "We are unable to harmonize the holdings of these cases."

The child-benefit theory has been criticized by several state courts on the ground that it proves too much. If the fact that a child is aided by an expenditure of public money insulates a statute from challenge, constitutional proscriptions on state aid to sectarian schools would be virtually eradicated. There is no logical stopping point. The doctrine may be used to justify any type of aid to sectarian schools because, as was stated in an Oklahoma case, "practically every proper expenditure for school purposes aids the child."[15]

It is impossible to predict how many states will rely on their own constitution to retain the traditional wall of separation, but some already have done so. Others will face the test in the near future. Many states have constitutional provisions more precise and sweeping than the First Amendment. Typical are these provisions in article XVI, section 5, of the California Constitution:

Neither the Legislature, nor any county, city and county, township, school district, or other municipal corporation, shall ever make an appropriation, or pay from any public fund whatever, or grant anything to or in aid of any religious sect, church, creed, or sectarian purpose, or help to support or sustain any school, college, university, hospital, or other institution controlled by any religious creed, church, or sectarian denomination whatever; nor shall any grant or donation of personal property or real estate ever be made by the state, or any city, city and county, town, or other municipal corporation for any religious creed, church, or sectarian purpose whatever.

Nebraska, Oregon, and other states have similar constitutional provisions and thus have been more strict than the

11. 392 U.S. 236 (1968).
12. *Committee for Public Education* v. *Nyquist*, 413 U.S. 756 (1973).
13. Respectively, 421 U.S. 349 (1975); 433 U.S. 229 (1977); 413 U.S. 472 (1973); 403 U.S. 602 (1971); 397 U.S. 664 (1970); 413 U.S. 455 (1973).
14. 632 P.2d 953 (Cal. 1981).
15. *Gurney* v. *Ferguson*, 122 P.2d 1002 (1942).

U.S. Supreme Court in enforcing church-state separation.[16]

MIRANDA

High on the constitutional agenda in the next few years will be *Miranda*[17] and what, if anything, to do about it. U.S. Attorney General Edwin Meese III has led a frontal charge against that bulwark of the Warren Court era. Will the Supreme Court capitulate?

Professor Yale Kamisar has written that the current Supreme Court believes that the *Miranda* ruling rejected "the more extreme position that the actual presence of a lawyer was necessary to dispel the coercion inherent in custodial interrogation."[18] Instead, the Warren Court settled for police-issued warnings that permit someone subjected to arrest and detention to waive his or her rights without actually receiving the guidance of counsel. Depending on one's viewpoint, says Kamisar, this is the *Miranda* case's great weakness or saving grace.

Attorney General Meese has taken a more extreme position, rejecting the right of suspects to terminate interrogation either by saying that they want to do so or that they desire to have the advice of a lawyer. Instead, the recent report of his office calls such persons uncooperative suspects and argues that the police should be able to undertake persuasion to induce the suspect to change his or her mind and talk—translation: to confess.

Many observers doubt that the attor-ney general will succeed in this effort. The overruling of precedent prevailing for two decades or more is a slow process. It is usually accomplished in a succession of cases. It is seldom done from the bully pulpit or by press release.

In short, to paraphrase Mark Twain, the death of *Miranda* is exaggerated. Reversals of former precedent are not unprecedented, however. Remember the fate of *Lochner* v. *New York*, *Pace* v. *Alabama*, *Plessy* v. *Ferguson*, *Minersville* v. *Gobitis*, *Swain* v. *Alabama*, and others.[19]

When *Miranda* was announced in 1966, many states were reluctant to accept it. Some were dragged kicking and screaming into conformity, but conform they did. The question will be, If *Miranda* expires, will some states revert to their pre-*Miranda* policy of anything goes at the station house, or will they insist on some form of *Miranda* warning under state constitutional authority?

Unless the U.S. Supreme Court rules that a *Miranda* warning is forbidden—which seems inconceivable—many, if not most, states will probably adhere to the state rules that they adopted to conform to *Miranda*. It has taken two decades, but law enforcement officers in the states have become reconciled to giving appropriate warnings to suspects. Trial judges also understand that they must reject statements obtained from defendants who were not warned. Many of the state decisions have been based on state constitutions.

For example, in *Harris* v. *New York*,[20] the U.S. Supreme Court permitted statements obtained in violation of *Miranda* to be used for impeachment purposes.

16. *Gaffney* v. *State Department of Education*, 220 N.W.2d 550 (Neb. 1974); *Dickman* v. *School District No. 62C, Oregon City*, 336 P.2d 533 (Ore. 1962); *California Teachers Association* v. *Riles*, 632 P.2d 953 (Cal. 1981).
17. *Miranda* v. *Arizona*, 384 U.S. 436 (1966).
18. *Los Angeles Times*, 11 Feb. 1987.
19. Respectively, 198 U.S. 45 (1905); 106 U.S. 583 (1882); 163 U.S. 537 (1896); 310 U.S. 586 (1940); 380 U.S. 202 (1965).
20. 401 U.S. 222 (1971).

California and several other states, however, have held that if a statement offends *Miranda*, it is useless for all purposes. Here is a forthright declaration of state independence in *People* v. *Disbrow*:

We therefore hold that the privilege against self-incrimination of Article I, section 15, of the California Constitution precludes use by the prosecution of any extrajudicial statement by the defendant, whether inculpatory or exculpatory, either as affirmative evidence or for purposes of impeachment, obtained during custodial interrogation in violation of the standards declared in *Miranda* and its California progeny. Accordingly, we . . . declare that *Harris* is not persuasive authority in any state prosecution in California.[21]

To the same effect are *State* v. *Santiago*, a Hawaii case, and *Butler* v. *State*, a Texas case.[22] Note this quotation from *Butler*: "*Harris*, of course, in no way obligates [state courts] to overturn prior decisions as a matter of state criminal procedure. . . . Therefore, we cannot agree with the [prosecution's] contention despite the natural temptation to rush to accept the *Harris* rationale. The beauty is only skin deep."

SEARCH AND SEIZURE

Another hole was dug in the exclusionary rule by the U.S. Supreme Court in 1984. In *United States* v. *Leon*,[23] the Court announced the good-faith exception to the exclusionary rule: in the absence of an allegation that the magistrate abandoned his or her detached and neutral role, suppression of evidence from the prosecution's case-in-chief is, as a matter of federal law, appropriate only if the officers were dishonest in preparing their affidavit for a search warrant or could not have harbored an objectively reasonable belief in the existence of probable cause.

In addressing the question of the proper remedy to be applied to a concededly unconstitutional search, the Court answered by "weighing the costs and benefits of preventing the use in the prosecution's case-in-chief of inherently trustworthy tangible evidence obtained in reliance on a search warrant issued by a detached and neutral magistrate that ultimately is found to be defective."

The good-faith doctrine was expanded to include reasonableness in the *Garrison* case, decided in February 1987.[24] There the Baltimore police invaded the wrong apartment, but in a 6-3 vote Justice John Paul Stevens held for the Court that the validity of the search depended on whether the officers' failure was "objectively understandable and reasonable."

Several state courts, on state constitutional grounds, have declined to follow *Leon* and probably will do the same with regard to *Garrison*. All the cases to date have involved searches conducted pursuant to a warrant later determined to be invalid.

In *State* v. *Novembrino*, the New Jersey Supreme Court, in a lengthy opinion, refused to follow *Leon* because (1) its long-run effect would be to undermine the integrity of the warrant process by diminishing the quality of evidence presented in search warrant applications; (2) it would "ultimately reduce respect for and compliance with the probable-cause standard"; (3) it is inconsistent with the state constitution as interpreted; (4) there was no evidence that the crim-

21. 545 P.2d 272 (Cal. 1976).
22. Respectively, 492 P.2d 657 (Hawaii 1971); 493 S.W.2d 190 (Tex. 1973).
23. 468 U.S. 897 (1984).

24. *Maryland* v. *Garrison*, 94 L. Ed. 2d 72 (Md. 1987).

inal justice system was impaired by the requirement of probable cause; and (5) there is no satisfactory alternative to the exclusionary rule.[25]

The New York court, in *People* v. *Bigelow*, declined to follow *Leon* because it (1) frustrates the exclusionary rule's purposes; (2) places a premium on the illegal police action; and (3) provides an incentive for "others to engage in similar lawless acts."[26]

The Michigan court, in *People* v. *Sundling*, rejected *Leon* because (1) the magistrate's decision would, as a practical matter, be insulated from appellate review; (2) the exception would result in increased illegal police activity; and (3) the Court's claim that the exclusionary rule is not working is not supported—indeed, is contradicted—by the evidence.[27]

Justice James L. Robertson in Mississippi declared that the exclusionary rule is necessary to guarantee that magistrates "take seriously their responsibilit[y] to ensure that people are free of unconstitutional searches" and that *Leon* undermines the integrity of the judicial process.[28] The Wisconsin Supreme Court refused to employ *Leon* because the state constitution and prior Wisconsin court decisions interpreting it hold that the receipt into evidence of the fruits of an invalid search warrant violates the defendant's state constitutional rights.[29]

It would appear that if state courts can find other ways of rejecting *Leon* and retaining the rule of excluding illegally obtained evidence, they will do so.

Automobile searches

Motor vehicles present a particular problem for courts as they grapple with the boundaries of permissible searches. If a motorist is stopped by a police officer for a simple traffic violation, the motorist may be subjected to a full body search, and the vehicle may be searched, too. There is no constitutional violation here, the U.S. Supreme Court has said.[30] But Hawaii and other states have found such police conduct to be offensive to state constitutional provisions unless the officer has articulable reasons to suspect illegal conduct other than the minor traffic infraction.

Most courts have difficulty ascertaining the limits, if any, of automobile searches in light of more recent federal opinions. If a vehicle is stopped on mere suspicion, may the car be searched without a warrant? What about the glove compartment, trunk, or a closed container in the trunk? If the vehicle is a van with a bed, kitchen, closet, curtained window, and so forth, does it have the qualities of an automobile because it is mobile, or is it entitled to the protections of a home because one lives in it? These are areas in which the states are likely to reach independent and varying conclusions.

The right of police to inventory the contents of an impounded motor vehicle results in another conflict between U.S. Supreme Court and state court decisions. In *South Dakota* v. *Opperman*,[31] the Court held inventory searches of automobiles to be consistent with the Fourth Amendment. In a recent case, the Court justified the inventory as a means to protect the police and garage attendants

25. *State* v. *Novembrino*, 519 A.2d 820 (N.J. 1987).

26. 497 N.Y.S.2d 630 (N.Y. 1985).

27. 395 N.W.2d 308 (Mich. 1986).

28. *Stringer* v. *State*, 491 So.2d 837 (Miss. 1986).

29. *State* v. *Grawien*, 367 N.W.2d 816 (Wis. 1985).

30. *United States* v. *Robinson*, 414 U.S. 218 (1973); *Gustafson* v. *Florida*, 414 U.S. 260 (1973).

31. 428 U.S. 364 (1976).

from subsequent false claims of theft.[32]

Colorado, however, reached a different conclusion, as did California.[33] Because property could conceivably disappear prior to or during an inventory, both states believed that a simpler solution would be to lock and seal the automobile in a secure parking facility. The *Mozzetti* case was particularly egregious: the woman was not a criminal suspect, she had been in an automobile accident, and had been taken to the hospital. It is difficult to justify the police searching her car trunk and examining a closed suitcase on the back seat, all on an inventory theory.

SELF-INCRIMINATION

Another significant federal-state conflict arises over the use of a defendant's pretrial silence. All jurisdictions agree that, as held in *Griffin* v. *California*,[34] the silence of a defendant, under a claim of privilege against self-incrimination, may not be admitted in the prosecution's case-in-chief. There is some divergence, however, as to the use of such silence for impeachment purposes.

Jenkins v. *Anderson*[35] approved the prosecutor's use for impeachment purposes of a defendant's failure to surrender for two weeks, when he claimed on the stand that his act of killing was in self-defense. Most state cases agree on a theory that the silence must amount to an invocation of Fifth Amendment rights in order to be excluded.

After arrest, however, the dichotomy depends on whether *Miranda* warnings

have been given. If so, *Doyle* v. *Ohio*[36] controls. Obviously, it would be unconscionable to penalize defendants for remaining silent after they have been told by the authorities that they have a right to refuse to talk.

If *Miranda* warnings have not been given, however, the U.S. Supreme Court held, defendants' constitutional rights are not violated by permitting them to be cross-examined about their pre-*Miranda* silence.[37] The Court reasoned that because there were no affirmative assurances as a result of the failure to give a *Miranda* warning, no fundamental unfairness would arise from allowing the defendants' silence to be used for impeachment purposes.

Courts in Washington, Connecticut, Alaska, New Jersey, Pennsylvania, Texas, and California have reached a contrary conclusion. The California court relied entirely on the state constitution. A fear was expressed in several of these state cases that to allow the defendant's silence to be used for any purpose would invite the police to dispense with *Miranda* warnings. These cases also expressed concern that silence used for impeachment would likely be used by the jury in determining guilt.

PEREMPTORY CHALLENGES

There is no better example of how the states can be laboratories for development of the law than the fate of *Swain* v. *Alabama*.[38] In that case, the majority of the U.S. Supreme Court held that there could be no limitations on the exercise of peremptory challenges. A modest concession was made if a defendant could demonstrate a long pattern of

32. *Colorado* v. *Bertine*, 93 L. Ed. 2d 739 (1987).

33. *People* v. *Bertine*, 706 P.2d 411 (Colo. 1985); *People* v. *Mozzetti*, 484 P.2d 84 (Cal. 1971).

34. 380 U.S. 609 (1965).

35. 447 U.S. 231 (1980).

36. 426 U.S. 610 (1976).

37. *Fletcher* v. *Weir*, 455 U.S. 603 (1982).

38. 380 U.S. 202 (1965).

discriminatory use of the challenges. Such demonstration, of course, is impossible. How can a defendant, while jury selection is under way, demonstrate that the prosecutor had employed discriminatory tactics in some number of previous cases in which, of course, the defendant was not involved and in which the racial characteristics of previous jurors were not recorded?

California specifically rejected *Swain*.[39] The state court held that there could be a limitation on peremptory challenges if they were employed for a discriminatory purpose. The method of ascertaining the systematic exclusion of a cognizable group was described in detail, and if a prima facie case of discrimination was evident, the trial judge could call on the prosecutor to explain each of his or her challenges. If the prosecutor failed the test, the entire jury panel was to be excused and a new panel brought in to start the proceedings over.

Massachusetts adopted much the same procedure, and a number of other states have acted similarly.

Last year, however, in *Batson* v. *Kentucky*,[40] the U.S. Supreme Court admitted that *Swain* is not workable and conceded that the use of peremptory challenges for racially discriminatory purposes must not be condoned. This ruling suggests that state courts can have a significant effect on the pattern of the law, even federal law.

OBSCENITY

A conflict is inevitable between national and state standards in the field of obscenity. Under the U.S. Supreme

Court's *Miller* rubric,[41] material is obscene if (1) it depicts sexual conduct in a patently offensive manner; (2) the average person, applying contemporary state standards, would find that it, taken as a whole, appeals to a prurient interest in sex; and (3) taken as a whole, it lacks serious literary, artistic, political, or scientific value.

Recently, in the case of *State* v. *Henry*,[42] a proprietor of an adult bookstore was convicted by a trial court after his entire inventory was seized in a police raid. The Oregon Supreme Court reversed, declaring that its state constitution was written by "rugged and robust individuals dedicated to founding a free society unfettered by the governmental imposition of some people's views of morality on the free expression of others." Oregon's pioneers intended to protect freedom of expression "on any subject whatever," including the subject of sex. In rejecting the *Miller* rule, the court declared: "In this state any person can write, print, read, say, show or sell anything to a consenting adult even though that expression may be generally or universally considered 'obscene.'"

FREE SPEECH IN SHOPPING MALLS

A very interesting and important federal-state dichotomy is in the history of a not uncommon factual situation: a small orderly group of citizens undertakes to pass out leaflets, or solicit signatures on petitions, in a privately owned shopping center. The mall owners seek to prohibit that activity.

Obviously there is a built-in tension here between two constitutional guaran-

39. *People* v. *Wheeler*, 583 P.2d 748 (Cal. 1978).
40. 90 L. Ed. 2d 69 (1986).
41. *Miller* v. *California*, 413 U.S. 15 (1973).
42. 732 P.2d 9 (Ore. 1987).

tees. On the one hand, the citizens assert their right of freedom of speech and the right to petition their government for a redress of grievances. On the other hand, the shopping center owner asserts his right to control his private property and to exclude all activity not related to the business of the shopping center. In that conflict, which right is to prevail?

The Supreme Court of California held in 1970, in *Diamond* v. *Bland*, that unless there is obstruction or undue interference with normal business operations, the bare title of the property owners does not outweigh the substantial interest of individuals and groups to engage in peaceful and orderly free speech and petitioning activities on the premises of shopping centers open to the public.[43] This, of course, is subject to reasonable time, place, and manner restrictions.

On four occasions the shopping center owner sought certiorari and a rehearing from denial of certiorari. In each instance he was rebuffed by the U.S. Supreme Court, with no votes noted to grant. The California court, therefore, had every reason to believe that *Diamond* v. *Bland* was acceptable law.

Two years later, however, the U.S. Supreme Court took over an almost identical case from Oregon, and in *Lloyd* v. *Tanner*[44] held that the owners had the right to prohibit distribution of political handbills unrelated to the operation of the shopping center.

Back to the California Supreme Court came the owner in *Diamond* v. *Bland*. He asked to be relieved from the previous orders. A 4-3 majority of the court agreed that the state was bound by *Lloyd* v. *Tanner*.

In its original opinion, the court had relied on the First Amendment to the U.S. Constitution and on related federal cases. On this second round, I urged the same result under "unmistakable independent non-federal grounds upon which our earlier opinion could have been based," but a majority of the court retained consistency with federal law.

Five years later, though, in 1979, a new majority of the court decided in *Robins* v. *Pruneyard* that the free-speech provisions of the California Constitution offer "greater protection than the First Amendment now seems to provide."[45]

When the U.S. Supreme Court granted certiorari in *Robins* v. *Pruneyard*, the California court sensed doom to its theory of state constitutionalism. But the Supreme Court agreed with the California ruling, 9-0. Justice William H. Rehnquist wrote the opinion, which declared that the reasoning in *Lloyd* v. *Tanner* "does not ex proprio vigore limit the authority of the State to exercise its police power or its sovereign right to adopt in its constitution individual liberties more expansive than those conferred by the Federal Constitution."[46]

CONCLUSION

No doubt there is growing interest in true federalism today. There was a time when states' rights were associated with Orval Faubus and George Wallace barring the entrance of blacks to public schools. We are long past that confrontational period.

Today, states' rights are associated with increased, not lessened, individual guarantees. There is every indication, particularly since *Pruneyard*, that the

---

43. *Diamond* v. *Bland*, 477 P.2d 733.
44. 407 U.S. 551 (1972).

45. 592 P.2d 341.
46. *Pruneyard Shopping Center* v. *Robins*, 447 U.S. 74, 81 (1980).

Rehnquist Court will defer to the states when they rely on state constitutional provisions.

At the top of any agenda for the bicentennial of the Constitution should be a consideration of James Madison's words in *Federalist* Number 45:

The powers delegated by the proposed Constitution to the federal government are few and defined. Those which are to remain in the State governments are numerous and indefinite. The former will be exercised principally on external objects, as war, peace, negotiation, and foreign commerce; with which last the power of taxation will, for the most part, be connected. The powers reserved to the several States will extend to all the objects which, in the ordinary course of affairs, concern the lives, liberties, and properties of the people, and the internal order, improvement, and prosperity of the State.

Sound policy 200 years ago. Sound policy today.

ANNALS, *AAPSS*, **496**, March 1988

Religion under
State Constitutions

By G. ALAN TARR

ABSTRACT: State constitutional provisions concerning church and state differ in specificity and substance from the First Amendment's establishment clause. In large part, these differences reflect the fact that the state provisions originated in concrete historical disputes. After the American colonies declared independence, conflict over established churches led states to adopt provisions safeguarding freedom of worship and prohibiting aid to religious institutions. During the nineteenth century, conflict between Protestants and Catholics over education resulted in the adoption in most states of provisions banning aid to parochial schools and prohibiting religious influences in schools receiving public funds. Reliance on either state or federal constitutional guarantees, therefore, should result in invalidation of religious exercises in public schools. In other cases, however, outcomes may depend on the constitutional basis for decisions. Whereas various indirect aids to parochial schools have survived scrutiny under the establishment clause, they may run afoul of state constitutional bans; and whereas the U.S. Supreme Court has upheld religious displays, some state courts have ruled that they violate state constitutional prohibitions.

G. Alan Tarr received his B.A. at the College of the Holy Cross and his M.A. and Ph.D. in political science at the University of Chicago. A former Constitutional Fellow of the National Endowment for the Humanities, he has published several books and numerous scholarly articles on constitutional law and on state courts. He is currently associate professor and chairperson of the Political Science Department at Rutgers University in Camden.

NOTE: The research for this article was supported in part by a fellowship from the National Endowment for the Humanities and a grant from the Rutgers University Research Council. The author gratefully acknowledges their generous support.

A MONG the most noteworthy legal
developments of the past two decades has been the rediscovery of state
bills of rights as bases for judicial rulings
safeguarding civil liberties. This phenomenon, which has been labeled the
new judicial federalism, has been chroni-
cled in numerous articles heralding the
emergence of state civil liberties law.[1]
Yet despite this renewed interest in state
constitutional law, commentators have
generally ignored state provisions and
judicial decisions dealing with church
and state. This is unfortunate because,
given the widespread dissatisfaction with
the U.S. Supreme Court's rulings on
church and state, it seems worthwhile to
consider whether state constitutional
guarantees might afford surer and more
consistent direction than can be found
in federal decisional law. Equally important, these state constitutional provisions, having grown out of particular
church-state conflicts in the states, provide a distinctive perspective on the
vexing problems of church and state.

THE DEVELOPMENT OF
STATE GUARANTEES

Virtually every student of American
constitutional law is familiar with the
battle, led by James Madison and
Thomas Jefferson, for religious freedom
in Virginia. Scholars and jurists have
usually focused on the implications of
the conflict for the interpretation of the
First Amendment's religion clauses. Yet

1. For a survey of literature on the new
judicial federalism, see Ronald K.L. Collins, "State
Constitutional Law," *National Law Journal*, 29
Sept. 1986, pp. S-9 to S-19. See also Ronald K.L.
Collins, Peter J. Galie, and John Kincaid, "State
High Courts, State Constitutions, and Individual
Rights Litigation since 1980: A Judicial Survey,"
Publius: The Journal of Federalism, 16:141
(Summer 1986).

the disestablishment struggle in Virginia
is also vitally important for the interpretation of state constitutional provisions.

Most obviously, this struggle illustrates that a state can devise its own
solution to the problems of church and
state. Indeed, this is what occurred.
Between the Declaration of Independence and the ratification of the U.S.
Constitution—that is, before the national
government addressed the issue—each
of the original 13 states reconsidered the
relationship between church and state
within its borders. In most instances,
this reconsideration led to the formal-
ization of new church-state arrangements
in the state constitutions.

Despite variation in the pace and
course of disestablishment, the overall
direction of change was, as in Virginia,
toward greater religious liberty. Typically, the states framed their constitutional bans on religious establishments
in repudiation of the most objectionable
features of the colonial experience,
namely, infringements on freedom of
worship, and taxation for the support of
an established church. Pennsylvania's
constitutional guarantee, adopted in
1776, is representative: "That all men
have a natural and indefeasible right to
worship Almighty God according to the
dictates of their own consciences; that
no man can of right be compelled to
attend, erect, or support any place of
worship, or to maintain any ministry,
against his consent."[2]

Yet disestablishment is not the whole
story of this first phase of state constitution making. The states eliminated coercion in religious matters largely out of
religious faith, in order to permit all
people to respond freely to what they
regarded as the call of God's grace. This

2. Pa. Const. art. II (1776).

is evident from the predominance of Baptists and members of other dissenting sects in the forefront of those championing disestablishment. Moreover, other provisions show that the state constitutions did not embody a secularist perspective on public life.

In marked contrast with their federal counterpart, most early state constitutions expressly recognized the existence of God, and most later state constitutions acknowledged the state's dependence on God's favor. The New Jersey Constitution of 1776, for example, decreed that "no person shall ever, within this Colony, be deprived of the inestimable privilege of worshipping Almighty God in a manner agreeable to the dictates of his own conscience"; and the state's constitution of 1844 added:

We, the people of the State of New Jersey, grateful to Almighty God for the civil and religious liberty which He hath so long permitted us to enjoy, and looking to Him for a blessing upon our endeavors to secure and transmit the same unimpaired to succeeding generations, do ordain and establish this CONSTITUTION.[3]

In addition, whereas the United States Constitution is silent on people's religious duties, several early state constitutions are not. The Massachusetts Constitution of 1780, for example, states that "it is the right as well as the duty of all men in society, publicly, and at stated seasons to worship the Supreme Being." Virginia's 1776 constitution notes that "it is the mutual duty of all to practice Christian forbearance, love, and charity towards each other."[4] Finally, in contrast to the U.S. Constitution, which forbids religious tests, several early state constitutions either prescribed beliefs to be held by officeholders or prohibited clergy from holding public office.[5]

As these provisions indicate, the early state constitutions did not seek to circumscribe the influence of religion in society or to eliminate religious influences on government but rather to prevent governmental intrusion into the religious sphere. The prevailing assumption was that government would continue to be supportive of religion in general and Protestant Christianity in particular, although this support would not take the form of direct subvention. Political and legal practice during the early nineteenth century was consistent with this assumption. State courts continued to recognize Christianity as part of the common law and to sustain convictions for blasphemy when speakers disparaged Christian beliefs.[6] Similarly, despite acknowledging the religious character of Sunday closing laws, state courts upheld them, noting in one case that "the Christian religion may be protected from desecration by such laws as the legislature in its wisdom may deem necessary."[7] Thus state constitutions were interpreted so as to protect Christianity and to enforce the prevailing, Protestant consensus.

If disputes over formal religious establishments supplied the initial impetus for state constitutional development, conflict over education provided the second. The institution of free public education forced educators and governmental officials to consider what

3. N.J. Const. art. XVIII (1776); ibid., preamble and art. I, § 3 (1844).
4. Mass. Const. pt. I, art. III (1780); Va. Const., declaration of rights, art. I, § 16 (1776).
5. See, for example, N.C. Const. art. XXXII (1776); S.C. Const. art. XXI (1778).
6. See, for example, *People* v. *Ruggles*, 4 N.Y.R. 545 (N.Y. 1811).
7. *Neuendorff* v. *Duryea*, 69 N.Y. 557, 563 (N.Y. 1887).

place religion should occupy in the newly founded public schools. Initially, the religious homogeneity of the populace encouraged public officials and teachers to give a Protestant orientation to public education. Prayer and Bible reading were used to inculcate morality, and the entire curriculum, from the materials used in teaching to the interpretation of religious conflicts in modern European history, reflected the perspective of Protestant Christianity. But the immigration of large numbers of Roman Catholics to America during the 1830s and 1840s prompted challenges to the schools' Protestant ethos. Catholic prelates in New York and other cities charged that the public schools were in reality tax-supported Protestant schools and demanded that Catholic schools share equally in tax revenues.

Even though these demands were not met, they did spark considerable constitutional activity. In states in which religious conflict was intense, constitutional provisions were adopted to end the conflict. In other states, constitution makers, mindful of the corrosive effect of religious conflict on public peace, adopted constitutional provisions to forestall conflict. In some religiously homogeneous states, in which aid to parochial schools never emerged as a serious issue, constitution makers nonetheless incorporated the constitutional language of sister states in their own constitutions. As a result, during the nineteenth century, most states addressed the issue of religion and education in their constitutions.

The states' treatment of this issue was strikingly uniform. As Anson Phelps Stokes and Leo Pfeffer have noted, "From 1844 on, all states amending their constitutions, and new states when admitted to the Union (except West

Virginia, which later corrected the omission), decreed in their fundamental laws against any diversion of public funds to denominational purposes."[8] Many states also prohibited religious practices in schools receiving public funds. The Washington Constitution of 1889 is representative. Its declaration of rights mandates that "no public money or property shall be appropriated for or applied to any religious worship, exercise or instruction, or the support of any religious establishment." The education article of the constitution requires that "all schools maintained or supported wholly or in part by the public funds shall be forever free from sectarian control or influence."[9]

This brief analysis of the two great periods of state constitutional activity regarding church and state permits several conclusions. First, whereas the constitutional provisions governing the relationship between church and state under the U.S. Constitution were adopted during the founding era and have not since been altered, the states have amended and revised their constitutions in recognition of changing views and in response to the emergence of new church-state issues. Second, because state constitutional provisions characteristically originated out of specific disputes, these provisions represent, for the most part, considered constitutional judgments about contentious issues of church and state. Third, state constitutional provisions tend to be concrete and detailed, because they are framed in language aimed at the specific evils that brought them forth. Consequently, they lend

8. Anson Phelps Stokes and Leo Pfeffer, *Church and State in the United States* (New York: Harper & Row, 1950), p. 271.
9. Wash. Const. art. I, § 11; ibid., art. IX, § 4 (1889).

themselves to direct application with only minimal interpretation. Finally, despite interstate variation, what is striking are the commonalities in how state constitutions deal with the relations between church and state.

Most state constitutions acknowledge the existence of God in their preambles, and some even encourage citizens to worship God. Yet almost all contain emphatic prohibitions on favoritism toward a particular religion and on aid to religious groups or institutions. These prohibitions generally are premised on the belief that it is important to avoid intrusion by government into the realm of freedom of conscience. Most state constitutions also seek to maintain a separation of church and state in the realm of education, in part by safeguarding public funds for public schools and by preventing their diversion to sectarian institutions or purposes, and in part by banning religious practices in schools receiving state funds.

Yet a few states in the late nineteenth and early twentieth centuries sought to ensure that these constitutional bans would not interfere with certain traditional practices, such as Bible reading in the public schools, by inserting provisions that either permitted or required such practices.[10] The very adoption of these provisions, however, implies that in their absence, such practices would be impermissible. Such provisions, therefore, direct our attention to how state constitutions have been interpreted and to how they should be interpreted in resolving long-standing and current issues of church and state.[11]

THE INTERPRETATION OF STATE CONSTITUTIONS

Because almost all state constitutions prohibit aid to schools that are controlled by religious denominations or that teach religious doctrines, few cases have arisen in state courts involving direct aid to such schools. State courts have often considered, however, the constitutionality of indirect aid to religious schools and their students, such as the provision of transportation or textbooks to children attending nonpublic schools. Because the U.S. Supreme Court has ruled that such programs do not transgress the First Amendment, the basis for challenge has typically been the state constitutions.[12]

Indirect aid to nonpublic schools

Given the no-aid language found in most state constitutions and the historical circumstances leading to its adoption, it seems reasonable to conclude that indirect aid to parochial schools should also be viewed as constitutionally suspect. Some states, recognizing this, have revised their constitutions to permit such aid. Thus in 1947, after the New Jersey Court of Errors and Appeals had upheld a program of bus transportation for parochial school students in *Everson*, the state sought to ensure that future judges would not reverse the decision. It therefore specifically authorized such programs in its new constitution.[13] After

---

10. See, for example, Miss. Const. art. III, § 18 (1890).

11. The next section draws upon material presented in G. Alan Tarr, "State Constitutionalism and 'First Amendment Rights,'" in *Human*

Rights in the States, ed. Stanley H. Friedelbaum (Westport, CT: Greenwood, 1988).

12. On provision of bus transportation, see *Everson* v. *Board of Education*, 330 U.S. 1 (1947); on the loaning of textbooks, see *Board of Education* v. *Allen*, 392 U.S. 236 (1968).

13. N.J. Const. art. VIII, § 4, para. 3 (1947), *confirming Everson* v. *Board of Education*, 44 A.2d 333 (N.J. 1945).

courts in Wisconsin and New York struck down public transportation programs for parochial school students, constitutional amendments were adopted to authorize their reinstitution.[14]

Most state constitutions, however, neither expressly permit nor prohibit the provision of bus transportation or the loaning of textbooks to students in nonpublic schools. Thus state courts have had to determine whether the general constitutional bans on aid to religious institutions likewise rule out programs of indirect aid. In ruling on these programs, state courts have divided almost evenly. For the most part, these differing outcomes cannot be attributed to textual differences, because the no-aid language in most state constitutions is clear and emphatic. Rather, the variation among state courts seems to reflect the willingness or unwillingness of the justices to read the applicable state provisions as independent constitutional judgments on the permissibility of aid to religious institutions.

Those state courts that have upheld the challenged programs have tended to assume, often without supporting analysis, that the state provisions impose no greater restriction than does the First Amendment. In addition, they have emphasized either that the challenged programs benefited the schoolchild rather than the religious school or that the valid public purposes served by the programs—ensuring the safety of schoolchildren, in transportation cases, or providing for their better education, in textbook cases—justified their continuation.

Snyder v. *Town of Newton* (1960), in which the Connecticut Supreme Court upheld a transportation program against constitutional challenge, is representative. The Connecticut Constitution provides that no one shall be compelled "to support any congregation, church or religious association" and that the school fund shall not be diverted "to any other use than the encouragement and support of public or common schools." The Connecticut court, however, focused on the benefits of the program rather than on the constitutional language, asserting that "a statute which serves a public purpose is not unconstitutional merely because it incidentally benefits a limited number of persons." Dismissing the contention that the program violated the constitutional ban on aid to religion, the court simply asserted that "in light of our history and policy, [the program] cannot be said to compel support of any church."[15]

In contrast, those courts that have invalidated programs of indirect aid have been more attuned to differences in language between federal and state constitutional provisions and to the distinctive historical experiences underlying these textual differences. A model of this sort of independent constitutional analysis is *Gaffney* v. *State Department of Education* (1974), which involved the constitutionality of Nebraska's textbook loan law. Eschewing the tripartite analysis pioneered by the U.S. Supreme Court in *Lemon* v. *Kurtzman* (1971), the Nebraska Supreme Court insisted that Nebraska's prohibition of any "appropriation in aid of any sectarian institution or any educational institution not owned

14. Wis. Const. Amend. art. I, § 21, *overturning Reynolds* v. *Nusbaum*, 115 N.W.2d 761 (Wis. 1962); N.Y. Const. Amend art. XI, § 4, *overturning Judd* v. *Board of Education*, 15 N.E.2d 576 (N.Y. 1938).

15. *Snyder* v. *Town of Newton*, 161 A.2d 770 at 774-75 and 779 (Conn. 1960), *commenting on* Conn. Const. art. VII, § 1, and art. VIII, § 2 (1818).

and controlled by the state" was clear on its face and admitted of no exceptions. Indeed, the records of the convention that drafted the provision indicated that a major aim of the delegates was to devise a precise prohibition that would prevent sectarian conflict over the funding of church-related schools. The court therefore concluded that the law violated the state's constitution.[16]

Other state courts have likewise relied on the distinctive language of state constitutional provisions to justify development of an independent constitutional position. The California Supreme Court, for example, concluded in 1981 that the state constitution's ban on expenditures for "any sectarian purpose" was designed to prevent the state from providing any benefits to sectarian schools that furthered their educational purposes. On that basis, the California court struck down a textbook loan program.[17] Similarly, in 1961 the Alaska Supreme Court ruled that, given the clear import of the state constitution's no-aid language, if the constitution's framers had wished to permit provision of transportation to students in parochial schools, they would have included a provision expressly indicating that intent.[18] Finally, the Massachusetts Supreme Judicial Court, noting that a challenged textbook loan program aided sectarian schools in carrying out their essential educational function, held that it violated a constitutional amendment that ruled out the "use" of money for "maintaining or aiding" sectarian schools.[19]

16. Gaffney v. State Department of Education, 220 N.W.2d 550 (Neb. 1974).
17. California Teachers Association v. Riles, 632 P.2d 953 (Cal. 1981).
18. Matthews v. Quinton, 362 P.2d 932 (Alaska 1961).
19. Bloom v. School Committee of Springfield, 379 N.E.2d 578 (Mass. 1978).

Taken together, the rulings banning indirect aid seem more faithful to the purposes and history of state constitutional guarantees than do those upholding aid. Should the United States Supreme Court decide that heretofore prohibited forms of indirect aid are compatible with the establishment clause, one can expect renewed challenge to such aid under state constitutions. In such circumstances, state courts will have both the opportunity and the constitutional basis to chart an independent course.

Religious practices in public schools

Many state constitutions not only prohibit governmental expenditures for sectarian religious purposes but also expressly forbid sectarian control or influence in schools supported by state funds. These provisions are designed not only to prevent public funding of parochial schools but also to allay Catholic concerns about the prevalence of Protestant religious practices and the inculcation of Protestant doctrine in public schools. Several state constitutions also guarantee an absolute freedom of worship and forbid government from compelling attendance at a place of worship. Both the narrow and the more general provisions in state constitutions provide a basis for invalidating religious practices in public schools and ensuring that state governments do not interfere with freedom of belief and worship.

At least initially, however, these restrictive provisions had little effect. In states whose constitutional guarantees of freedom of worship and belief antedated the establishment of systems of public education, these constitutional provisions did not prevent the institution of Bible reading and daily prayer in the public schools. In states that banned sectarian influences in state-funded schools, the constitutional guarantees did not eliminate religious practices as standard elements in the public school curriculum. Nonetheless, the adoption of these constitutional provisions, despite the continuation of practices incompatible with them, was important because they furnished a weapon for litigants who would later challenge the states' sponsorship of religious practices.

These challenges began during the nineteenth century. Five state courts anticipated the U.S. Supreme Court's 1963 ruling in *School District of Abington Township* v. *Schempp* by striking down Bible reading in public schools under their state constitutions.[20] Most state courts, however, rejected constitutional challenges to Bible reading and other sectarian observances in the public schools. To do so, they were forced to deny that the Bible is sectarian, arguing that its "adopt[ion] by one or more denominations as authentic . . . or inspired, cannot make it a sectarian book."[21] They also had to contend that use of a version of the Bible favored by a particular sect did not constitute governmental endorsement of, or preference for, a particular religion. Finally, they had to deny that school prayer and Bible

reading transformed the classroom into a place of worship, insisting that the constitutional ban on compelled attendance at a place of worship applied only to places where people met for that express purpose.[22]

These assertions, unconvincing though they are, demonstrate the commitment that many state courts had to upholding Bible reading in the schools. Paradoxically, they also underline the strength of state constitutional strictures on governmental sponsorship of religious practices. Because the clarity of the provisions precluded interpreting them in an accommodationist fashion, state courts were forced to misrepresent the situations they confronted in order to uphold the practices they favored. Should new issues arise involving religious practices in the public schools or the introduction of religious perspectives into their curricula, these constitutional provisions can and should serve as a barrier to efforts to compromise the secular character of the public schools.

Religious practices in public places

A more difficult question is posed by state sponsorship of religious practices or displays outside the school context, where constitutional restrictions on sectarian influences in public schools do not apply. Controversy in recent years has centered on the erection and/or maintenance of religious displays on public property. Prior to 1984, when the United States Supreme Court ruled that the inclusion of a Nativity scene in a Christmas display on public property did not violate the establishment clause,

20. *School District of Abington Township* v. *Schempp*, 374 U.S. 203 (1963). Rulings prior to *Schempp*, which either struck down Bible reading in public schools or upheld laws banning it, include *People* v. *Board of Education of District 24*, 92 N.E. 251 (Ill. 1910); *Herold* v. *Parish Board of School Directors*, 68 So. 116 (La. 1915); *State* v. *Scheve*, 91 N.W. 846 (Neb. 1902); *Weiss* v. *District Board*, 44 N.W. 967 (Wis. 1890); *Board of Education* v. *Minor*, 23 Ohio St. 322 (Ohio 1872).

21. *Hackett* v. *Brookville Graded School District*, 87 S.W. 792, 794 (Ky. 1905).

22. *Church* v. *Bullock*, 109 S.W. 115 (Tex. 1908).

the courts in five states had addressed the issue.[23] In only two instances, however, did the courts base their rulings on independent interpretation of their states' bills of rights.

Acknowledging that expenditures to support or benefit a religious sect would violate the state constitution, the Oklahoma Supreme Court insisted in 1972 that, despite the city's maintenance and illumination of a Christian cross, no use of public moneys was involved. Furthermore, argued the court, the display of the cross did not entail forbidden governmental support for religion, because the commercial setting of the cross "stultif[ied] its symbolism and vitiate[d] any use, benefit, or support for any sect, church, denomination, system of religion, or sectarian institution as such."[24]

Considerably more convincing is the California Supreme Court's opinion in *Fox* v. *City of Los Angeles* (1978). The court pointed out that the sectarian religious character of the display in question was apparent in both the selection of the cross, a symbol particularly pertinent to the Christian religion, and in the efforts of Greek Orthodox Christians to ensure that the cross would be displayed on their Easter as well. It thus concluded that the state's special recognition of one religion, at least where others were not similarly recognized, violated the state's constitutional ban on any governmental preference for religious sects.[25]

State support for religion in general

These decisions, however, leave a broader question unanswered: is it valid under state constitutions for states to recognize and support religion in general? Although much depends on the text of a state's constitution, some observations are possible.

First, the constitutions of the American states are far from neutral on the question of religious belief. The preambles of over forty current state constitutions expressly recognize the existence of God, often admitting the state's dependence on his blessings. Some state constitutions also acknowledge a duty of religious worship.

Second, far more than the analogous provisions in the U.S. Constitution, the provisions on church and state in state constitutions, read in the light of the circumstances of their adoption, offer support for Justice William O. Douglas's claim that "we are a religious people, whose institutions presuppose a Supreme Being." From this claim Douglas drew the conclusion that "when the state encourages religious instruction or cooperates with religious authorities . . . it follows the best of our traditions."[26]

Third, this dual recognition of the religious character of the American populace and of the existence of a Supreme Being, even when tied to a duty of religious worship, neither imposes on the states an obligation to provide financial assistance to religion nor authorizes such support. Indeed, many state constitutions, responding to the evils generally associated with religious establishments, preclude such support in no uncertain terms.

23. The U.S. Supreme Court upheld inclusion of a crèche in a Christmas display on public property in *Lynch* v. *Donnelly*, 465 U.S. 668 (1984).

24. *Meyer* v. *Oklahoma City*, 496 P.2d 789, 792-93 (Okla. 1972).

25. *Fox* v. *City of Los Angeles*, 587 P.2d 663 (Cal. 1978).

26. *Zorach* v. *Clauson*, 343 U.S. 306, 313-14 (1952).

Finally, from the foregoing observations, it appears that state constitutions would not be violated by governmental recognition of religion and religious practices as long as this recognition (1) did not entail favoritism to particular sects or religions; (2) did not involve financial aid to religion; and (3) did not interfere with the freedom of religious belief, sentiment, or worship. Whether policies could be devised that would meet these exacting requirements is a real question. There is a further concern that such policies might run afoul of the establishment clause of the First Amendment. Nonetheless, the fact that such criteria can be developed underscores once again the fact that state constitutions tend to incorporate a different perspective on church and state from that found in the U.S. Constitution, leading, at least potentially, to different outcomes depending on whether litigants invoke federal or state guarantees.

PROSPECTS FOR THE
NEW JUDICIAL FEDERALISM

Our analysis reveals that state constitutional guarantees differ markedly in form and substance from their federal counterparts. For some states, these guarantees register considered constitutional judgments on such contentious issues as the maintenance of religious establishments and aid to sectarian schools. For others, they represent efforts to prevent sectarian conflict over church and state. For still others, they reflect a borrowing of provisions from sister states. Yet, whatever their basis, the result has been that many states have enshrined in their constitutions a distinctive perspective on the claims of religious liberty and on the separation of church and state, thus affording ample

justification for states to develop their own jurisprudence of church and state.

Whether state courts will seize the opportunity available to them to pursue an independent course remains unclear. Still, some general observations are possible. First, the relatively frequent litigation of claims under the states' religion guarantees shows that some jurists and litigants have recognized that these provisions offer a basis for independent constitutional development. Indeed, the beginnings of a state jurisprudence of church and state can be found, even before the turn of the twentieth century, in early state judicial rulings banning Bible reading in public schools. Perhaps surprisingly, the U.S. Supreme Court's incorporation of the establishment clause in 1947, instead of eliminating serious consideration of state constitutional guarantees, actually increased the level of state constitutional litigation.[27] As a result, state courts entered the era of the new judicial federalism with a body of precedent upon which they could build.

Second, at least since incorporation, the litigation of church-state claims under state constitutions has usually been reactive. That is, litigants have typically resorted to state law in order to attack programs or practices that had been validated by the U.S. Supreme Court. For example, in the two decades after the Court upheld public transportation of students to parochial schools, litigants in eight states mounted state constitutional challenges to such programs. Similarly, in the wake of the Court's 1967 ruling upholding New York's textbook loan program, litigants brought suit in nine states, attacking similar programs

27. It should be noted that the incorporation of the establishment clause increased the level of church-state litigation in federal courts even more than it did in state courts.

on state constitutional grounds. If this pattern of reactive litigation continues, it can be expected that movement toward a more accommodationist stance by the U.S. Supreme Court will promote an increased willingness to look to state courts and state constitutions for vindication.

Finally, insofar as a trend can be detected, it appears that state courts are moving toward a more separationist reading of their state constitutional guarantees on church and state. Some evidence for this can be found in the courts' rulings on indirect aid to parochial schools. Since 1970, seven state courts have struck down programs involving either the transportation of students to parochial schools or the lending of textbooks to them, and no state court has upheld such a program. Yet this is hardly conclusive—some state courts have not always been consistent in their rulings, and others may decide to reconsider their positions.[28] What is clear is that the new judicial federalism has led jurists and scholars to give renewed attention to state bills of rights. This can only have a beneficial effect on the prospects for an independent state jurisprudence of church and state.

28. For an example of apparent state court inconsistency, compare *Weiss* v. *Bruno*, 509 P.2d 973 (Wash. 1973), with *Washington Health Care Facilities Authority* v. *Spellman*, 633 P.2d 866 (Wash. 1981). The possibility of a reversal of position is particularly strong on the California Supreme Court, because three justices who had endorsed a no-aid reading of the state constitution were denied reelection to the court in 1986.

ANNALS, *AAPSS*, **496**, March 1988

State Courts and Economic Rights

By PETER J. GALIE

ABSTRACT: The recent movement among state supreme courts to affirm rights not protected by the United States Supreme Court has occasioned much favorable commentary. In one area of this new judicial federalism—economic rights protection—the response has been less enthusiastic. State courts used various clauses of their respective constitutions to protect these rights even before the Civil War and have continued to do so despite the U.S. Supreme Court's abdication of any serious role in the realm of economic rights. This persistence by state courts is justified by a historically valid substantive content of the due process clause, the numerous clauses in state constitutions concerned with the protection of property, and the role of the state courts in the American constitutional system. The arguments frequently invoked by critics of judicial activism on the part of the federal judiciary do not apply with the same force to the state judiciary. State courts can contribute to American constitutional liberties by actively protecting an area of rights that would otherwise find no forum for vindication.

Peter J. Galie has a Ph.D. from the University of Pittsburgh. He is professor and chair of the Political Science Department at Canisius College, Buffalo, New York. He is the author of numerous articles on state constitutional law.

NOTE: The author would like to thank John D'Amato, his student assistant, for his assistance in collating the data, and Paulette Kirsch for preparing the manuscript.

T HE most controversial area of state court activism, the new judicial federalism, as it has been named, is in the use of state due process, equal protection, and right-to-remedy clauses to strike down economic regulations interfering with property interests. The movement to grant greater protection to individual rights on state constitutional grounds than the U.S. Supreme Court has granted under the federal Constitution has generally met with favorable responses.[1] When it comes to economic rights, however, the reaction has been less enthusiastic.[2]

This tepid response, though understandable, given the association of protecting economic rights with the *Lochner* era of substantive due process, is not without its ironies. For one, the new judicial federalism is not new in the area of economic rights. State supreme courts relied on various provisions of their constitutions to protect such rights well before the U.S. Supreme Court discovered substantive due process, and the state courts have continued to do so since the national Court discarded that doctrine as a means to protect economic rights. This state court persistence in protecting economic rights, it will be argued, is justified in terms of both state constitutional provisions and the differ-

ent role state supreme courts play in the structure of state governments.

STATE COURTS AND ECONOMIC RIGHTS IN THE NINETEENTH CENTURY

Substantive due process arose first among state courts; this fact was influential in its adoption by the U.S. Supreme Court.[3] Edward S. Corwin, after analyzing state and federal cases prior to the Civil War, credits *Wynehamer* v. *State of New York*[4] as the beacon case whose doctrine "less than twenty years from the time of its rendition . . . was far on the way to being assimilated into the accepted constitutional law of the country."[5] There were numerous other cases, enough to allow the conclusion that the development of substantive due process was as much a function of state judges' interpreting state constitutions as it was the creation of federal judges.[6]

The adoption of the Fourteenth Amendment, in 1868, did not give immediate impetus to the development of economic due process as far as the Supreme Court was concerned, but state courts were quick to add it to their constitutional arsenals. Exemplary in this respect is the case of *In re Jacobs* (1885).[7] The New York Legislature had

1. See, for example, A.E. Dick Howard, "State Courts and Constitutional Rights in the Day of the Burger Court," *Virginia Law Review*, 62:873 (1976); Bradley McGraw, ed., *Developments in State Constitutional Law* (St. Paul, MN: West, 1985); the articles in *Publius: The Journal of Federalism*, vol. 17, *New Developments in State Constitutional Law* (Winter 1987).

2. See Hans Linde, "Due Process of Lawmaking," *Nebraska Law Review*, 55:197, 237 (1976); James C. Kirby, Jr., "Expansive Judicial Review of Economic Regulations under State Constitutions," in *Developments in State Constitutional Law*, ed. McGraw, pp. 118-19.

3. Edward Corwin, "Due Process of Law before the Civil War," as reprinted in *American Constitutional History*, ed. A. T. Mason and G. Garvey (New York: Harper Torchbooks, 1964); Benjamin Twiss, *Lawyers and the Constitution: How Laissez Faire Came to the Supreme Court* (Princeton, NJ: Princeton University Press, 1942).

4. 13 N.Y. 378 (1856).

5. Corwin, *Liberty against Government* (Baton Rouge: Louisiana State University Press, 1948), pp. 114-15.

6. See, for example, *Taylor* v. *Porter*, 4 Hill 140 (N.Y. 1843); *In re Dorsey*, 7 Porter 293 (Ala. 1838).

7. 98 N.Y. 98 (1885).

prohibited the manufacturing or preparation of tobacco in tenements in cities of 500,000 or more residents. The Court of Appeals voided the law as a deprivation of liberty without due process of law. In doing so, the court wrote:

Liberty, in its broad sense as understood in this country, means the right, not only of freedom from actual servitude, imprisonment or restraint, but the right of one to use his faculties in all lawful ways, to live and work where he will, to earn his livelihood in any lawful callings, and to pursue any lawful trade or avocation. All laws, therefore, which impair or trammel these rights, which limit one in his choice of a trade or profession, or confine him to work or live in a specified locality, or exclude him from his own house, or restrain his otherwise lawful movements (except as such laws may be passed in the exercise by the legislature of the police power, which will be noticed later), are infringements upon his fundamental rights of liberty, which are under constitutional protection.[8]

This attitude is one that survived the nineteenth century among many state courts and remains an important principle guiding their decisions in this area. New York was not alone. Between 1885 and 1894, ten states adopted the same general approach. Bernard Siegan has suggested that the U.S. Supreme Court decision in *Allegeyer* v. *Louisiana*, in which the liberty of contract was constitutionalized, beginning the era of substantive due process, was not unexpected "because the federal judiciary was in fact following trends already established in many states."[9] Protection of property and economic rights was not foisted on the country by the judiciary; doctrines

of vested rights and economic due process were developed out of a commitment to protecting property and economic liberties that are part of the constitutional and political tradition of the United States.[10]

STATE COURT ACTIVITY AND ECONOMIC RIGHTS, 1897-1987

The heyday of federal substantive due process, roughly 1897 to 1937, has been well studied.[11] The reaction to substantive due process as it was interpreted in *Lochner* and its progeny was so intense that the U.S. Supreme Court has for all intents and purposes abandoned any serious review of the kind of economic regulation that had been the prime target of the doctrine. Oliver Wendell Holmes's stinging dissent to *Lochner* became the definitive understanding of *Lochner*. Holmes's view that *Lochner* was no more than an attempt to read into the Constitution a particular economic philosophy derived from Adam Smith and, more immediately, Herbert Spencer, became the dominant view among academic commentators as well as judges. In its place emerged a view that the due process clause means what its words suggest, namely, procedural but not substantive protection against government action.[12] While the Supreme

8. Ibid., pp. 106-7.
9. Bernard Siegan, *Economic Rights and the Constitution* (Chicago: University of Chicago Press, 1980), pp. 58-59.
10. Ibid., pp. 27-40, provides a history of this commitment.
11. Lawrence Tribe, *American Constitutional Law* (New York: Foundation Press, 1978), pp. 421-55, provides a summary overview; cf. the treatment in Siegan, *Economic Rights*, pp. 110-55.
12. The view that the due process clause has only a procedural content is put forth strongly in John Ely, *Democracy and Distrust: A Theory of Judicial Review* (Cambridge, MA: Harvard University Press, 1980), pp. 14-21; Linde, "Due Process of Lawmaking," passim.

Court has revived the general notion of substantive due process and has recently indicated that it may become more solicitous of property rights, there has been no attempt to revive substantive due process as a basis for stricter review of economic and social regulation.[13]

What follows is a look at the extent to which state courts adopted a similar doctrine; how rigorously they applied it and in what areas; and to what extent these state courts followed the U.S. Supreme Court in rejecting substantive due process. To get some idea of state court involvement in protecting economic rights, an examination was made of eight studies that collected cases in this area.[14] To the cases noted therein, I added decisions collected from lists provided by state courts themselves. Finally, to these cases were added cases collected since 1980 from the regional reporters. A total of 357 cases were discovered

using this method. While this figure by no means represents all the cases decided by state high courts in this area, it is believed that it is representative of the activity of state courts in the period from 1897 to 1987.[15]

During the period of 1897-1937, state courts definitely emphasized substantive due process, with 70 percent of the cases being decided on this basis. (See Table 1.) This figure increased to 81 percent during the next period, 1938-68, but dropped significantly to 23 percent during the years 1969-87. There was a corresponding shift from due process to equal protection over the same time spans. The increases in state legislative activity involving social and economic regulation may account for part of the shift but do not seem to be the primary factor. Decisions as far back as the end of the nineteenth century decided on due process grounds would today almost certainly be decided on equal protection grounds.[16] The discrediting of due pro-

13. See, for example, *First English Evangelical Lutheran Church of Glendale* v. *County of Los Angeles*, — U.S. — (1987); property owners must be compensated when use of their land is restricted even temporarily.

14. The studies used are as follows: M. Paulsen, "The Persistence of Substantive Due Process in the States," *Minnesota Law Review*, 24:91 (1950); Note, "State Views on Economic Due Process: 1937-1953," *Columbia Law Review*, 53:827 (1953); John A. Hoskins and David A. Katz, "Substantive Due Process in the States Revisited," *Ohio State Law Journal*, 18:384 (1952); Robert Carpenter, "Economic Due Process and the State Courts," *American Bar Association Journal*, 45:1027 (1959); John A. Heatherington, "State Economic Regulation and Substantive Due Process of Law," *Northwest University Law Review*, 53:226 (1979); Note, "State Economic Substantive Due Process: A Proposed Approach," *Yale Law Journal*, 88:1487 (1979); Note, "Counter Revolution in State Constitutional Law," *Stanford University Law Review*, 15:309 (1963); James C. Kirby, Jr., "Expansive Judicial Review of Economic Regulation under State Constitutions," in *Developments in State Constitutional Law*, ed. McGraw, pp. 94-145.

15. Generally these articles exclude cases involving public utilities rates, the validity of state taxation, and zoning. I have followed this exclusionary policy to keep the added cases consistent with those in the studies. One major caveat: most of the research on state courts and economic regulation has focused on the 1937-87 period, with little done on the period 1890-1910. The results presented in Table 1 probably underrepresent the activity that occurred between 1910 and 1937. The disproportionate number of cases after 1937, however, also represents state court reactions to increasing activity by state legislatures, and the fact that the U.S. Supreme Court generally refused to review or strike down social and economic legislation passed by the states after 1937.

16. *Bailey* v. *People*, 60 N.E. 98 (Ill. 1901), is typical of many cases. In *Bailey*, the Illinois court struck down a statute that limited the number of people a lodging housekeeper could sleep in one room while exempting keepers of inns, hotels, and boarding houses from that limit. The court reasoned on equal protection terms, and the case clearly involved invidious or irrational classifica-

TABLE 1
STATE SUPREME COURT ACTIVITY AND ECONOMIC RIGHTS, 1897-1987

	Local Regulations or Miscellaneous		Judicial Remedy		Anticompetitive		Totals	
	%	N	%	N	%	N	%	N
1897-1937								
Substantive due process	40.5	(15)	2.7	(1)	27.0	(10)	70.3	(26)
Equal protection	8.1	(3)	2.7	(1)	5.4	(2)	16.2	(6)
Substantive due process and equal protection	5.4	(2)	0	(0)	8.1	(3)	13.5	(5)
Total								(37)
1938-68								
Substantive due process	13.0	(27)	0	(0)	67.8	(141)	80.8	(168)
Equal protection	3.4	(7)	1.4	(3)	6.3	(13)	11.1	(23)
Substantive due process and equal protection	1.4	(3)	0.5	(1)	3.4	(7)	5.3	(11)
Miscellaneous	0.5	(1)	0.5	(1)	1.9	(4)	2.9	(6)
Total								(208)
1969-87								
Substantive due process	8.9	(10)	3.6	(4)	10.7	(12)	23.2	(26)
Equal protection	8.0	(9)	34.8	(39)	5.4	(6)	48.2	(54)
Substantive due process and equal protection	3.6	(4)	5.4	(6)	4.5	(5)	13.4	(15)
Miscellaneous*	0	(0)	14.3	(16)	0.9	(1)	15.2	(17)
Total								(112)
Total cases	22.7	(81)	20.2	(72)	57.1	(204)		(357)

*All but one case in this category concern open-court or right-to-remedy provisions of state constitutions.

cess as a basis for examining social and economic regulation and the rise of equality as a constitutional value have combined to make judges and scholars feel more comfortable with equal protection analysis, even though the outcomes are the same.[17]

---

tion questions, but the court voided the statute on substantive due process grounds. 60 N.E. at 99.

17. Philip B. Kurland, *Politics, the Constitution and the Warren Court* (Chicago: University of Chicago Press, 1970), esp. chap. 4; Alexander Bickel, *The Supreme Court and the Idea of Progress* (New York: Harper Torchbooks, 1970), pp. 103 ff.

A second significant aspect of the data is the existence of a consistent philosophy governing this judicial activism that persists throughout the periods in question. Approximately 57 percent of all the cases examined fell into the anticompetitive category. State court judges struck down measures that either overtly or covertly tended to create monopoly and/or interfere with the operation of the marketplace. In decision after decision, judges concluded that the real as opposed to the ostensible purpose of the legislation in question was anticompetitive. In doing so, the judges were being true to what one scholar has demonstrated was one of the historically valid purposes of the due process clause, namely, protection against monopoly.[18]

The most recent period, 1969-87, reveals a development of some promise in the use of open-court or right-to-remedy clauses contained in most state constitutions. These clauses typically take the form of guaranteeing that all courts shall be open and that all persons shall have a remedy for injuries suffered to their persons, property, or reputations. In conjunction with equal protection clauses, they have been used to strike down guest statutes, which preclude liability for nonpaying passengers in private vehicles; statutes of repose; caps on malpractice awards; and similar measures. The U.S. Supreme Court has not directly addressed any of these issues. Assuming that at least some of these statutes are open to legitimate challenge, the only available forums for those challenges have been the state judiciaries. In fact, the single most striking development among state supreme courts in protecting economic rights since 1980 has been the increasing use of these right-to-remedy clauses, frequently in conjunction with equal protection clauses, to strike down a variety of legislative schemes.[19]

The protection of economic rights extends beyond the confines of the business world and involves a variety of groups and interests. These range from widows of workmen denied access to courts for claims to compensation,[20] to suppliers of materials denied the special exemption from liability granted to architects.[21] These decisions have protected minors from statutes of limitation that would make suit impossible when those minors reached legal age[22] and consumers from attempts by legislatures arbitrarily to limit entry into professions, fix prices, or otherwise lessen competition.[23]

ECONOMIC RIGHTS:
CONSTITUTIONAL CHARGE OR
REACTIONARY RESIDUE?

State supreme courts continue to rely on their due process, equal protection, and, increasingly, their right-to-remedy clauses to grant greater protection to economic rights than would be forthcoming from the federal judiciary. All but three states have refused to follow the lead of the U.S. Supreme Court in its rejection of substantive due process and equal protection in the area of economic regulation.[24] There is no doubt about

18. See the discussion of the history of due process in the following subsection of this article, "Argument 1: The Distorted History Argument."
19. The importance of these clauses has been recognized by commentators. See O. Schuman, "Oregon's Remedy Guarantee," *Oregon Law Review*, 65:1063 (1986); Comment, "State Constitutions' Remedy Guarantee Provisions Provide More than Mere 'Lip Service' to Rendering Justice," *University of Toledo Law Review*, 16:585 (1985); Note, "Medical Malpractice Statute of Repose: An Unconstitutional Denial of Access to Courts," *Nebraska Law Review*, 63:150 (1984).

20. *Alvarado* v. *Industrial Com'n of Arizona*, 716 P.2d 18 (Ariz. 1986).
21. *Henderson Clay Products Inc.* v. *Edgar Wood & Associates Inc.*, 451 A.2d 174 (N.H. 1982).
22. *Mominee* v. *Sherbarth*, 503 N.E.2d 717 (Ohio 1986).
23. For example, *Batton-Jackson Oil Co. Inc.* v. *Reeves*, 340 S.E.2d 16 (Ga. 1986); *Finocchiaro* v. *Nebraska Liquor Control*, 351 N.W.2d 710 (Neb. 1984); *San Antonio Retail Grocers* v. *Lafferty*, 297 S.W.2d 813 (Tex. 1985); *Vaughan* v. *State Bd. of Embalmers etc.*, 82 S.E.2d 618 (Va. 1954).
24. See Note, "State Views on Economic Due Process," p. 827. Kirby reports that 35 states have specifically refused to follow the lead of the Supreme Court. Kirby, "Judicial Review of Economic Regulation," pp. 109, 122.

the continued solicitude for economic rights on the part of state supreme courts; there are doubts about the justifications for that activism. Six arguments have been put forth in opposition to judicial activism in this area. Some apply only to the use of substantive due process, but most would apply to any attempt by courts to scrutinize economic and social regulations, though there does seem to be less opposition to the use of the equal protection and right-to-remedy clauses to protect economic rights.

Argument 1: The distorted history argument

This view is based on a reading of the due process clause as exclusively procedural. The claim is that substantive due process had very little pre-Civil War basis: substantive due process was essentially the invention of the judiciary in its ideologically based determination to protect property interests. This position seemed so obvious to Leonard Levy that he would write that what the U.S. Supreme Court did was a "miraculous transubstantiation of process into substance and human rights into vested rights. . . . The accomplishment was bizarre, haphazard, and unplanned."[25]

It has already been noted that early in the nineteenth century, state courts had construed their due process clauses so as to provide substantive protection to property rights. Was there any justification for these states to do so? Or, putting the question a bit differently, if there is no indication whatsoever that the framers of the Fourteenth Amendment meant to

provide for substantive due process, is that evidence conclusive insofar as the state due-process-of-law and law-of-the-land clauses are concerned? In the most recent work on the history of the due process and law-of-the-land clauses, Frank Strong shows that articles 39 and 52 of the Magna Carta were meant to provide "a substantive ban on invasion of ancient rights of personal liberty and feudal property."[26]

It was Edward Coke who successfully fused the law-of-the-land provision of the Magna Carta with due process of law and in doing so provided a historical basis for a substantive content to the due process clause that would be handed down to the colonists in the New World. Strong shows that government-granted monopolies and expropriation by public conversion were regarded as denials of due process. Due process was the ancient enemy of monopoly: a shield against publicly granted monopolies but at the same time a sword bolstering state power to deal effectively with private monopolies.[27]

Strong concludes his analysis of due process by asserting that the inherited content of substantive due process embraces two more meanings: antiexpropriation of property interests and antimonopoly in economic enterprise.[28] He contends therefore that the perversions of due process occurred not with reading into the clause a substantive content but with *Allegeyer* v. *Louisiana* and *Lochner* v. *New York*.

The substantive due process the Court now unanimously embraced was of an utterly

25. Leonard Levy, ed., *American Constitutional Law: Historical Essays* (New York: Harper Torchbooks, 1966), p. 129.

26. Frank R. Strong, *Substantive Due Process of Law: A Dichotomy of Sense and Nonsense* (Durham, NC: Carolina Academic Press, 1986), p. 7.

27. Ibid., p. 14.
28. Ibid., p. 72.

different order from that espoused by Bradley and Field. They had stood for opposition to monopoly, a position with deep historical roots in Due Process increasingly articulated as espousal of freedom of trade. The essence of freedom of trade was the general right of all to engage in the common calling free from constrictions or prohibitions on entry. In severing this right from its tie with anti-monopoly the Court in one sentence catapulted into an uncharted domain in which substantive due process could become the obstacle to endless instances of legal, economic and social reform.[29]

The reading of liberty of contract into the due process clause was not consistent with the historical meaning of substantive due process. The reaction of the U.S. Supreme Court and scholars to this perversion was to read out of the clause any substantive content, thus throwing the proverbial baby out with the bathwater. The notion of due process has historically been not only a shield against arbitrary expropriation and monopolies but also a sword enabling the state to destroy or regulate private monopolies. Whether or not this revisionist history provides sufficient reason for the Supreme Court to reenter the arena, it is certainly relevant to any argument about the appropriateness of state supreme courts' so doing.

Argument 2: Lack of textual basis

Leonard Levy succinctly summarizes this position in responding to the arguments by Robert McCloskey for protecting economic rights: "The problem, rather, is that the Constitution quite explicitly protects religious liberty, but radiates from the vague contours of due process no visible protection to bar-

29. Ibid., p. 91.

tenders—nor riverboat pilots, oculists, nor any other occupation."[30]

To the extent there is force to this argument, it applies to the United States Constitution. The same argument, however, cannot be made with regard to state constitutions. In addition to a due process clause found in almost every state constitution, a majority of the state constitutions explicitly protect the "inalienable right of acquiring, possessing and protecting property."[31] Some states explicitly grant the judiciary review power any time a taking for public purposes is an issue.[32] The clauses in state constitutions concerning the protection of property are more numerous and more explicit than in the United States Constitution. For example, Colorado's constitution, in addition to the due process clause, contains nine other provisions dealing with the protection of

30. Levy, ed., *American Constitutional Law*, p. 157.
31. Colo. Const. art. II, § 3. See also Ala. Const. art I, § 35; Alaska Const. art. I, § 1; Ark. Const. art. II, § 22; Idaho Const. art. I, § 1; Ill. Const. art. I, § 1; Iowa Const. art. I, § 1; La. Const. art. I, § 4; Mass. Const. art. I, § 1; Mo. Const. art. I, § 2; Mont. Const. art. I, § 3; Neb. Const. art. I, § 1; Nev. Const. art. I, § 1; N.D. Const. art. I, § 1; N.H. Const. pt. I, art. 2; N.J. Const. art. I, para. 1; N.M. Const. art. II, § 4; N.C. Const. art. I, § 1; Ohio Const. art. I, § 1; Okla. Const. art. II, § 2; Pa. Const. art. I, § 1; S.D. Const. art. VI, § 1; Utah Const. art. I, § 1; Vt. Const. chap. I, art. 1; Va. Const. art. I, § 1; W.Va. Const. art. III, § 1; Calif. Const. art. I, § 1.
32. For example, Ariz. Const. art. II, § 17; Miss. Const. art. III, § 17. Six states add to their just compensation clauses for property "taken" the phrase "or damaged." Neb. Const. art. I, § 21; Hawaii Const. art. I, § 20; Mo. Const. art. I, § 26; Tex. Const. art. I, § 27; Va. Const. art. I, § 11. Finally, a majority of states have right-to-remedy or open-court clauses that generally read like the Idaho constitutional provision: "Courts of justice shall be open to every person and a speedy remedy afforded for every injury of person, property or character." Idaho Const. art. I, § 18.

property.[33] By virtue of their quantity and explicitness, property rights under state constitutional law cannot be placed in a subordinate position to personal rights, at least not on textual grounds.

Argument 3: Conservation of judicial resources

This argument is most forcefully made by Robert McCloskey.[34] The U.S. Supreme Court, he argues, has all it can do to handle the delicate and intractable problems involved in protecting and promoting political and civil liberties. Because the Court cannot do everything, it best serves our constitutional order by concentrating on the protection of personal rights.

To the extent that this argument has force, that force is attenuated if not completely dissipated in state constitutional history. Indeed, to the extent that it is accepted by the Supreme Court so as to eschew any role in policing economic regulations, a stronger case can be made for state judiciaries to provide a forum in which redress may be obtained. Levy himself, while rejecting any role for the U.S. Supreme Court, suggests that "the remedy may properly lie with state courts and state constitutional law."[35]

Argument 4: Lack of judicial competence

This argument, applied to the federal courts by a number of scholars, has also been applied to the state judiciaries. But this transfer is questionable. State courts may well be in a better position to assess and judge local conditions and problems than is the U.S. Supreme Court. State court decisions do not encompass national issues or problems, and the scope of their decision making is limited to individual states. The Supreme Court of Pennsylvania put the argument most effectively when it wrote:

This difference [between federal and state constitutional law] represents a sound development, one which takes into account the fact that state courts may be in a better position to review local economic legislation than the Supreme Court, since their precedents are not of national authority, may better adapt their decisions to local economic conditions and needs. . . . And where an industry is of basic importance to the economy of the state or territory, extraordinary regulations may be necessary and proper.[36]

It may well be that the U.S. Supreme Court ought not to spend time on, and lacks the expertise to adjudge, antiscalping ordinances in Indiana, but this cannot be said with the same degree of persuasiveness about state courts. James Kirby, in addressing this issue, wrote, "State courts . . . do not appear to have thrust themselves into unmanageable situations. Review of an economic regulation may well be simpler than an apportionment case, a voting rights case, or a product liability appeal."[37]

    33. Colo. Const. art. II, §§ 3, 6, 7, 9, 11, 13, 14, 15, 27.
    34. Robert McCloskey, "Economic Due Process and the Supreme Court: An Exhumation and Reburial," in *American Constitutional Law,* ed. Levy, pp. 185-87. A variation on this argument is found in Jesse Choper, *Judicial Review and the National Political Process: A Functional Reconsideration of the Role of the Supreme Court* (Chicago: University of Chicago Press, 1980).
    35. Levy, ed., *American Constitutional Law,* p. 157.
    36. *Pennsylvania State Bd. of Pharmacy* v. *Pastor,* 272 A.2d 487, 300 (Pa. 1971).
    37. Kirby, "Judicial Review of Economic Regulation," p. 120.

Argument 5: Antidemocratic character of judicial review

One of the most serious objections to judicial activism is that it conflicts with the basic assumptions of a self-governing polity. This argument applies, *a fortiori*, when courts are dealing with protecting economic rights rather than rights that involve the political process. Judicial activism involves judges deeply and directly in the political process and preempts large areas of policy from decision by the people or their elected representatives.[38] Judges are not elected; they serve for life. As with the previous arguments, however, this objection applies with less force to the state judiciaries.

First, the image of the state legislature as the model of democracy and the state high court as the model of an antidemocratic institution is overdrawn. State legislatures are subject to powerful special interests and lack of time and resources. It is not too great an exaggeration to call much state legislative output the state-enforced power of small groups.[39]

Even conceding that legislatures are in theory and often in practice more representative than courts, the argument needs modification when applied to state courts. The concern that life-tenured judges are frustrating the will of the

majority has much less force in the states because the overwhelming majority of states require election of judges in some form. An elected judiciary adds a democratic element to state court decision making.

A second factor is the nature of state amendment processes. State constitutions are more easily amended and are amended more frequently than the U.S. Constitution. Between 1970 and 1979, states adopted a total of 976 amendments to their constitutions.[40] Amendment by initiative is even allowed by 17 states.[41] A judicial branch that thwarts the will of a persistent majority is not nearly as likely to exist in a state as it might in the national government. Both the open and accessible constitutional amendment process and the elective character of state judiciaries significantly weaken the charge that state judicial activism thwarts or stultifies the democratic process.

Of course, none of these responses to the arguments against judicial activism is meant to be a definitive refutation. What they are meant to suggest is that the arguments against judicial activism apply with less force when the arena is shifted from the federal to the state judiciaries.

Argument 6: Lack of workable standards for review

In spite of the fact that the preceding arguments against judicial activism apply with less force to state courts, there

---

38. For a statement of the antidemocratic character of the judiciary, esp. in the area of economic rights, see M. Paulsen, "The Persistence of Substantive Due Process in the State," *Minnesota Law Review*, 24:91, 118 (1950); John A. Hoskins and David A. Katz, "Substantive Due Process in the States Revisited," *Ohio State Law Review*, 18:384, 400-401 (1952).

39. Heatherington, "State Economic Regulation," pp. 248-49. Even critics of judicial review of economic regulations like Paulsen recognize these defects. Paulsen, "The Persistence of Substantive Due Process," p. 118.

40. Note, "Developments in the Law—The Interpretation of State Constitutional Rights," *Harvard Law Review*, 95:1324, 1354, n. 106 (1982).

41. David Magleby, *Direct Legislation: Voting on Ballot Propositions in the United States* (Baltimore, MD: Johns Hopkins University Press, 1984), p. 36.

remains a final objection, namely, that the contours of the various state constitutional clauses in question are so undefined as to enable, and perhaps require, judges to read a particular economic philosophy into the clauses—one at variance with, but no more legitimate than, the one adopted by the legislature.[42]

A first response to this charge is to note that in state constitutions, many of the clauses protecting property rights are as specific as the specific provision in the national Bill of Rights and that others are no less vague than the most important clauses of the Fourteenth Amendment. This argument becomes even more strained in the face of the U.S. Supreme Court's adoption of substantive due process to protect personal rights.

A corollary to this argument is that when state judges do apply the more general or vague phrases of their constitutions to protect economic rights, they adopt more conservative social and economic theories, thus placing a stranglehold on attempts by the people to deal with their social and economic problems.[43] There is evidence, however, that when state courts did resort to substantive due process, during the Progressive era (1890-1910), to strike down economic reform legislation, no consistent philosophy or theory governed the cases decided during that period.[44] Melvin Urofsky's study of state courts and protective legislation during this era

concluded that "with few exceptions, state courts moved consistently towards approval of a wide range of reform legislation. . . . Progressives although occasionally delayed in court, were not blocked there."[45] State courts balanced legal doctrines, contract, and police power and, in most instances, deferred to legislative judgment in policy matters.[46] A study of more recent decisions in the same area concluded, "On balance, most of the economic legislation which state courts have invalidated during the past twenty-five years is arbitrary."[47]

Judges should not be allowed to substitute personal prejudice or their own economic philosophies for that of the legislatures; the public ought to have the right to adopt economic and social policies through their elected representatives. Nonetheless, the legislature is not the people, and the policies legislators adopt cannot be automatically equated with the will of the people. In the American tradition, the existence of a constitution means that courts are expected to protect the people from their legislatures when those legislatures act arbitrarily. Some balance must be struck between the competing values involved. With the U.S. Supreme Court unable or unwilling to play a role, state courts need to develop workable standards of review that will enable them to hold the competing interests in a creative balance. There are a number of approaches or criteria that could provide the guidance

42. Paulsen, "Persistence of Due Process," p. 117; Hoskins and Katz, "Substantive Due Process Revisited," p. 401.
43. Hoskins and Katz, "Substantive Due Process Revisited," p. 401.
44. Lawrence Friedman, "Freedom of Contract and Occupational Licensing 1890-1910: A Legal and Social Study," *California Law Review*, 53:487, 525 (1965).
45. Melvin Urofsky, "State Courts and Protective Legislation during the Progressive Era: A Reevaluation," *Journal of American History*, 72:63, 64 (1985).
46. Ibid., p. 91.
47. Note, "Counter Revolution in State Constitutional Law," *Stanford Law Review*, 15:309, 330 (1963). See also Heatherington, "State Economic Regulation," pp. 250-51; Note, "State Economic Substantive Due Process," p. 1510.

to enable state supreme courts to steer a course between the Scylla of judicial abdication and the Charybdis of judicial arrogance.[48]

CONCLUSION

While the problems and policy responses will change—from legislative

---

48. Among those who have proposed standards for the judiciary are Siegan, *Economic Rights and the Constitution*, pp. 322-31; Gerald Gunther, "The Supreme Court 1971 Term, Foreword: In Search of Evolving Doctrine on a Changing Court: A Model for a Newer Equal Protection," *Harvard Law Review*, 86:1, 20 ff; Note, "State Economic Substantive Due Process," pp. 1504-10; Strong, *Substantive Due Process of Law*, pp. 79-80, 94, 205-7, 297-99; Kirby, "Judicial Review of Economic Regulation," pp. 118-22.

attempts to hold railroads strictly liable in tort actions involving injury to livestock, to attempts to limit court remedies for victims of medical malpractice—the importance of having a judicial forum in which constitutional challenges can be heard is readily apparent. The tests to be used and the extent of judicial activity are legitimate matters for dispute; what is not disputable is the need for some judicial forum in which constitutional challenges can be heard. The U.S. Supreme Court's decision to deny hearings on these questions provides both the opportunity and the obligation for state courts to play an important role in protecting economic rights and, in doing so, to make a signal contribution to American constitutionalism.

ANNALS, *AAPSS*, **496**, March 1988

The Public Employee's Stake in
State Constitutional Rights

By JENNIFER FRIESEN

ABSTRACT: The idea that public employees are able to assert any constitutional rights against their government employers is a relatively recent development in American law. Federal constitutional law no longer permits the wholesale invasion of public employee rights to free speech, though it still reflects a tendency to treat public employees as second-class citizens. State constitutional law is just beginning to make contributions to the public employee's rights of privacy, equality, and free speech. State constitutional guarantees that protect these three interests tend to be more explicit and, therefore, potentially more protective of employee liberties than federal law. Enforcement of these state guarantees, however, is seriously hampered by lack of legislative enthusiasm. State legislators should fulfill their solemn oath to protect and defend the state constitution by enacting laws that provide compensation for victims of unconstitutional acts.

Jennifer Friesen is associate professor of law at Loyola Law School in Los Angeles, teaching labor law and constitutional rights. She was counsel to the Oregon House Labor Committee in 1983 and for three years practiced law with a firm specializing in the employment rights of public employees. She received her juris doctor degree from the University of Oregon in 1978 and served as law clerk for one year to Justice Hans A. Linde of the Oregon Supreme Court.

T HE two things most important to human beings, it has been said, are love and work. Certainly each has the capacity infinitely to enrich, or to impoverish, human existence. This article is not about love, except, to be sure, our historic love of liberty. It is about one aspect of work in the United States—the constitutional rights of the women and men who work for us, the people.

THE DUAL STATUS OF PUBLIC EMPLOYEES

Unlike most rights claimants—prisoners would be another exception—public employees have a dual status vis-à-vis the local or state government that employs them. First, they are members of the public, often even voters and taxpayers in that government's constituency; second, of course, they are hired to do a job. The first relationship is common to all of the governed and carries no obligations other than the usual ones of paying taxes and obeying the laws. The second is a concrete relationship that carries numerous duties, some clear and others only vaguely described as loyalty and efficiency in service to the public.

Not long ago, constitutional law viewed public employees almost exclusively in their second role. The rights they had possessed as citizens they lost as servants. Thus, in 1892, Justice Oliver Wendell Holmes could make his deathless observation about a policeman discharged for holding office in a political party organization: "The petitioner may have a constitutional right to talk politics, but he has no constitutional right to be a policeman. There are few employments for hire in which the servant does not agree to suspend his constitutional right of free speech, as well as idleness, by the implied terms of his contract."[1]

The United States Supreme Court's preference for apolitical public servants held firm until barely 35 years ago, when the anti-Communist loyalty oaths required of public school teachers and others began to fail First Amendment tests.[2] Now placing the accent on the first, constituent role of the public employee, the Warren Court developed the doctrine of "unconstitutional conditions," which holds that "public employment . . . may [not] be conditioned upon the surrender of constitutional rights which could not be abridged by direct government action."[3]

The expansion of employee rights to include constitutional rights required the corollary premise that the public employer—the school district or the city sanitation district—was in fact government. As one constitutional scholar commented in the middle 1960s, when this crucial change occurred, "If personnel policies in the public sector are seen as issues of government, they will be judged by principles invoked from the law of constitutional rights rather than the law of master and servant."[4] The law of public employment has, ever since, been a tightrope stretched between these two sources of rights.

Currently the battle in the United States Supreme Court is not so much over efforts to neutralize public employees' private beliefs and political associations, but rather over how much consti-

1. *McAuliffe* v. *Mayor of New Bedford*, 155 Mass. 216, 29 N.E. 517, 517-18 (1892).
2. Hans A. Linde, "Justice Douglas on Freedom in the Welfare State: Constitutional Rights in the Public Sector," *Washington Law Review*, 39:4, 31-44 (1964).
3. *Keyishian* v. *Board of Regents*, 385 U.S. 589, 605-6 (1967).
4. Linde, "Justice Douglas on Freedom," p. 39.

tutional protection is owed to their job-related expression, conduct, and privacy. The dual status of the employee as both constituent and worker still figures prominently in the Court's opinions. Now, however, the justices are engaged in inventing formulas intended to accommodate—or balance—the qualified constitutional freedoms of the employed with the ancient prerogatives of the employer—usually phrased as needs for "loyalty" and "efficiency."

The dilemma posed by dual status—constituent and employee—is not fictional. Consider the question of what kinds of employee speech are legitimate subjects for discipline. Doubtless a government employee's statements, even if unaccompanied by punishable conduct, can sometimes harm government functions in a way that an outside critic's cannot. Imagine a city planner who discloses the city's top price to the landowner during condemnation negotiations. When the employee's expected job performance consists itself of speech, as with schoolteachers or lawyers, other problems are raised. Still, much employee speech is addressed to government performance and genuine workplace concerns. The ability freely to criticize the government is a value highly prized in all American constitutions, even if the value of simple self-expression by the public worker is more controversial. Many observers, including several of the justices themselves, believe the present Court has done too much to relieve the public employer of perceived troublemakers and too little to protect the employees' rights to protest and communicate.[5]

As has been well documented by now, rights independently secured by the rediscovered state constitutions often exceed the federal constitutional floor.[6] In state courts that no longer feel bound to decide constitutional cases solely according to the dictates of the United States Supreme Court, state bills of rights may begin to reclaim governance of civil liberties for public employees. If so, the opinions in employment cases are bound to contribute generally to state constitutional theory and practice. Such cases upholding, for example, privacy and speech rights of public employees, though still sparse, are made doubly important by the fact that so few civil cases are brought to the courts under state bills of rights at all. Civil suits resulting in the recovery of damages—as for wrongful discharge—are rarer still. Apart from the familiar cases on public expression in private shopping centers,[7] the majority of opinions and scholarly work still stops with the application of state guarantees to criminal law and procedure. One reason for the scarcity of civil cases is the lack of civil remedies at the state level for violations of bills of rights, a theme that is amplified later in this article.[8]

STATE CONSTITUTIONAL CONTRIBUTIONS ON NONSPEECH EMPLOYMENT ISSUES

State constitutional rights for public employees are most likely to differ from

5. *Connick* v. *Meyers*, 461 U.S. 138, 156 (1983) (dissenting opinion of Justices Brennan, Marshall, Blackmun, and Stevens).

6. Ronald K.L. Collins, Peter J. Galie, and John Kincaid, "State High Courts, State Constitutions, and Individual Rights Litigation since 1980: A Judicial Survey," *Publius: The Journal of Federalism*, 16:141 (Summer 1986).

7. See, for example, Sanford Levinson, "Freedom of Speech and the Right of Access to Private Property under State Constitutional Law," in *Developments in State Constitutional Law*, ed. B. McGraw (St. Paul, MN: West, 1985), p. 51.

8. Jennifer Friesen, "Recovering Damages for State Bills of Rights Claims," *Texas Law Review*, 63:1269 (1985).

federal rights in the areas of equality, privacy, and free speech. What little case law exists in these three areas comes mostly from the courts of Oregon and California.

Interests in equality or equal treatment

Because public as well as private employees have statutory rights to be free of invidious discrimination in the workplace, the additional invocation of a constitutional equality guarantee will normally be unnecessary. Two questions not necessarily answered by equal opportunity statutes concern (1) affirmative action, or so-called reverse discrimination; and (2) discrimination against persons, such as nonheterosexuals, who are still denied the "equal protection" of the federal Fourteenth Amendment.

Most states have some form of equality provision in their bills of rights. The diversity of these texts is enormous, and the 11 states that have an equal protection clause are distinctly in the minority. Naturally, the guarantee of equal protection in some states can mean things that the United States Supreme Court has said it cannot mean. With respect to gay workers, for example, the California Supreme Court decided that denying employment opportunities because of a job applicant's sexual preference violated the California equal protection clause.[9] The court also broke new ground when it said that its equal protection rule had to be respected by even a nongovernment employer, like a monopolistic, privately owned utility, because the California clause does not, by its terms, forbid government discrimination only.

Other states go about protecting equality interests in different ways. Eighteen state constitutions explicitly prohibit gender discrimination, and some of them, like Pennsylvania's, do so in words that echo the rejected federal Equal Rights Amendment.[10] The constitution of Oregon, along with those of 16 other states, simply targets unequal distribution of government's benefits and burdens: "No law shall be passed granting to any citizen or class of citizens privileges, or immunities, which upon the same terms, shall not equally belong to all citizens."[11]

The equal "privileges or immunities" clause is sometimes invoked when employees charge discrimination in hiring, firing, and job benefits. In an important case invalidating a worker's compensation scheme that favored females over males, Oregon's Justice Betty Roberts wrote that this clause made legislative classifications based on gender "inherently suspect." The suspicion may be overcome if the reason for the classification reflects specific biological differences between men and women, but not when consequences are assigned to men or women because of their gender and for no other reason.[12]

Assuming that the same standard applies to, say, individualized promotion decisions, does it cast a cloud on voluntary employer affirmative action plans? Santa Clara, California's plan was

9. *Gay Law Students Association* v. *Pacific Telephone & Telegraph Company*, 24 Cal.3d 458, 156 Cal. Rptr. 14 (1979).

10. See Ronald Collins, "Bills and Declarations of Rights Digest," in *The American Bench* (Sacramento, CA: Reginald, Bishop, Forster, 1985), pp. 2494-95.

11. Ore. Const. art. I, § 20. See Hans A. Linde, "E Pluribus—Constitutional Theory and State Courts," *Georgia Law Review*, 18:165, 182, n. 43 (1984).

12. *Hewitt* v. *SAIF*, 294 Ore. 33, 653 P.2d 970 (1982).

recently much in the national news after a United States Supreme Court opinion said it was legal under federal equal opportunity law.[13] The plan became controversial because it had resulted in the promotion of a qualified female to a skilled position—in which women were completely unrepresented—over a male applicant with greater seniority and a slightly better score on subjective evaluations. According to the Oregon rule, would such a plan be fatally suspect because consequences were assigned to men or women on account of their gender? Or is erasing the effects of historical disadvantage one of the other reasons that the state may consider in granting privileges or immunities, even if it is not compelled to do so? This difficult question remains unanswered by state law.

Privacy on and off the job

Explicit rights to privacy are spelled out in modern amendments of a number of state bills of rights.[14] The United States Constitution does not mention privacy in so many words. What is labeled a privacy right under the federal Bill of Rights—for example, a woman's right to choose abortion—is under attack precisely because it lacks such a textual foundation.

Of course, privacy, as a legal matter, has come to mean a multitude of conceptually distinct ideas: freedom from disclosure of true but damaging facts; freedom to make intimate deci-

sions without government interference; freedom from unreasonable searches of one's mind, body, effects, or personal territory.

As a state constitutional matter, privacy means, in New York, that public school teachers cannot be forced to submit their urine or blood to authorities for drug tests, at least not without prior reason to suspect a particular individual of drug abuse.[15] In Montana and California, use of polygraph examinations to screen or investigate public employees has been held illegal on privacy and equal protection grounds.[16] A California court also found that a city employee was deprived of his constitutional right to privacy when his supervisors posted a notice in an employee workroom that he had been terminated for "unauthorized absence, failure to observe department rules, and dishonesty."[17] Thus, aside from forbidding some means of obtaining information about employees, a privacy clause may also forbid "improper use of information properly obtained."[18]

Does the public employer ever have a legitimate reason to invade constitutional privacy interests? The same California court said that the employer could prevail if it had some—unspecified—"compelling public interest" in posting the embarrassing memorandum. That is a very disappointing answer for policymakers and lawyers alike. "Compelling public interest" is a familiar judicial exit line in constitutional opinions. It sounds well intentioned enough, but because

13. Civil Rights Act of 1964, 42 U.S.C. § 2000 et seq., popularly known as Title VII; *Johnson* v. *Transportation Agency*, — U.S. —, 107 Sup. Ct. 1442 (1987).
14. Robert Gerstein, "California's Constitutional Right to Privacy," *Hastings Constitutional Law Quarterly*, 9:385 (1982).

15. *Patchoque-Medford Congress of Teachers* v. *Board of Education*, 70 N.Y.2d 57 (1987).
16. *Oberg* v. *City of Billings*, 674 P.2d 494 (Mont. 1983); *Long Beach City Employees* v. *City of Long Beach*, 41 Cal.3d 937, 719 P.2d 660 (1986).
17. *Payton* v. *City of Santa Clara*, 132 Cal. App. 3d 152, 183 Cal. Rptr. 17 (1982).
18. Ibid., 132 Cal.App.3d p. 154.

there is generally no textual premise whatsoever for it, its meaning is impossible to predict or to contain. It might mean that employees whose jobs entail a high degree of public visibility and accountability will have no private lives. In Montana, for example, the state's compelling interest in maintaining the public image of a police force justified punishing an officer who committed sexual misconduct in his private hypnosis practice.[19]

Clearly we would prefer that our police officers never commit any kind of misconduct anywhere. Many Americans would also prefer to have police officers who could pass some sort of psychological test to certify them free of subconscious racism. Some would strongly prefer that none of their police officers father children out of wedlock, or cohabit with members of the opposite sex, or commit a host of other presumably immoral acts that create a negative image for some part of the public. But, measured against privacy, which objectionable acts should the government rightly feel most compelled to discourage? "Compelling public interest," by itself, is not an adequate description of what acts or attitudes fall inside or outside of privacy or any other constitutional zone of protection.

WHEN CAN A PUBLIC EMPLOYEE "FREELY SPEAK"?

Reading judicial opinions about what constitutions mean in the context of particularized disputes is one way to study constitutional law but not necessarily the best or most interesting way. Another obvious way, though in fact routinely ignored by lawyers, is parsing the actual words of the drafters. State freedom-of-speech clauses illustrate the value of looking closely at the text; they also form the core of public employee civil liberties.

Starting with
fidelity to the text

Freedom-of-speech clauses in state constitutions show a surprising degree of uniformity. Most are phrased in terms much more detailed and emphatic than the terse First Amendment to the United States Constitution. These state clauses are ripe for independent interpretation. It is particularly frustrating, therefore, that almost no one pays attention to their precise texts.

About forty states employ language similar to California's article 1, section 2(a), which reads: "Every person may freely speak, write and publish his or her sentiments on all subjects, being responsible for the abuse of this right. A law may not restrain or abridge liberty of speech or press." Of these state provisions, 26 stipulate that "no law" may restrain speech. In the remainder, the right to speak is simply affirmed without identifying precisely who must refrain from abridging it. This omission has given rise to a fascinating debate about whether such a clause is intended to bind private parties as well as government.[20] In most states, however, very little in case law or commentary illuminates the meaning of these strongly worded speech rights in ordinary, modern applications.

What is the probable minimum content of a right so described? Naturally,

19. *In re Paynes*, 698 P.2d 856 (Mont. 1985).

20. Cf. James M. Dolliver, "The Washington Constitution and 'State Action': The View of the Framers," *Willamette Law Review*, 22:445 (1986), and Robert Utter, "The Right to Speak, Write, and Publish Freely," *University of Puget Sound Law Review*, 8:157 (1985).

the different states can interpret this language according to their own lights; what is good law in Georgia might not be good law in Michigan, despite a near identity of texts. Arguments drawn from history, structure, and the expressed intent of the drafters of the constitution might require exceptions or unusual interpretations of particular phrases or words. Nevertheless, at least some consequences can be made to flow logically from the English words chosen.

First, the language makes no distinctions between natural speakers: "every person" may freely speak. Thus noncitizens should be on the same footing as citizens. The press should enjoy no special privileges that ordinary persons do not also enjoy. Likewise, the speech of government employees should be no less protected than that of nonemployees, although the speaker's situation might be relevant to whether the right has been "abused." The speech of corporations would not be protected at all as a matter of state law, unless a corporation is considered a "person" for these purposes.

Second, the language itself makes no distinctions in subject matter: "all subjects" qualify for protection, so long as a person is expressing his or her "sentiments" on that subject. Thus the right to speak, write, and publish should embrace everything from political commentary to obscenity.[21] Again, history might show that certain types of expression were not intended to be shielded, despite the broad language. The Oregon Supreme Court, which has pioneered the modern interpretation of these clauses, allows that certain historically established crimes and torts, such as perjury and fraud, are such exceptions, even when committed by means of speech.[22]

Incidentally, most of what I have just stated is directly contrary to received First Amendment doctrine, past and present. Federal law is mired in troublesome distinctions. Until recently, even experts assumed that federal law shielded newspapers, but not ordinary persons, when they negligently defamed private persons.[23] Presently, the First Amendment, according to the United States Supreme Court, grants a higher level of protection in suits for defamation to untrue remarks that are on a subject of "public concern" than to remarks that are not.[24] Likewise, public employees fired for speaking out at the office can claim some degree of privilege against reprisal if their complaints were of public concern, but none at all if they were merely discussing workplace "grievances," which, the Court says, are of purely private concern.[25] Even employee statements deemed worthy of public concern are grounds for discharge if a supervisor "reasonably believes" the employee is disrupting the office by defying the supervisor's authority.[26] Finally, corporations are treated as persons for free-speech purposes,[27] and certain subjects, like obscenity, are simply none of the First Amendment's concern.[28]

21. *State* v. *Henry*, 302 Ore. 510, 732 P.2d 9 (1987), regarding obscenity included within the subjects on which a person may "speak, write, or print freely."

22. *State* v. *Robertson*, 293 Ore. 402, 649 P.2d 569 (1982).
23. See, for example, Steven Shiffrin, "Defamatory Non-Media Speech and First Amendment Methodology," *University of California, Los Angeles Law Review*, 25:915, 935-36 (1978).
24. *Dun & Bradstreet* v. *Greenmoss Builders*, 472 U.S. 749 (1985).
25. *Connick* v. *Meyers*, 461 U.S. 138 (1983).
26. Ibid., p. 154.
27. *First National Bank of Boston* v. *Bellotti*, 435 U.S. 765 (1978).
28. *Miller* v. *California*, 413 U.S. 15 (1973).

I mention these intricacies only to show that state constitutionalists cannot comfortably borrow free-speech doctrine from federal precedents, which draw on a different text, history, and set of institutional constraints. Fidelity to the text and history of the state bills of rights, will, I believe, dictate a much more cautious approach to censoring public employee expression than the approach in use by the Supreme Court.

The state clauses in employment situations

First it is necessary to give some content, in the employment context, to the qualification in article I, section 2, of the California and other state constitutions that every speaker is "responsible for the abuse of the right" to speak. Leaving aside for now any demonstrable historical exceptions to the right to speak, it appears that California public employees simply cannot be disciplined for speaking, writing, or publishing on any subject, unless they have abused their right.

No consensus exists on the meaning of "abuse" even in nonwork situations. Constitutional language that grants a right to speak freely, while preserving responsibility for the consequences, might mean only to forbid prior restraints upon publication and leave the government free to impose even criminal sanctions afterward. This was Sir William Blackstone's narrow view of the liberty of the press. American thinking about free expression, however, has gone far beyond this view.

Remaining "responsible for the abuse" could also mean that the speaker can be made to pay compensation for actual harm done to another's reputation but not punitive damages or criminal penal-

ties. That is the law in Oregon for defamation suits.[29] The importance of this rule for public employee speech problems lies in its limitation of abuse to actual harm done by the speech. Thus an employee's statement, to lose its otherwise absolute protection, would have to be more than simply controversial, annoying, or embarrassing to supervisors. It would have to cause a measurably, or at least a very likely, harmful effect.

In fact, when the Oregon Supreme Court later had occasion to define the abuse of expression for which a public official can be disciplined, it made incompatibility of the expression with the employee's job responsibilities the essence of the test.[30] Beyond the notion of actual harm, this indicates the precise kind of harm that matters. It also means that the public employee relinquishes absolute rights to speak while holding a government position only to the minimum extent logically required to fulfill the duties of that position.

To illustrate, consider the facts in the Oregon case. A lawyers' disciplinary rule, aimed at preserving fair criminal trials, forbade prosecutors from making public statements in regard to the arrest or prosecution of suspects. A prosecuting attorney was accused of violating the rule by issuing certain statements to the press. The court packed a lot of theory into the following explanation:

The rule addresses the incompatibility between a prosecutor's official function, including his responsibility to preserve the conditions for a fair trial, and speech that, though privileged against other than professional sanctions, vitiates the proper performance of that function under the circum-

29. *Wheeler* v. *Green*, 286 Ore. 99, 593 P.2d 777, 788-89 (1979).

30. *In re Laswell*, 296 Ore. 121, 673 P.2d 855, 857 (1983).

stances of the specific case. In short, a lawyer is not denied freedom to speak, write, or publish; but when one exercises official responsibility for conducting a prosecution according to constitutional standards, one also undertakes the professional responsibility to protect those standards in what he or she says or writes.[31]

The prosecutor was ultimately found not guilty because he neither intended to prejudice the suspects' rights nor did he act with indifference to a serious and imminent risk that his remarks would have that effect.

The lesson of history is that, with respect to freedom of expression, caution is always the right approach. Government employees need the solicitude of free-speech theorists not less, but more, than others, because loss of employment is for most a sanction more serious even than a criminal prosecution.

THE POLITICAL DUTY TO ENFORCE THE CONSTITUTION

Justice Hans Linde, in a 1979 speech about state bills of rights, said: "It is common knowledge that the rights all Americans prize, whether or not they wish to see them enforced, come from the first ten amendments of the United States Constitution. It is common knowledge, but of course it is false."[32] This issue of The Annals should scuttle, for its readers, what remains of the common knowledge that Justice Linde lamented. Yet it is equally common knowledge that the rights all Americans prize, when they do wish to see them enforced, can be safeguarded only by the courts. Of course, it is equally false.

Any notion that the state or federal courts are the only, or even the chief, champions of constitutional liberties is a disservice to honest legislators and a service to dishonest ones. All state legislators and, for that matter, all high executive officers normally pledge as a condition of office to support and defend the constitution of their states and of the United States, "against all enemies, foreign and domestic."[33] Yet those who regularly observe statutes being made hear legislators say, in response to doubts that a bill is constitutional, "That's not our department—let's leave that up to the courts." The policymaker may in fact not know whether the bill is constitutional, but it is certainly his or her department, according to the oath of office.

Lowering our expectations of legislators in this way also places unfair, even intolerable, pressure on elected state judges. A lawmaker who supports a popular bill that he or she knows to have serious constitutional problems receives the political credit for its passage, while the court receives the political heat for its ultimate demise.

All this is standard civics. The enforcement of civil liberties for public workers requires that a stronger claim be made on legislatures than merely to avoid the enactment of unconstitutional laws. It is equally their duty, in my view, to pass laws affirmatively granting those injured by unconstitutional acts a right to sue for damages and other appropriate relief, as well as to recover their attorney fees if they win. Beyond that fairly modest demand, granted by Congress over 100 years ago for state violations of federal rights,[34] I want to make a political claim

31. Ibid., 673 P.2d p. 857.
32. Hans A. Linde, "First Things First," *University of Baltimore Law Review*, 9:379, 380-81 (1980).

33. See, for example, Cal. Const. art. 20, § 3.
34. Civil Rights Act of 1871, 42 U.S.C. § 1983.

on legislators, that they pass laws that attempt to define substantive content for state bills of rights in sufficient detail that officials in charge can be expected to understand and satisfy them.

My first, modest demand is far from being the law of these United States. As of 1985, only seven states had permitted suits, under their common law, for damages for violations of state constitutional rights.[35] Only one state—Massachusetts—has enacted a general right of access to the courts for deprivation of all state constitutional rights, providing a remedy in damages and attorney fees to successful plaintiffs.[36] Oregon law grants prevailing parties their attorney fees in cases involving "discrimination" forbidden by the state constitution.[37] Finally, Connecticut, in an interesting twist that equalizes the speech rights of public and private employees, recently made all employers liable for damages if they discharge their employees for exercising constitutional free-speech rights. According to the Connecticut law, an employee's expression is cause for discharge only when it seriously interferes with his or her job performance or working relationship with the employer.[38]

Civil liberties do not get enforced without civil remedies. It is unrealistic to expect that ordinary citizens can bear on their own the high cost of litigation against public bodies. State legislators who fail to offer effective, compensatory remedies to persons injured by unlawful acts are simply not protecting and defending the constitution against its domestic enemies.

My other demand, less modest but still reasonable, is a political rather than a legal claim. Bills of rights are not commonly expressed in enough detail to allow responsible officials to ensure compliance with them. The federal Fourth Amendment search-and-seizure clause is a conspicuously woeful example. What is to prevent legislatures from spelling out, for example, the narrow circumstances under which a public employee's speech is incompatible with the employee's function? The answer may be different in every state, and there is no guarantee that the state supreme court will agree with it when it is tested by a disciplined employee or his or her union. Surely, though, a good-faith attempt is preferable, on fairness grounds alone, to forcing employees, employers, and courts to hammer out the answers case by case. Or perhaps legislators are still, as they have been in the past, "short-tempered with such claims of freedom, if not to bite, at least to bark at the hand that feeds one."[39]

35. Friesen, "Recovering Damages," pp. 1275-76.

36. Massachusetts Civil Rights Act, Mass. Gen. Laws Ann. chap. 12, §§ 11-H to 11-I (West Supp. 1984-85).

37. Ore. Rev. Stat. 20.107 (1985).

38. Conn. Gen. Stat. Ann. § 31-51q (West 1986).

39. Hans A. Linde, "Constitutional Rights in the Public Sector: Justice Douglas on Liberty in the Welfare State," *Washington Law Review*, 40:10, 19 (1965).

ANNALS, *AAPSS*, **496**, March 1988

Lockstep Analysis and the Concept of Federalism

By EARL M. MALTZ

ABSTRACT: Commentators on state constitutional law have been generally critical of those state courts that follow lockstep analysis. Often these criticisms have relied heavily on the concept of federalism. This reliance is misplaced; lockstep analysis is entirely consistent with basic notions of state autonomy. Instead, it is courts using other approaches that have at times ignored the basic theory of federalism.

Earl M. Maltz is professor of law at Rutgers University in Camden, New Jersey. He graduated with highest distinction from Northwestern University in 1972 and cum laude from Harvard Law School in 1975. At Harvard, he was an editor of the Harvard Law Review. *After graduation he clerked for the Honorable Judge Harrison Winter and practiced law in Milwaukee, Wisconsin, before entering academia. Prior to coming to Rutgers in 1980, he taught at the University of Oklahoma and the University of Arkansas at Little Rock.*

THE rhetoric of federalism has played an important role in the discussion of current developments in state constitutional law. In particular, it has dominated criticism of those courts that have adopted lockstep analysis—the theory that state constitutional provisions should be interpreted to provide exactly the same protections as their federal constitutional counterparts. Commentators have consistently contended that adoption of the lockstep approach is inconsistent with basic principles of state autonomy.

This article will challenge that assertion. The article will begin by describing one of the most controversial lockstep cases and the reaction to the case. It will proceed to demonstrate that lockstep analysis is entirely consistent with the basic concept of American federalism. The article will conclude by arguing that concerns of state autonomy are in fact more heavily implicated when courts adopt other approaches to state constitutional adjudication.

THE LOCKSTEP APPROACH

The Montana case of *State* v. *Jackson*[1] engendered a heated dispute over the desirability of adopting the lockstep approach. *Jackson* began as a prosecution for drunk driving; at issue was the admissibility into evidence of the defendant's refusal to take a breathalyzer test at the time of his arrest. The defendant claimed that such a refusal was testimonial and that, therefore, the admission of the evidence would violate his right to be free from self-incrimination. This right was guaranteed by both the federal and the state constitutions.

Initially, the state supreme court found

the evidence inadmissible by a 4-3 vote.[2] The dissenters argued that Montana had adopted the lockstep approach to self-incrimination issues and that federal constitutional law did not bar the use of the evidence.[3] The majority opinion, by contrast, concluded that the evidence was inadmissible under the Fifth Amendment and that "the issue is also controlled by the [self-incrimination provision] of our own constitution." The majority did not specifically address the question of whether the state constitutional protections might differ from those provided by federal law; in its discussion of the state provision, however, the opinion cited only federal cases to support its conclusion.[4]

The state petitioned the U.S. Supreme Court for a writ of certiorari. Prior to disposition of the writ, the Court held in *South Dakota* v. *Neville* that admission of the type of evidence at issue in *Jackson* did not violate any federal constitutional norms.[5] The Court then vacated *Jackson* and remanded the case for further consideration in light of *Neville*.[6] The action clearly presaged the adoption of the much-maligned rule of *Michigan* v. *Long*:

When . . . a state court decision fairly appears to rest primarily on federal law, or to be interwoven with federal law, and when the adequacy of any possible state ground is not clear from the face of the opinion, we will accept as the most reasonable explanation that the state court decided the case the way it did because it believed that federal law *required* it to do so.[7]

2. 637 P.2d 1 (1981).
3. Ibid., pp. 5-10 (C. J. Haswell, dissenting).
4. Ibid., pp. 4-5. The majority did cite one Montana case for the purpose of distinguishing it from *Jackson*.
5. 459 U.S. 553 (1983).
6. 460 U.S. 1030 (1983).
7. 463 U.S. 1032, 1040-41 (1983).

1. 637 P.2d 1 (1981), *vacated*, 460 U.S. 1030, *rev'd*, 672 P.2d 255 (1983).

On remand, the Montana Supreme Court reversed its earlier stance by a 5-2 margin.[8] All members of the majority firmly embraced the lockstep approach to self-incrimination issues, concluding that in this area of law "'the Montana constitutional guaranty affords no greater protection than that of the Federal constitution.'"[9] This conclusion brought a bitter dissent from Justice Daniel J. Shea, the author of the original majority opinion in *Jackson*. He asserted that "the majority has abdicated [its] responsibility by . . . permit[ting] the United States Supreme Court to tell us what our state constitution means."[10]

Advocates of other approaches have often relied on the concept of state autonomy in criticizing cases such as *Jackson*. Echoing Justice Shea, for example, Robert F. Williams has charged that the lockstep approach "constitutes an unwarranted delegation of state power to the Supreme Court and a resultant abdication of state judicial responsibility."[11] Similarly, Ronald K.L. Collins has accused the second *Jackson* majority of "the abdication of an obligation duly imposed on state judges to be the final

arbiters of state law."[12] In essence, these and other critics claim that the pure independent approach is a necessary corollary of the theory that each state is a quasi-sovereign entity.

To understand the flaw in this argument, one must first analyze the relationship between state court activism generally and the concept of state autonomy. A minority of commentators seems to believe that such activism per se advances the values of federalism. For example, Justice William J. Brennan claimed that "every believer in our concept of federalism . . . must salute this development [of an increasingly activist posture] in our state courts."[13] Similarly, Donald E. Wilkes has described state court protection of rights not protected by federal law as "a cornerstone of federalism."[14] This argument necessarily rests on the premise that a refusal by a state court to be activist implies that the court is allowing the U.S. Supreme Court to control the interpretation of the state constitution. Given this premise, the negative implications of a lack of judicial activism for the principle of state autonomy are obvious.

The difficulty with the argument is that the premise reflects a fundamental confusion between the decision to take an activist posture and the power to choose whether or not to be activist. Plainly, principles of state autonomy guarantee to the state courts the right to

---

8. *State* v. *Jackson*, 672 P.2d 255 (Mont. 1983). In part, this decision was a vindication of the *Long* approach to the relationship between the federal courts and state supreme courts. Justice Frank B. Morrison, Jr., whose vote was essential to the original decision, averred explicitly that he had originally voted to suppress only because he had misunderstood the applicable federal law, later authoritatively construed in *Neville*. Thus review by the Supreme Court had served its proper function—correction of state court mistakes in the application of a federal standard.

9. 672 P.2d at 260, quoting *State* v. *Armstrong*, 552 P.2d 616, 619 (1976).

10. Ibid., p. 262.

11. Robert F. Williams, "In the Supreme Court's Shadow: Legitimacy of State Rejection of Supreme Court Reasoning and Result," *South Carolina Law Review*, 35:353, 404 (1984).

12. Ronald K.L. Collins, "Reliance on State Constitutions—The Montana Disaster," *Texas Law Review*, 63:1095, 1137 (Mar.-Apr. 1985).

13. William J. Brennan, "State Constitutions and the Protection of Individual Rights," *Harvard Law Review*, 90:489, 503 (Jan. 1977).

14. Donald E. Wilkes, Jr., "The New Federalism in Criminal Procedure in 1984: Death of the Phoenix?" in *Developments in State Constitutional Law—The Williamsburg Conference*, ed. B. D. McGraw (St. Paul, MN: West, 1985), pp. 166, 183.

adopt any rule of law not inconsistent with the United States Constitution. In exercising this choice, however, a state court may refuse to take a more activist position than that of the U.S. Supreme Court for a variety of reasons. The state court may be persuaded by the reasoning of the Supreme Court on the issue; it may believe that the state constitution provides less protection than the U.S. Constitution; it may even believe that the state constitution does not deal with the relevant issue at all. In any of those cases, the state court will be bound to apply the law as enunciated by the U.S. Supreme Court. This obligation does not imply, however, that the state court accepts the doctrine of the Supreme Court as a binding interpretation of state law; instead, the obligation is derived from the supremacy clause, which binds the state court to honor applicable federal law.

Once this point is understood, it becomes clear that state court activism in and of itself does not advance the cause of federalism. Federalism is concerned with the allocation of authority between the state and the federal governments. Thus considerations of federalism are important when the U.S. Supreme Court reviews state legislation; the question in such cases is whether a state can retain its locally established rule or whether that rule must yield to a paramount national principle enunciated by the Court. By contrast, state court review under the state constitution raises no such issues. The only question is whether the controlling rule will be that established by the legislature or a court-made substitute. In either case, the relevant decision will be made at the state level.

The decision of the Utah Supreme Court in *Malan* v. *Lewis*[15] illustrates this

15. 693 P.2d 661 (Utah 1984).

point. *Malan* was a challenge to a Utah statute that severely limited the right of nonpaying passengers injured in automobile accidents to maintain negligence actions against their hosts. The U.S. Supreme Court has clearly indicated that such statutes do not violate the equal protection clause of the federal Constitution.[16] The Utah court conceded that the state constitutional provision requiring that "all laws of a general nature shall have uniform operation" embodied the same basic principles as the equal protection clause; indeed, the court purported to derive the appropriate standard of review from federal as well as state case law.[17] Nonetheless, the court found the guest-passenger statute to be inconsistent with the state constitution.

One searches in vain for any enhancement of the autonomy of the state of Utah by the *Malan* decision. The federal government had left Utah free to have a guest statute or not to have a guest statute, at the option of the state. The state legislature had deemed such a statute desirable; the state court found the legislative classification unreasonable. In neither case was any element of the concept of federalism implicated.

Once the link between the concepts of federalism and activism is broken, lockstep analysis emerges in quite a different light. Basically, a decision by a state court to follow such analysis reflects the view that there is no need for additional judicial review in a system where some judicial review is already available in the federal courts. Such a decision does not enhance federal power in any respect; instead, it simply takes account of an unalterable reality—the existence of

16. *Hill* v. *Garner*, 434 U.S. 989 (1977) *dismissing mem.* 561 P.2d 1016; *Silver* v. *Silver*, 180 U.S. 117 (1929).

17. 693 P.2d at 669-74.

federal judicial review—in determining the allocation of authority among state governing bodies. As in *Malan*, the choice is not between federal judicial power and state judicial power, but rather between state judicial power and state legislative power. The courts that advocate lockstep analysis simply choose to allocate maximum power to the state legislature.

In short, the substance of lockstep analysis is entirely consistent with the basic concept of state autonomy. Of course, one can still attack the standard verbal formulations of the lockstep approach, which seem to suggest that U.S. Supreme Court decisions somehow create state constitutional law. For lockstep courts, however, these flaws in articulation have little impact on the practical results reached.

By contrast, analogous difficulties create very real federalism-related problems for more activist state courts. These difficulties revolve around the application of the concept that federal constitutional decisions create a minimum standard for state court analysis. The remainder of this article will explore the problems that this description has created for some state courts.

THE PROBLEM OF THE FALSE FLOOR

The image of federal constitutional law as a floor in state court litigation pervades most commentary on state constitutional law. Commentators contend that in adjudicating cases, state judges must not apply rules that fall below this floor; courts may, however, appeal to the relevant state constitution to establish a higher ceiling of rights for individuals. Elsewhere I have argued that the entire idea that courts can somehow add to the total volume of rights available to members of society is faced with insuperable analytic difficulties.[18] Even leaving these difficulties aside, however, the concept of the federal floor must be carefully circumscribed.

Certainly, as a matter of federal law, state courts are bound not to apply any rule that is inconsistent with decisions of the U.S. Supreme Court; the supremacy clause of the federal Constitution clearly embodies this mandate. It would be a mistake, however, to view federal law as a floor for state constitutional analysis; principles of federalism prohibit the U.S. Supreme Court from dictating the content of state law. In other words, state courts are not required to incorporate federally created principles into their state constitutional analysis; the only requirement is that in the event of an irreconcilable conflict between federal law and state law principles, the federal principles must prevail.

This distinction creates no problems for those courts that follow lockstep analysis. As already noted, this approach rests on the conclusion that judicial activism based on state law is simply inappropriate in the area under consideration. Thus the state court need not speculate on what rights would be guaranteed if such activism were appropriate.

State courts following other models are faced with far more difficult problems. Unlike lockstep courts, they cannot claim to be deferring to the state legislatures except when forbidden to do so by the supremacy clause of the federal Constitution; instead, they must make an independent determination of the merits of each claim based solely on

18. Earl M. Maltz, "The Dark Side of State Court Activism," *Texas Law Review*, 63:995, 1007-11 (Mar.-Apr. 1985).

principles of state constitutional law. If that analysis begins with the federal floor, the state court is allowing a federal government body—the U.S. Supreme Court—to define, at least to some extent, the rights guaranteed by the state constitution. Thus, to avoid conflict with fundamental principles of state autonomy, a state court deciding whether to expand federal protections as a matter of state law must employ a two-stage process. It must determine independently whether the federal protections themselves are incorporated in the state constitution and only then determine whether those protections are more expansive under state law.[19]

THE PERFORMANCE OF THE COURTS

The plurality opinion of the Oregon Supreme Court in *State* v. *Smith*[20] provides a classic example of proper state court methodology. In *Smith*, two deputy sheriffs came upon the defendant when responding to a report of a vehicle off the road. Prior to either being arrested or receiving his *Miranda* warnings, the defendant admitted that he had been drinking but denied owning the disabled vehicle. After the sheriffs were informed by their dispatcher that the defendant did indeed own the vehicle, the defendant admitted ownership and was then arrested for driving under the influence of intoxicants and given his *Miranda* warnings.

The issue in *Smith* was whether the defendant's prewarning statements were inadmissible as evidence against him. Under the U.S. Supreme Court's ruling

in *Berkemer* v. *McCarty*,[21] federal law was no bar to the admission of the statements. Thus the defendant's only viable argument was that the protection against self-incrimination in the Oregon Constitution prevented the statements from being used against him.

The state supreme court rejected this contention. After an extensive review of the Oregon precedents on the subject, Justice J. R. Campbell concluded that state law required only that confessions be voluntary in order to be admitted as evidence.[22] The fact that the defendant incriminated himself prior to receiving *Miranda* warnings thus became irrelevant; because the confession had plainly been voluntary, it could be used against him in court.

The *Smith* result shocked some of those who had hitherto been strong supporters of independent state court analysis. Collins, for example, characterized the decision as "one of the most devastating blows to state constitutional law."[23] Yet the *Smith* opinion merely adopted an approach that reflects the fact that the United States Supreme Court cannot determine the content of state law. Justice Campbell examined the historical development of Oregon law and determined that the federal rule was inconsistent with established state practice. Thus he rejected the federal approach in favor of a different theory.

The *Smith* plurality also demonstrated a commendable sensitivity to the circumstances in which state courts develop their jurisprudence. The opinion suggested that in the absence of a widely applicable federal rule, a different state approach might appropriately be fash-

19. Paul M. Bator, "The State Courts and Federal Constitutional Litigation," *William & Mary Law Review*, 22:605, 605-6 n. 1 (1981).

20. 725 P.2d 894 (1986).

21. 468 U.S. 420 (1984).

22. 725 P.2d at 901-4.

23. *National Law Journal*, 20 Oct. 1986, p. 10, col. 1.

ioned.[24] This observation reflected Campbell's recognition of the reality that state constitutional law does not exist in a vacuum; instead, judges must be aware of the context in which they operate. An important part of this context is the existence of a body of federal constitutional law, which the state courts are powerless to change. In making their decisions, state judges quite properly take the existence of this body of law into account. They cannot, however, allow federal judges to dictate the content of state constitutional doctrine. In short, however one views the precise result in *Smith*, one should admire Justice Campbell's understanding of the basic methodology underlying pure independent analysis.

Unfortunately, the performance of state courts in analyzing search and seizure problems generally has not risen to the same level of excellence. Prior to the decision in *Mapp* v. *Ohio*,[25] state courts were free to consider evidence that was seized in a manner inconsistent with the requirements of the Fourth Amendment. Exercising the discretion available to them under this regime, many states expressly held that as a matter of state law the exclusionary rule did not apply in state criminal prosecutions.[26] *Mapp* changed the rule, holding that evidence seized in violation of the federal Constitution could not be used in any criminal prosecution. In recent years, the U.S. Supreme Court has rendered a variety of decisions that have limited the scope of the *Mapp* requirements. Not surprisingly, litigants often argue that state courts should give a broader reading to the exclusionary rule

as a matter of state constitutional law.

These arguments necessarily involve two related but analytically distinct claims. The first claim is that, as a matter of state law, the evidence was seized illegally. The second is that state law requires that illegally seized evidence be suppressed. Given the state of the pre-*Mapp* law and the generally controversial nature of the exclusionary rule itself, one would expect both extensive discussion of the latter issue and substantial disagreement among state courts regarding the appropriate conclusion.

In fact, post-*Mapp* state courts have paid virtually no attention to the question of whether state law bars the admission of illegally seized evidence. Instead, they have generally assumed without discussion that the exclusionary rule should be applied to state constitutional violations as well as their federal counterparts. Even those state courts that had refused to adopt the exclusionary rule prior to 1960 seem to believe that the *Mapp* holding requires that the exclusionary rule be applied to state constitutional claims as well as their federal counterparts.[27] Some of these courts have extended the exclusionary rule beyond the requirements of federal law.

The recent New Jersey Supreme Court decision in *State* v. *Novembrino*[28] provides a dramatic example. In *Novembrino*, the relevant evidence had been seized under a warrant that the court found had been issued without probable cause; the police, however, had acted on the good-faith belief that the warrant was valid. Under these circumstances, the U.S. Supreme Court had held in

---

24. 725 P.2d at 906.
25. 367 U.S. 643 (1961).
26. See *Elkins* v. *U.S.*, 364 U.S. 206, 224-25 (1960).

27. See, for example, *Wilson* v. *The People*, 398 P.2d 35 (1965); *State* v. *Wood*, 457 So. 2d 206 (La. App. 1984).
28. 519 A.2d 820 (1987).

United States v. *Leon*[29] that the federal Constitution was no obstacle to the admissicn of the evidence. The New Jersey court was asked to rule that as a matter of state law the evidence should be excluded.

One difficulty with this argument is that prior to *Mapp* the New Jersey courts had consistently held that state law did not embrace the exclusionary rule.[30] Indeed, the 1947 state constitutional convention had explicitly rejected an attempt to write the exclusionary rule into the state constitution. Hostility to the basic principle was not the sole motive for rejection of the constitutional provision; some delegates were simply reluctant to bind the state courts to any position on the subject.[31] Nonetheless, it is fair to say that, prior to 1960, all indications in New Jersey bespoke a hostility to the exclusionary rule.

Nonetheless, the court in *Novembrino* refused to apply the *Leon* principle to state law claims and held that the trial court acted properly in suppressing the evidence. In rejecting the dissent's claim that "New Jersey has no historical attachment to the exclusionary rule," Justice Gary S. Stein's majority opinion cited a number of cases.[32] Primarily, however, Justice Stein relied on *State* v. *Valentin*[33] as having "[e]mbedded [the exclusionary rule] in our jurisprudence."[34]

Obviously, there would be nothing untoward about a state court holding either that pre-*Mapp* case law should be reconsidered in the light of subsequent

developments,[35] or even that the case law had been overruled *sub silentio* by later decisions.[36] The heavy reliance on *Valentin*, however, reflects a fundamental misconception regarding the relationship between state and federal law. *Valentin* was an appeal from a denial of a motion to suppress evidence that had allegedly been seized illegally. At the time the motion was denied, New Jersey had no exclusionary rule; thus the prosecuting attorney had submitted no evidence to demonstrate that the search had been reasonable. Before disposition of the appeal, *Mapp* established that state courts were required to suppress evidence seized in violation of federal constitutional norms. Thus the *Valentin* court remanded the case for development of a record on the issue of the legality of the seizure.

Admittedly, *Valentin* made passing reference to the fact that the defendant had raised both state and federal claims[37] and noted that in devising new procedures the courts should consider "the provisions of the constitutions of both sovereignties."[38] The mandate of the court, however, directed only that "both parties [should be permitted] to introduce all relevant proof on the new issue generated by *Mapp*."[39] Thus the *Valentin* decision did not embed the exclusionary rule in New Jersey state constitutional law; it simply purported to apply the rule of federal law established in *Mapp*. Yet that rule by its nature could only apply the exclusionary rule to cases in which the federal Con-

29. 468 U.S. 897 (1984).
30. For example, *Eleuteri* v. *Richman*, 141 A.2d 46, *cert. denied*, 358 U.S. 843 (1958); *State* v. *Alexander*, 83 A.2d 441 (1951), *cert. denied*, 343 U.S. 908 (1952).
31. 519 A.2d at 851.
32. Ibid., p. 851, n. 30.
33. 174 A.2d 737 (1961).
34. 519 A.2d at 851.
35. Ibid., pp. 851-53.
36. For this point, the New Jersey Supreme Court might have relied on *State* v. *Hunt*, 450 A.2d 952 (1982).
37. 174 A.2d at 737.
38. Ibid., p. 738.
39. Ibid.

stitution had been violated; the U.S. Supreme Court is powerless to mandate that the exclusionary rule apply to state constitutional claims. It was thus the obligation of the New Jersey state courts to explore independently the question of whether state law generally required the exclusion of evidence in cases where state law was violated but federal law did not require its suppression. By simply assuming that as a matter of state law *Mapp* and *Valentin* automatically overruled previous state court rejections of the exclusionary rule, the *Novembrino* court acted inconsistently with basic premises of state autonomy and federalism.

In short, the concept of federalism suggests constraints on judges who would adopt some approach other than lockstep analysis in state constitutional adjudication. These constraints are, however, relatively minor. The only necessity is that state courts consult their own pre-existing law rather than mindlessly adopting federal constitutional standards as a floor for state constitutional analysis. Once this requirement is satisfied, considerations of state autonomy are simply irrelevant to the ultimate result.

CONCLUSION

Discussions of state autonomy have played far too large a role in state constitutional analysis. Upon close examination, most of the expressed federalism-related concerns prove groundless. Moreover, by focusing on such considerations, courts and commentators divert attention from the real issues involved, issues concerning the allocation of decision-making authority within each state's government.

Analysis of this problem should begin by reference to general constitutional theory.[40] Application of such theory, however, must also take into account the special context in which state courts operate. Many commentators point to state-specific characteristics that they claim should lead state courts to assume greater power in the governing process.[41] These activists typically ignore the central point recognized by the plurality in *Smith*: that state courts operate in an environment in which the legislature will always be constrained by federal judicial review.

This fact generates the central issue of state constitutional theory: do we wish to construct a system in which the judgment of state legislatures is subordinated to the sense of fairness of not one but two sets of judges? The activist response has often been that such a system is a necessary corollary to the American concept of federalism. As I have tried to demonstrate, this argument is totally unsound. Thus, until a more persuasive justification is put forth, the case for state court activism will remain unproven.

40. Some commentators have recognized this point. See David R. Keyser, "State Constitutions and Theories of Judicial Review," *Texas Law Review*, 63:1051 (Mar.-Apr. 1985); Hans A. Linde, "E Pluribus—Constitutional Theory and State Courts," *Georgia Law Review*, 18:165 (Winter 1984); Maltz, "Dark Side."

41. See, for example, Lawrence G. Sager, "Foreword: State Courts and the Strategic Space between the Norms and Rules of Constitutional Law," *Texas Law Review*, 63:959 (Mar.-Apr. 1985); Williams, "In the Supreme Court's Shadow," pp. 389-402.

ANNALS, *AAPSS*, **496**, March 1988

Intergovernmental Relations in
State Constitutional Law:
A Historical Overview

By MICHAEL E. LIBONATI

ABSTRACT: In the aftermath of the American Revolution, the relationship between local governments and their states could have been conceptualized in terms of four competing models of legitimacy: (1) custom and practice, (2) community autonomy, (3) corporate status, and (4) subordination to the sovereign. The implications for local autonomy and state-local relations of accepting each of these models is discussed in this article. Historically, the triumph of the theory of state hegemony over local government was reflected in judicial adoption of Dillon's Rule, the doctrine of implied preemption, and the idea that local governments have no rights under a state constitution. Recent state-court cases recognizing the capacity of local governments to assert procedural, dignitary, and substantive claims against the state, however, may signal the demise of the theory that local governments are merely creatures of their states and may herald a reconceptualization of the meaning of local autonomy.

Michael E. Libonati received bachelor's and master of law degrees at Yale University. Currently professor of law at Temple University, Philadelphia, he has served as visiting professor of law at the University of Alabama, Cornell University, and the College of William and Mary. He has served on the editorial board of the American Journal of Legal History *and on the Council of the American Bar Association's Urban, State and Local Government Law Section. In 1982, he completed publication of the four-volume* Local Government Law, *coauthored with the late C. Dallas Sands.*

NOTE: The research support of the Temple Law School Foundation is gratefully acknowledged.

107

AFTER 1787, the United States had national, state, and local government. Only national and state government, however, enjoyed "constitutional legitimacy."[1] The failure of the framers of either the U.S. Constitution or the state constitutions to include provisions "separating powers vertically (state-local) as well as horizontally (executive-legislative-judicial)"[2] had pervasive consequences for local government. An intellectual milieu quickly developed in which policy questions about intergovernmental structure and functions were forestalled and engrossed by debates concerning the constitutional legitimacy and autonomy of local government. The purpose of this article is to identify and appraise four competing constitutional models of local government—conceptions that were already at hand during the intellectual ferment attending the American Revolution—to sketch their evolution and transformation during the nineteenth century, and to depict briefly their contemporary impact. These models are custom and practice, community autonomy, corporate status, and subordination to the sovereign.

CUSTOM AND PRACTICE

Claims to local rights emerging out of custom ought to be congenial to the common-law mind, even in the field of public law.[3] Towns in Massachusetts, for example, exercised a variety of regulatory and entrepreneurial functions

during the colonial period without any firmer warrant than custom and practice.[4] Demophilus, a revolutionary pamphleteer, invoked the usage of free Saxon communities when urging the framers of Pennsylvania's constitution to purge a reconstituted commonwealth of the pernicious accretions of Norman centralization in the allocation of power.[5] Judge Thomas M. Cooley's assertion of an inherent right to local self-government is grounded on the notion that there are "powers which from time immemorial have been locally possessed and exercised."[6]

The arguments furnished by Demophilus and by Cooley are, however, skewed by the pervasive ideology of constitutionalism. Neither was interested in fashioning the kind of ingenious gloss on custom that allowed medieval jurists to reconcile state sovereignty with the de facto independence or autonomy of cities.[7] Demophilus called for the incorporation of the details of a mythicized Saxon public customary law into a written constitutional text. But what if the state constitution is silent? Cooley argued that the custom and practice of local government is so pervasive that local autonomy from state legislative

1. James E. Herget, "The Missing Power of Local Government: A Divergence between Text and Practice in Our Early State Constitution," *Virginia Law Review*, 62(5):999, 1001 (June 1976).

2. Ibid.

3. J.G.A. Pocock, *The Ancient Constitution and the Feudal Law* (New York: Norton, 1967), pp. 30-55.

4. Oscar Handlin and Mary F. Handlin, *Commonwealth: A Study of the Role of Government in the American Economy: Massachusetts, 1774-1861*, rev. ed. (Cambridge, MA: Harvard University Press, Belknap Press, 1969), pp. 87-88.

5. Demophilus, *The Genuine Principles of the Ancient Saxon or English Constitution* (Philadelphia: Robert Bell, 1776). See generally H. Trevor Colbourn, *The Lamp of Experience: Whig History and the Intellectual Origins of the American Revolution* (Chapel Hill: University of North Carolina Press, 1965).

6. *People* v. *Hurlbut*, 24 Mich. 44, 109 (1871).

7. Joseph Canning, *The Political Thought of Baldus de Ubaldis* (New York: Cambridge University Press, 1987), pp. 64-65, 67-68, 93-158.

interference must be read into a state constitutional document even when it does not expressly speak to the issue. A subsequent state court decision, however, summarized and disposed of Cooley's contentions in the following language:

The principal circumstances from which the court there found in the constitution of that state implied restrictions upon the power of the legislature, as regards local government, were, first, that the constitution was adopted in view of a well-understood and tolerably uniform system of local government existing from the earliest settlement of the country, and secondly, that the liberties of the people were generally supposed to spring from and to depend upon that system.

With respect to the second point, whatever may be the historical origin of the liberties of the people, they seem to be dependent at the present day upon the right of the people to participate by suffrage and by representation in the government which they themselves have established under the guaranties of a written constitution. The absence from such written constitution of any guaranty of local self-government is a cogent argument against its existence as a right.

With respect to the first point, the constitution of this state was not adopted in view of any uniform system of local governments, for we have had none such; certainly no uniform recognition of the right of local self-government that is here contended for.[8]

Although Cooley's formulation is no longer taken seriously in the field of state constitutional law,[9] it may linger, like the smile of the Cheshire cat, in a mood or predisposition in favor of local autonomy, such as that sketched by Richard Briffault.[10]

8. *Attorney General ex. rel. Booth* v. *Mc-Guinness*, 78 N.J.L. 346, 355 (1909).

9. C. Dallas Sands and Michael E. Libonati, *Local Government Law* (Wilmette, IL: Callaghan, 1981), chap. 3.

10. Richard Briffault, "Localism in State

COMMUNITY AUTONOMY

A robust practice of civic republicanism[11] based on the dispositive powers of local juries and on local militia flourished during the Revolutionary War. Thus a Connecticut town was deemed empowered to pay an enlistment bonus to those who had served in the Continental Army.[12] In 1814, a coastal town unanimously voted to levy a tax to defray expenditures for its defense during a British invasion. A taxpayer challenging the legality of the tax contended that

the practice of towns during the revolutionary war may perhaps be cited in support of the act of the town. . . . [b]ut that was a period of confusion and anarchy, from which precedents cannot be drawn in times of settled government. Towns then at one time or another, exercised almost all the powers of sovereignty. By the constitution of the United States, the power of raising and supporting armies, and all necessary concomitant powers, are vested exclusively in Congress. The common defense is committed to that body, and all necessary means for that object. It can, then, make no portion of the necessary expenses of our towns.[13]

In ruling in the challenger's favor, Chief Justice Isaac Parker rejected the communitarian notion that the town could assume a duty to defend itself against the incursions of an enemy in

Constitutional Law," this issue of *The Annals* of the American Academy of Political and Social Science.

11. J.G.A. Pocock, *The Machiavellian Moment: Florentine Political Thought and the Atlantic Republic Tradition* (Princeton, NJ: Princeton University Press, 1975); Forrest McDonald, *Novus Ordo Seclorum: The Intellectual Origins of the Constitution* (Lawrence: University Press of Kansas, 1985), pp. 71-72, 289-91.

12. *Hitchcock* v. *Town of Litchfield*, 1 Root 206 (1790).

13. *Stetson* v. *Kempton*, 13 Mass. 272, 274 (1816).

time of war, as towns are "creatures of legislation . . . enjoying only the powers which are expressly granted them."[14] Thus a thick, rich, and complex practice of civic community was rejected and replaced by an abstract juridical entity— a municipality whose powers are derived from and subject to the sovereign state legislature.

In the last quarter of the nineteenth century, the idea of community reengaged leading academic thinkers.[15] Similarly, under the aegis of the home-rule movement, state constitutional provisions according local governments meaningful autonomy were enacted. The Ohio Constitution conferred on municipalities "all powers of local self-government,"[16] that is, the capacity to initiate actions over a wide range of issues in terms of the municipality's own goals.[17] The California Constitution conferred not only policymaking initiative but also immunity from state legislative interference in "municipal affairs."[18]

In retrospect, it is apparent that the resurgent communitarian commitment of the home-rule movement recapitulated a characteristic vice of American thinking about government—the ideology of constitutionalism. Home rule on the Ohio and California model sought to legitimate local autonomy by constitutionalizing a rigid formula allocating power within the polity. The constitutionalization of local rights had the effect of turning policy debates about the scope of local initiative and the

allocation of powers between state and local decision makers into constitutional questions resolvable only by the state judiciary. The dream of local autonomy realized itself in a regimen of "judicial home rule" in which state courts demonstrated their inability to draw sensible boundaries between state and local functions.[19] Most modern state constitutional provisions on home rule reject the *imperium in imperio* model. Instead, the formulation of the American Municipal Association and the National League of Cities, under which the state legislature retains full control over the scope of local powers, predominates.

The contemporary rediscovery of the value of community and decentralization will perform a useful service to the extent that it shifts the focus of attention from historical, philosophical, and political controversies about legitimation to concrete questions of institutional policy analysis, that is, questions concerning which functions of government are most appropriately handled by particular governments—federal, state, or local. Contemporary communalism has, unfortunately, little to say about the limits of community autonomy or about the circumstances under which the broader polity may be obliged to scrutinize, review, or overturn local initiatives. The prevalence of two complementary remedial devices—claims under the Civil Rights Act for violation of federally created rights, and the taxpayer's action, which affords individuals standing to challenge the legality of a wide variety of official decisions under state law—seems to go a long way toward answering the

---

14. Ibid., p. 284.
15. R. Jackson Wilson, *In Quest of Community: Social Philosophy in the United States, 1860-1920* (New York: John Wiley, 1968), pp. 26-31.
16. Ohio Const. art. XVIII, §§ 3, 7.
17. Gordon L. Clark, *Judges and the Cities* (Chicago: University of Chicago Press, 1985), p. 6.
18. California Const. art. XI, § 5(a).

19. Jefferson B. Fordham and Joe F. Asher, "Home Rule Powers in Theory and Practice," *Ohio State Law Journal*, 9(1):18 (1948); Sho Sato, "'Municipal Affairs' in California," *California Law Review*, 60(4):1055 (June 1972).

suspicions that local governments are dominated by "discrete and insular majorities." Such suspicions have dominated much of elite discourse about the decentralization of power since *The Federalist.*

Communalism can also be criticized for its failure to face the fact that local governments cannot be confined to a purely representative role that simply mirrors the consensus preferences of the majority. As Gordon Clark has reminded us, local governments are also bureaucratic organizations with their own agendas of power and continuity, which may or may not correspond to the interests of their putative constituents.[20]

CORPORATE STATUS

A third vision for legitimating local government rights derives from the ambiguous status of local government as a corporate entity that performs governmental and proprietary functions. Prior to the Revolution, most corporations were entities such as towns, parishes, and common fields, "created in order to enable individuals to pool their wealth for community purposes."[21] Chartered municipal corporations were instruments for stimulating commercial development and promoting trade. Their aims were narrow: preserving monopolies in the hands of licensed tradesmen and artisans; regulating markets; price fixing; and setting standards of quality, weight, and measure for commodities authorized to be sold in the city.[22] The corporation was self-supporting, raising revenues by collecting import or sales duties, licensing fees, and rents from the commercial facilities that it owned and operated. Holding fast to the doctrine of the inviolability of the corporate charter then prevalent in England, the municipal corporation of Philadelphia, for example, refused to accept new responsibilities in the areas of public health, safety, and welfare.[23]

Had the doctrine of charter inviolability, which frustrated the attempt of the New Hampshire legislature to assert control over the corporation of Dartmouth College,[24] been extended to municipal corporations, qualifying municipalities would have possessed enforceable autonomy rights against the state. At minimum, a municipal corporation acting in a proprietary capacity would have received the same protections under the U.S. Constitution as that vouchsafed to their private sector brethren. This approach was decisively rejected by the United States Supreme Court when it sanctioned the New Jersey legislature's policy of expropriating municipally owned water-diversion rights without compensation while paying for identical rights in private ownership.[25]

At the state level, Hendrik A. Hartog's masterful monograph on the evolution of New York's law of municipal corporations demonstrates that the city of New York was transformed from a protagonist with significant powers of initiative and immunity into a dependent

20. Clark, *Judges and the Cities,* p. 6.

21. William E. Nelson, *Americanization of the Common Law: The Impact of Legal Change on Massachusetts Society, 1760-1830* (Cambridge, MA: Harvard University Press, 1975), p. 6.

22. Jon C. Teaford, *The Municipal Revolution in America* (Chicago: University of Chicago Press, 1975), pp. 16-34.

23. Judith M. Diamondstone, "Philadelphia's Municipal Corporation, 1701-1776," *Pennsylvania Magazine of History and Biography,* 90:183 (Apr. 1966).

24. *Trustees of Dartmouth College* v. *Woodward,* 4 Wheat. (17 U.S.) 518, 4 L.Ed. 629 (1819).

25. *Trenton* v. *State of New Jersey,* 262 U.S. 182 (1923).

Caliban under the tutelage of the state legislature.[26] Even less protection against state legislative intervention was afforded by other state courts. For example, the Pennsylvania Supreme Court vigorously rejected the city of Philadelphia's claims that a state statute impermissibly stripped it of powers or franchises held in its proprietary capacity. The court held that the city charter was "in no sense a contract with the state—and therefore fully subject to the control of the legislature."[27]

What the Pennsylvania Supreme Court sustained was an early example of what came to be known as ripper legislation—state statutes that divested a city of its power to administer its parks or police force or personnel matters. Such legislation typically sought to remove as many areas of decision making as possible from local political control by vesting power over municipal functions in state appointees carrying out a state-formulated agenda.[28]

These developments have most clearly affected local government not through constitutional discourse but through the application of what Peter J. Steinberger calls the "ideology of managerialism."[29]

Our legacy from managerialism is significant. It has yielded a harvest of innovations. To the managerial approach we owe these structural forms: the council-manager form of government, the independent board, and metropolitan

government. On the procedural front, civil service, the merit system, and the creation of a rationalized and professional local administrative system are products of managerialism. Substantively, managerialism stands for rational planning and social engineering. At its best, managerialism represents a skilled and committed elite of experts in service to a broadened vision of community. At its worst, managerialism squeezes the citizenry out of the public space in which decisions are made. The commitment to expertise and professionalism on the part of managers also breeds careerism, job hopping, and a failure to commit to the community for the long, slow process of implementing any innovation. The triumph of managerialism imports a transformation of local law into a subordinate topic within the field of hyperextended administrative law stretching from the federal government to the smallest local government. As Steinberger observes, managerial principles, such as centralization, hierarchy, and formal coordination, are inimical to claims for an autonomous city government.[30]

SUBORDINATION TO THE SOVEREIGN

The most influential patrimony shaping dominant American conceptions about the allocation of powers in society crystallized at the close of the eighteenth century. The natural-rights approach stemmed from an earlier intellectual and political movement in Europe in which the sovereign state and the sovereign individual allied themselves against the corporation.[31] No room was left for

26. Hendrik A. Hartog, *Public Property and Private Power: The Corporation of the City of New York in American Law, 1730-1870* (Chapel Hill: University of North Carolina Press, 1983).

27. *Philadelphia* v. *Fox*, 64 Pa. 169, 180-81 (1870).

28. Martin J. Schiesl, *The Politics of Efficiency* (Berkeley: University of California Press, 1977).

29. Peter J. Steinberger, *Ideology and the Urban Crisis* (Albany: State University of New York Press, 1985), pp. 28-36.

30. Ibid., p. 133.

31. Otto Gierke, *Associations and the Law* (Buffalo, NY: University of Toronto Press, 1977), pp. 43-44.

intermediate bodies in the amalgam of individualism, natural law, and statism that prevailed during the Enlightenment.[32] As Otto Gierke pointed out in his magisterial summation of the natural-rights tradition as of 1650, local polities were regarded as "no more than administrative institutions" that "the sovereign could create, transform or abolish in light of his own free judgment of their utility."[33]

Two centuries later, Judge John F. Dillon identified the state legislature as the sovereign and reiterated the natural-rights orthodoxy concerning the subordinate status of local government in the following words: "Municipal corporations owe their origin to, and derive their powers and rights wholly from, the legislature. It breathes into them the breath of life, without which they cannot exist. As it creates, so it may destroy. If it may destroy, it may abridge and control."[34] The message of this text is blunt: the state legislature is the boss; the state legislature commands, localities obey. There is no room for disharmony or plurality of governmental interests within the structure of state government. The judiciary acknowledges, supports, and legitimizes the intellectual construct of a unitary, centralized sovereign endowed with the arbitrary and despotic power of Uranus over his children.

The normative effects of Dillon's approach go beyond the rejection of local government claims to immunity from state legislative control. First, the unitary theory of sovereignty entails a positivist stance toward claims of local initiative.

That is, the scope of local structural and programmatic initiatives must be confined to that which is granted by state enabling legislation. Second, statutes empowering local government units are in derogation of sovereignty and hence must be construed narrowly. Thus Dillon's rule of interpretation flows from his concept of sovereignty.[35] Third, because local governments are subordinate and the state is dominant, any jurisdictional conflict must be resolved in favor of the hierarchically superior governmental unit. Because courts serve as the lions under the sovereign's throne, they undertake to safeguard the primacy of the state not only when a statute directly ousts local jurisdiction but also when a local exercise of power conflicts with a state statute. Thus courts have fashioned and applied a doctrine of implied preemption that quashes, in the interest of the sovereign, local initiatives sanctioned by enabling legislation deemed discordant with other state statutes.[36] Fourth, because the state constitution confers no rights upon a local government unit against the state sovereign, a local government unit has no capacity to assert state constitutional claims against the state sovereign.

Each of these four effects of the natural-rights theory of sovereignty has left its mark on state constitutional law. In Georgia, a legislative attempt to confer home-rule powers on the city of Atlanta was struck down as an unconsti-

32. Ibid., p. 5.
33. Otto Gierke, *Natural Law and the Theory of Society 1500 to 1800* (Boston: Beacon, 1960), p. 67.
34. *Clinton v. Cedar Rapids and Missouri River Railroad*, 24 Iowa 455 (1868).

35. *State v. Thompson*, 149 Wis. 488, 505, 137 N.W. 20 (1912); Sands and Libonati, *Local Government Law*, sec. 13.05.
36. The fallacious reasoning underpinning the doctrine of implied preemption as conventionally formulated is discussed in *Commonwealth of Pennsylvania, Department of General Services v. Ogontz Area Neighbors Association*, 505 Pa. 614, 483 A.2d. 448 (1984).

tutional delegation of sovereign legislative powers, thus necessitating an amendment to the state constitution in order to permit home rule. The Iowa Constitution had to be amended to overturn Dillon's rule of strict and niggardly interpretation of legislative grants of power to municipalities.[37] The home-rule provision of the Illinois Constitution contains an elaborate set of rules addressing the question of preemption,[38] as well as a provision mandating that the "powers and functions of home rule units shall be construed liberally."[39]

LOCAL GOVERNMENT'S CAPACITY TO SUE

I should like to close this article with an extended discussion of emerging trends in state court decisions on the problem of local government's capacity to sue, because these decisions and their ramifications bode well for a resurgent commitment to local self-government.

The laurel for the most sensible approach in reported cases goes to the Utah Supreme Court.[40] A county sought to challenge the constitutionality of a state assessment of mining properties because the assessment level did not reflect the full cash-value standard embedded in the state constitution. The Utah Supreme Court enunciated two criteria, one aimed at the objective of assuring a full and vigorous adversarial presentation of the claim and another

designed to vindicate the public interest in assuring the rule of law. The county was held to have capacity to sue on the basis of traditional standing criteria: that the interests of the parties be adverse, and that the challenging party have a legally protectable interest in the controversy. The Utah court did not succumb to the blandishments of the notion that the county, as a creature of the state, was irrebuttably presumed to exist in happy harmony with the state. The court held that the assessment determinations of the state tax commission directly and adversely affect county budget and taxing functions to the extent that mining properties are underassessed.

The court also delineated a second, separate standing test, which is germane to the creation of a sound public-law doctrine. According to that criterion, a local government unit is afforded standing to raise issues of great public importance that are susceptible to judicial resolution. Under this criterion, the county can sue because, otherwise, underassessments could be effectively insulated from challenges that would not likely be brought by a property owner benefiting from underassessment, the state agency making the underassessment, or a county taxpayer. That is, county standing is recognized on the pragmatic footing that only the local government unit has the will and resources to check constitutional misconduct in state administration of the assessing function.

The Utah test recognizes that localities have interests different from those of the state. It further recognizes that localities are not servants of the state but potential protagonists in the ongoing process by which power is shaped and shared. Note the tack that the Utah court could have taken. The state lawmaking process is the exclusive forum for working out

37. Iowa Const. art III, § 40. The state constitutions of Alaska, New Jersey, Michigan, and Montana contain similar provisions that require local government powers to be liberally interpreted. Sands and Libonati, *Local Government Law*, sec. 13.05, n. 23.

38. Ill. Const. art. VII, § 6(g), (h), (i).

39. Ibid., § 6(m).

40. *Kennecott Corporation* v. *Salt Lake County*, 702 P.2d 451 (1985).

controversies between centralization and localism. Because citizens are the only bearers of participatory rights, and they are fully represented in the legislature, there can be no judicially cognizable conflict between the generalized interest represented by the state and the parochial interests asserted by local governments. If localities are aggrieved, their grievances are resolvable exclusively by the centralized decision-making apparatus known as the state legislature. The structure of this argument mirrors the U.S. Supreme Court's reasoning in *Garcia*.[41] Just as states have no claims against the national government because their interests are fully represented in the national legislature, so localities cannot be heard to complain of actions by the states.

It is now time to turn from capacity and standing questions to the trend of decisions concerning specific allegations of infringement of state constitutional norms.

One significant cluster of claims has to do with the procedural validity of state statutes affecting units of local government. These challenges involve purported violations of such state constitutional arcana as the subject-title rule and the prohibition of local or special legislation. As a practical matter, much state legislation having to do with local government takes the form of pure public law, that is, statutes that address themselves to the internal processes or routines of local public administration.[42]

Consequently, no individual rights or entitlements are affected by such statutes, and there is no probability that an individual or private organization or taxpayer will be inclined to contest them. Unless the affected local entity can challenge their validity, statutes that are at root unconstitutional will be controlling. Recent state court decisions recognize successful challenges by local government units against statutes with a defective title, local or special legislation, and even statutes violating separation-of-powers principles.

Some courts are tacitly recognizing the dignitary interests of local governments, that is, their right to procedural and substantive fair treatment. A municipality subject to the regulatory authority of a state land-use development agency was held to be constitutionally entitled to notice and to an opportunity to be heard on a development application pending before the agency. An intermediate appellate court in Ohio ruled that the equal protection provision of the Ohio Constitution applies to a municipality exercising proprietary functions. The court held that a state agency acted unconstitutionally when it imposed obligations on the city of Cleveland not imposed on other public or private sector entities. Other courts have employed a rational basis standard for appraising the validity of local government challenges to state statutory classifications.

---

41. *Garcia* v. *San Antonio Metropolitan Transit Authority*, 469 U.S. 528 (1985).

42. The skeptical reader is invited to peruse the statutes pertinent to local government units in his or her own jurisdiction. Unless he or she has some familiarity with the field, the reader will be astonished to note the utter absence of annotations to judicial decisions glossing an enormous body of law except, of course, insofar as the statute speaks to powers affecting the private rather than the public sector. Many annotations emerge out of controversies submitted to the attorney general or the comptroller concerning the construction of statutes bearing on local public administration given that a judicial forum for the resolution of such disputes is not normally available because of the law of standing.

Several other recent cases show a willingness to apply substantive constitutional protections to local governments. Thus a Pennsylvania constitutional provision prohibiting the taking of property without just compensation was held to invalidate the uncompensated expropriation of a city-owned park. A Tennessee appellate court ruled that retroactive application of a statutory provision holding the statute of limitations applicable to actions against governmental entities impermissibly stripped a governmental entity of a vested right.

A fascinating set of cases traces the implementation of state constitutional provisions in Michigan and Missouri, which prohibit the state both from mandating new or expanded activities by local governments without full state financing of the additional costs and from reducing the state financing proportion of the costs of existing mandates.[43] Accordingly, a state statute imposing new duties on localities with respect to solid-waste management resulting in increased costs was unconstitutional. A state statute increasing the salaries of county employees was held to violate the Missouri version of this significant new guarantor of local fiscal autonomy.

CONCLUSION

The recognition of procedural, dignitary, and autonomy interests of local governments has significant implications for state-local relations. In the first place, state courts have begun to undo the unitary theory of sovereignty whereby localities are presumed not to have interests adverse to those of the state that created them. Second, local gov-

43. Mich. Const. art. 9, § 26; Mo. Const. art. X, §§ 16-24.

ernments are viewed not as mere servants of the state but as potential protagonists in the ongoing process by which state legislative claims to omnipotence are checked and balanced by judicial review. Third, a significant new class of potential plaintiffs is now empowered to vindicate the rule of law in a variety of public-law areas hitherto unscrutinized by the state judiciary. Fourth, state courts have indicated an increased willingness to resolve conflicts that inevitably arise between the general interests represented by the state and the particular interests represented by local governments within the overriding framework of the state constitution.

Obviously, the decisions reviewed here do not rest easily within the frameworks provided by the four models of legitimacy that have been sketched. At the same time, however, recent state court decisions do not yet reflect a resurgent commitment to a robust autonomy for local governments. Instead, the decisions seek largely to enlist local communities in holding the state accountable to the rule of law as embedded in the state constitution. Most of the court decisions do not rest upon the distinction between governmental and proprietary functions that underlies the corporate-status approach to intergovernmental questions arising under the state constitution. The doctrine of state hegemony over the activities and affairs of local government is neither repudiated nor, for the most part, addressed directly and forthrightly. It is generally ignored or sidestepped. Nevertheless, the impact of these decisions forces a reopening of problems and questions slighted by that peculiar congeries of statism, individualism, and natural rights that has ruled the conceptual roost for the past century in state constitutional law.

ANNALS, *AAPSS*, **496**, March 1988

Localism in
State Constitutional Law

By RICHARD BRIFFAULT

ABSTRACT: It is a truism of state constitutional law that states have plenary authority over local governments. Some scholars believe that giving local governments more power would be an appropriate reform. A review of the school finance and exclusionary zoning litigations of the past two decades, however, indicates that local governments have considerable autonomy and that many state courts are committed to notions of local control. This state court commitment to localism has frequently been grounded in concerns for protection of the home and family. Such localism is problematic given the limited fiscal capacity of many localities and the external effects of certain local actions. Many localities would, in fact, be better off if the states were compelled to assume greater oversight and fiscal responsibility for local affairs.

Richard Briffault is associate professor of law at the Columbia University School of Law. He has published articles in the Columbia Law Review *and the* Texas Law Review.

A persistent theme in the literature of state-local relations has been that states enjoy plenary power in their dealings with local governments, while local governments are legally powerless. The black-letter rules of state-local relations are that states have complete hegemony over their political subdivisions; local governments are mere creatures of the states, possessing only those powers delegated by the states; and there is no such thing as an inherent right of local self-government.[1] Many scholars have been critical of these rules and have called for greater local power.[2] While proponents of local autonomy recognize that the states have delegated substantial powers to local governments, these critics contend that the legal foundations of local autonomy are insecure and ultimately insubstantial.

This notion of plenary state power with inherent local powerlessness significantly understates the degree to which state courts have supported the concept of strong local governments, and it misses the substantial amount of real power enjoyed by many local governments. The force of localism in state jurisprudence was dramatically underscored by two major law reform initiatives pursued in state courts during the last two decades: challenges to the local property-tax-based system of funding public education and to suburban exclusionary zoning.

The school finance and exclusionary zoning litigations are of central signifi-

cance in understanding the structure of contemporary state-local relations. Education is the leading service provided by local governments, and zoning is the principal regulatory activity of local governments. The litigations were pursued in state courts and framed in terms of state constitutional doctrines.[3] Moreover, these lawsuits addressed weaknesses in the concept of local autonomy that even advocates of local power recognize: the limited fiscal capacity of many localities to provide basic public services, and the extra-local effects of local actions.

Nevertheless, neither initiative actually did much to alter local responsibility for financing education or to weaken local power over land use. The state courts displayed a localist orientation, regularly assenting to the delegation of significant powers and duties to localities and treating the challenges as an unwelcome threat to local autonomy. The role of localism in maintaining social and economic inequities was often acknowledged, but the commitment to local autonomy was usually given primacy. These cases indicate that the states' abdication of oversight and fiscal responsibility for delegated functions is at least as much of a dilemma as city powerlessness.

THE SCHOOL FINANCE AND EXCLUSIONARY ZONING LITIGATIONS

The school finance and exclusionary zoning litigations grew out of several

1. Chester Antieau, *Municipal Corporation Law* (New York: Matthew Bender, 1986), sec. 2.00; Eugene McQuillen, *Law of Municipal Corporations*, 3rd ed. (Wilmette, IL: Callaghan, 1971), secs. 1.21, 1.42; C. Dallas Sands and Michael Libonati, *Local Government Law* (Wilmette, IL: Callaghan, 1981), sec. 2.03.

2. See, for example, Gerald Frug, "The City as a Legal Concept," *Harvard Law Review*, 93:1057 (1980).

3. Both challenges were initially brought as federal constitutional claims, but these were rejected by the U.S. Supreme Court. See, for example, *Warth* v. *Seldin*, 422 U.S. 490 (1975); *Village of Belle Terre* v. *Boraas*, 416 U.S. 1 (1974); *San Antonio Independent School District* v. *Rodriguez*, 411 U.S. 1 (1973); *James* v. *Valtierra*, 402 U.S. 137 (1971).

underlying conditions in state-local relations. The states have generally delegated to local governments the responsibility for providing many basic public services, including elementary and secondary education and the authority to control land use. Local governments derive most of their own-source revenues from the real property tax, and the quality of local public services is significantly determined by taxable wealth. Due to the uneven distribution of industrial facilities and upper-income residential properties, there is an enormous variety in taxable wealth among localities.[4] Although all states provide some fiscal assistance to their localities, wealthier communities are able to spend far more on services like public education than can poorer ones. Moreover, local units have an incentive to maintain their taxable wealth per capita in order to keep taxes down and keep property values up while providing desired levels of public services.

Many suburbs have used their zoning authority to protect the local fisc. Zoning ordinances excluding multifamily housing or requiring that homes be of large size and built on large lots are widespread. These devices tend to assure that new residents have wealth as great as or greater than the current residents, to prevent lower-income families from moving to these communities, and to drive up the cost of housing throughout the region. Exclusionary zoning limits housing opportunities and exacerbates the interlocal gap in the quality of public services.

The local property-tax-based system of school finance and suburban exclu-

4. See, for example, Robert Inman and Daniel Rubinfeld, "The Judicial Pursuit of Local Fiscal Equity," *Harvard Law Review*, 92:1662 (1979).

sionary zoning reflect and reinforce social and economic inequities. Starting in the 1960s, serious legal challenges to these practices were mounted by reformers. Advocates of school finance reform sought to sever the link between local wealth and the quality of local education by requiring states to assume a significant degree of responsibility for financing public schools. The attack on exclusionary zoning was aimed at opening the suburbs to lower-cost housing. The goals of the two movements were interrelated. Reducing the local role in school financing would ease local tax burdens and reduce the incentive to zone out lower-income residents. Opening the suburbs to lower-income families would mitigate interlocal disparities in property wealth, thereby reducing the differences in local ability to spend on education.

The school finance cases

Courts in 18 states have considered challenges to the local property-tax-based system of funding public education. Plaintiffs usually made two arguments: interlocal spending inequities violate state equal protection clauses, and the low level of spending in poorer districts violates the articles on education in state constitutions—the requirements, variously phrased, that the state provide for "the maintenance and support of a system of free common schools" or "a thorough and efficient system of free schools" or "a general and uniform public school system."

The resulting decisions may be grouped into three categories. Both the state equal protection and the education article claims were rejected outright by high courts in ten states: New York, Pennsylvania, Ohio, Michigan, Arizona, Colorado, Georgia, Idaho, Maryland,

and Oregon.[5] An eleventh state, Wisconsin, also affirmed the traditional local finance system in a case that arose in a slightly different setting.[6] Three states—New Jersey, Washington, and West Virginia—rejected the equal-protection-clause attack but found for plaintiffs under their education articles.[7] Four states—Arkansas, California, Connecticut, and Wyoming—determined that the traditional financing system denied children in poorer districts equal protection.[8]

The state supreme courts in the first, and largest, category grounded their decisions on a strong commitment to local self-government, which they defined as requiring local control of the funding and provision of basic governmental services. These courts saw the challenge to local school funding as necessarily having implications for police, fire, roads, and other local services. Yet unequal levels of local services and taxation were deemed characteristic of the American system of local government. Differences in the cost and quality of local services were seen as inherent in the structure of local government. "We are all aware," observed the Arizona Supreme Court, "that the citizens of one county shoulder a different tax burden than the citizens of another and receive varying degrees of governmental service."[9] Notwithstanding these disparities, "this tradition of local government providing services paid for by local taxes," wrote the Oregon Supreme Court, "continues to be a basic accepted principle of Oregon government."[10] These courts denied that local control could survive if the state were required to fund education or to equalize local fiscal capacities. The New York Court of Appeals, for example, concluded that there was "a direct correlation" between the implementation of local interests and the local control of school budgets. Only through local fiscal responsibility could local residents "exercise a substantial control over the educational opportunities made available in their districts."[11]

Several courts acknowledged that disparities in local wealth existed, leading to "significant inequalities in the availability of financial support for local school districts"[12] and implying that poorer districts would have "less fiscal control than wealthier districts."[13] Yet these courts determined that so long as a minimally adequate education was provided in each district, the state had met its responsibilities. A uniform level of support of education, regardless of district wealth, was not required. The inability of poorer districts to fund programs comparable to those offered in

5. *Board of Educ., Levittown Union Free School Dist.* v. *Nyquist*, 57 N.Y.2d 27 (1982); *Danson* v. *Casey*, 399 A.2d 360 (Pa. 1979); *Board of Educ.* v. *Walter*, 390 N.E.2d 813 (Ohio 1979); *Milliken* v. *Green*, 212 N.W.2d 711 (Mich. 1973); *Shofstall* v. *Hollins*, 515 P.2d 590 (Ariz. 1973); *Lujan* v. *Colorado State Bd. of Educ.*, 649 P.2d 1005 (Colo. 1982); *McDaniel* v. *Thomas*, 285 S.E.2d 156 (Ga. 1981); *Thompson* v. *Engelking*, 537 P.2d 635 (Idaho 1975); *Hornbeck* v. *Somerset Co. Bd. of Educ.*, 458 A.2d 758 (Md. 1983); *Olsen* v. *State*, 554 P.2d 139 (Ore. 1976).

6. *Buse* v. *Smith*, 247 N.W.2d 141 (Wisc. 1976).

7. *Robinson* v. *Cahill*, 303 A.2d 273 (N.J. 1973); *Seattle School Dist. No. 1* v. *State*, 585 P.2d 71 (Wash. 1978); *Pauley* v. *Kelly*, 255 S.E.2d 859 (W. Va. 1979).

8. *Dupree* v. *Alma School Dist. No. 30*, 651 S.W.2d 90 (Ark. 1983); *Serrano* v. *Priest*, 135 Cal. Rptr. 345 (1976); *Horton* v. *Meskill*, 376 A.2d 359 (Conn. 1977); *Washakie Co. School Dist. No. 1* v. *Herschler*, 606 P.2d 310 (Wyo. 1980).

9. *Shofstall*, 515 P.2d at 593.

10. *Olsen*, 554 P.2d at 147.

11. *Levittown*, 57 N.Y.2d at 45.

12. Ibid., p. 38.

13. *Lujan*, 649 P.2d at 1023.

richer communities did not give rise to a constitutional claim. Indeed, several courts expressly vindicated the right of school districts to spend more than the state required or than their neighbors could afford.

The most striking confirmation of local control came in Wisconsin, where the supreme court invalidated state legislation designed to ameliorate spending disparities. The Wisconsin plan directed, *inter alia*, that districts with spending or wealth above a certain ceiling make payments into a state fund, which would be used to supplement the state's own revenues for providing aid to poorer districts. Acknowledging that school districts, like other political subdivisions, are "but arms of the state, carrying out state duties," the Wisconsin court nevertheless placed local rights with respect to education on a par with state power. The court concluded that "local districts retain the control to provide educational opportunities over and above those required by the state."[14] The legislature could not limit district spending in the name of interlocal equality and could not require one district to aid a poorer neighbor.

The three state courts that relied on education articles to uphold challenges to the school finance system shared many of these assumptions about the inevitability, and acceptability, of interlocal wealth and public service differences. These courts stressed the exemplary position of education among all public services and denied that their decisions had any implications for the inequalities in the funding of other local services or in local taxation. Even within the context of education, these courts limited their holdings by denying that the state had to fund education wholly or to equalize interlocal wealth or spending differences.

In the leading education article case, *Robinson* v. *Cahill*, the New Jersey Supreme Court gave thoughtful attention to the equal protection argument but ultimately rejected it. The court concluded that local fiscal incapacity and interlocal inequities are inherent in local self-government and that the localist interest should prevail: "A signal feature of home rule as we know it is that the residents of a political subdivision are permitted within substantial limits to decide how much to raise for [local] services. . . . How much will be done by local government may, of course, depend upon the size of the tax base. . . . It is inevitable that expenditures per resident will vary among municipalities, resulting in differences as to benefit and tax burden."[15]

The New Jersey Supreme Court, surely one of the most activist and liberal in the nation, after giving a full accounting of the costs of local fiscal responsibility in terms of interlocal inequality and inadequately met local needs, was willing to pay the price for interlocal disparities in order to preserve the system of local self-government. Indeed, in a later case, the court denied an equal protection challenge to the requirement that counties pay for local welfare and judicial administration costs out of the local property tax. Local fiscal responsibility for local services was, according to the court, an "implicit premise of local government" notwithstanding differences in local ability to pay.[16]

14. *Buse*, 247 N.W.2d at 151.

15. *Robinson*, 303 A.2d at 283.
16. *Bonnet* v. *State*, 382 A.2d 1175 (N.J. Super. 1978); *aff'd*, 395 A.2d 194 (N.J. 1978).

The *Robinson* court construed the thorough and efficient clause of the New Jersey Constitution as requiring the state to define the content of a "thorough and efficient" education and to see to it that such an education was provided in all districts. While the state could delegate that function to localities, it had an obligation to oversee local school districts to assure that the "thorough and efficient" commitment was met. The court found that the state had failed to undertake these definitional and supervisory functions, and it treated the relatively low levels of spending in poorer districts as evidence that a "thorough and efficient" education was not being provided in those districts. Nevertheless, the court did not mandate equalization, and it accepted that richer districts would spend above the constitutional minimum.

The four remaining state supreme courts found that their states had violated state equal protection clauses in making the quality of educational opportunity dependent on the "fortuitous circumstance" of the assessed valuation of the district in which each child resided. These courts rejected the conclusion of the other courts that local authority over the scope and content of local education programs required local fiscal responsibility, and they found that greater equalization and greater state support need not reduce local school autonomy.

These courts did not clearly indicate what role their state constitutions would allow local wealth inequalities to continue to play under a reformed system, and there is some indication from later cases that, despite the strong language about equalization, these courts would be satisfied with a remedy comparable to that in *Robinson*, that is, increasing

the resources available to the poorest districts without either capping the richest districts or compelling full equalization of district tax bases.[17] Moreover, none of these courts required either full state funding or complete equality in district spending. District residents could decide the rate at which they desired to tax themselves for the support of local schools. So long as spending differences were not the product of disparities in wealth, school expenditures could vary.[18] Although these four courts disagreed with the others over the connection between local control and local fiscal responsibility and on the importance of equalizing local fiscal capacities, they shared the common judicial commitment to some measure of local autonomy.

The exclusionary zoning cases

Efforts on the part of local communities to control their own social and economic demography originally received the imprimatur of state courts. Ironically, in view of its current position as the leading critic of exclusionary zoning, it was the New Jersey Supreme Court that most prominently affirmed local power to determine community composition. In a series of decisions between 1949 and 1962, that court upheld efforts by New Jersey suburbs to exclude industry, apartment houses, and mobile homes and to impose costly minimum floor space, building frontage, and large-lot requirements.[19] The court indicated

17. See, for example, *Horton v. Meskill*, 486 A.2d 1099 (Conn. 1985).
18. *Serrano*, 135 Cal. Rptr. at 370.
19. See *Duffcon Concrete Products, Inc.* v. *Borough of Cresskill*, 64 A.2d 347 (N.J. 1949); *Lionshead Lake, Inc.* v. *Wayne Township*, 89 A.2d 693 (N.J. 1952); *Fischer* v. *Bedminster Township*, 93 A.2d 378 (N.J. 1952); *Fanale* v. *Borough of Hasbrouck Heights*, 139 A.2d 749

that it would sustain local zoning measures that were "reasonably calculated
to advance the community as a social,
economic or political unit."[20] An element
of community advancement could be
the protection of community "character."
The court endorsed the efforts of New
Jersey's communities to secure for themselves the blessing of suburban life:
"more land, more living room, indoors
and out, and more freedom in their scale
of living than is generally possible in the
city."[21] Lower courts were directed to
"allow fullest flexibility to the range of
well-informed local judgment as to the
precise way in which local zoning can
best serve the welfare of the particular
community."[22]

During the last two decades, suburban
exclusionary zoning and the consequent
increased housing costs and metropolitan-
area segregation have been challenged
in court, and the handful of victories
won by exclusionary zoning plaintiffs
have drawn considerable scholarly attention. These cases have been seen as part
of the quiet revolution in which state
institutions are said to be asserting
greater responsibilities over land use.
The judicial limitation of exclusionary
zoning, however, has been overstated.

Only four state supreme courts have
undertaken a significant review of exclusionary zoning—California, New
Jersey, New York, and Pennsylvania.
These courts have pointed to the regional
effects of local zoning decisions, have
directed local zoning bodies to consider
these effects, and have urged the states

to monitor local zoning. With the exception of New Jersey, however, each court
has left the structure of local zoning
largely intact and has permitted the
states to continue to abdicate an effective
oversight role.

In a pair of decisions in the mid-
1970s, the New York Court of Appeals
and the California Supreme Court determined that because local zoning "often
has a substantial impact beyond the
boundaries of the municipality,"[23] the
propriety of local land-use regulation
"must be measured by its impact not
only upon the welfare of the enacting
community, but upon the welfare of the
surrounding region."[24] But these decisions also affirmed the legitimacy of the
"local desire to maintain the status quo
within the community,"[25] and the California court found that "suburban residents . . . may assert a vital interest in
limiting immigration to their community."[26] Regional needs would not displace local self-interest; rather, local
zoning bodies and reviewing courts
would be required to balance these
competing interests, with little indication
given as to how that balance should be
struck.

The New York court invalidated a
local ordinance excluding multifamily
housing, where it was plain that the
defendant town had given no consideration to regional needs. Subsequently,
that court upheld a five-acre minimum-
lot ordinance,[27] and a town zoning process that tended to exclude low cost multi-

(N.J. 1958); *Vickers* v. *Gloucester Township*, 181
A.2d 129 (N.J. 1962).

20. *Vickers*, 181 A.2d at 137.

21. *Lionshead Lake*, 89 A.2d at 697.

22. *Clary* v. *Eatontown*, 124 A.2d 54, 66 (N.J.
1956).

23. *Berenson* v. *Town of New Castle*, 38
N.Y.2d 102, 110-11 (1975).

24. *Associated Home Builders of the Greater
East Bay, Inc.* v. *City of Livermore*, 135 Cal. Rptr.
41, 51 (1976).

25. *Berenson*, 38 N.Y.2d at 110.

26. *Livermore*, 135 Cal. Rptr. at 56.

27. *Robert E. Kurzius, Inc.* v. *Incorporated
Village of Upper Brookville*, 51 N.Y.2d 338 (1980).

family housing.[28] The defendant municipalities had apparently given some attention to the region but were reasonable in striking the balance in favor of local interests.

Similarly, the California court placed the burden of proof on challengers seeking to upset a moratorium on residential growth, presumed that the defendant city had balanced local and regional interests in good faith, and directed that the ordinance be measured by the "liberal standards that have traditionally tested the validity of land use restrictions enacted under the zoning power."[29] The court also protected use of the voter initiative to zone, despite the voters' proclivity for exclusionary measures.[30]

The Pennsylvania Supreme Court, which pioneered the judicial attack on exclusionary zoning, has invalidated large-lot requirements and bans on multifamily housing,[31] although, more recently, it upheld municipal exclusion of townhouses.[32] The court declared that a "political subdivision cannot isolate itself and ignore the needs of the areas surrounding it" and that, in the absence of state or regional planning, a community that is "a logical area for development and population growth"

may not totally exclude such growth.[33]

The Pennsylvania court, however, has permitted municipalities to continue to restrict residential development without any new state or regional legislative or administrative oversight. While the court has been vigorous in reviewing certain exclusionary ordinances, it has proceeded on a case-by-case basis, allowing localities to initiate such zoning and putting the onus on prospective developers to come forward and plead and prove their cases—a time-consuming and costly process. The burden is on the plaintiff to demonstrate that the community is "in the path of growth"—neither fully developed nor still outside the area of imminent metropolitan population expansion—and that it has sought to avoid its fair share of regional housing development. The court's most recent decisions suggest that although the municipality's legal interest in exclusion has been rejected, individual communities have not been stripped of authority to regulate and control growth.

Only the New Jersey Supreme Court has mounted a sustained assault on exclusionary zoning. In *Mount Laurel*, the court declared that it would take a "non-local approach to the meaning of 'general welfare'" in zoning cases, so that if an ordinance has "a substantial external impact, the welfare of the state's citizens beyond the borders of the particular municipality cannot be disregarded and must be recognized and served." The court invoked the basic premise of state-local relations in declaring it "fundamental and not to be forgotten that the zoning power is a police power of the state and the local authority is acting only as a delegate of that

28. *Suffolk Hous. Serv.* v. *Town of Brookhaven*, 70 N.Y.2d 122 (1987).

29. *Livermore*, 135 Cal. Rptr. at 52-53, 56-57.

30. See, for example, *Building Indus. Ass'n of So. California* v. *City of Camarillo*, 226 Cal. Rptr. 81, 88-89 (1986); *Arnel Devel. Co.* v. *City of Costa Mesa*, 169 Cal. Rptr. 904 (1980); *Livermore*, 135 Cal. Rptr. at 44-49.

31. *Appeal of Kit-Mar Builders, Inc.*, 268 A.2d 765 (Pa. 1970); *Appeal of Girsh*, 263 A.2d 395 (Pa. 1970); *National Land & Inv. Co.* v. *Kohn*, 215 A.2d 597 (Pa. 1965).

32. *Appeal of Elocin, Inc.*, 461 A.2d 771 (Pa. 1983); *Appeal of M. A. Kravitz Co.*, 460 A.2d 1075 (Pa. 1983).

33. *Surrick* v. *Zoning Hearing Bd.*, 382 A.2d 105, 108, 110 (Pa. 1977).

power." Municipalities may not zone for fiscal or character goals. Moreover, the mere elimination of exclusionary devices would not suffice. A community must "affirmatively plan and provide, by its land use regulations, the reasonable opportunity for an appropriate variety and choice of housing, of course including low and moderate cost housing."[34]

Despite *Mount Laurel*'s strong language, the New Jersey court initially acted cautiously and preserved a substantial measure of local autonomy over zoning. The court determined that it was "the local function and responsibility, in the first instance at least, rather than the court's to decide on the details" of a proper zoning ordinance, and it did not order that any developer be given permission to build. The court expressed a strong preference for legislation to determine and allocate regional housing needs.[35] Only after eight years of local resistance and legislative inaction did the New Jersey court conclude that it would no longer defer to local decision making or wait for the state to come up with comprehensive regional plans. In *Mount Laurel II*, the court held that lower courts could make regional housing allocations; localities would be required to remove all excessive restrictions and exactions; suburbs would be directed to provide incentives for the construction of low-income and moderate-income housing; and trial courts would be authorized to enter remedial orders permitting prevailing developer-plaintiffs to begin to build.[36]

Mount Laurel II, especially its provision of a builder's remedy, galvanized the legislature into action. In the Fair Housing Act of 1985, the legislature adopted the *Mount Laurel* doctrine while also toning it down. Localities would retain authority to zone, and a moratorium on builders' remedies was imposed, but a new state agency would set criteria and guidelines, monitor local actions, and, through its power to immunize municipalities from *Mount Laurel*-style lawsuits, affect the content of local zoning and housing plans. While acknowledging the need for more low-income and moderate-income housing, the Fair Housing Act also directed that the state respect "the established pattern of development in the community" and consider the costs of improving public facilities. The New Jersey Supreme Court upheld the act.[37]

LOCAL CONTROL AS A STATE
CONSTITUTIONAL VALUE

State supreme courts clearly place a premium on local control, even against a legal background of presumptive state power. Why? The courts have said surprisingly little about the value of local control. Scholars of local government have put forward two normative arguments for local autonomy: allocational efficiency in the provision of public services,[38] and expansion of opportunities for political participation.[39] While

---

34. *Southern Burlington County NAACP v. Township of Mount Laurel*, 336 A.2d 713, 726, 728 (1975).

35. Ibid., p. 734. See also *Oakwood at Madison, Inc.* v. *Township of Madison*, 371 A.2d 1192 (N.J. 1977).

36. *Southern Burlington County NAACP v.*

Township of Mount Laurel, 456 A.2d 390, 436-53 (N.J. 1983).

37. *Hills Development Co.* v. *Township of Bernards*, 510 A.2d 621, 632-33 (1986).

38. See, for example, Charles Tiebout, "A Pure Theory of Local Expenditures," *Journal of Political Economy*, 64:416 (1956).

39. See, for example, Frug, "City as a Legal Concept."

localist courts have been attentive to these values, a third explanation more closely captures the tenor of judicial reasoning: the courts apparently equate local autonomy with individual or family autonomy and are protective of local power because of their intuitive linkage of the community to the home and the family.

Thus local control of land use has been supported by state courts not because local units are considered more efficient or more representative than regional or state agencies but because local control is seen as better for protecting the home. Local responsibility for public education is maintained not because school districts are more responsive to local needs or better able to meet them but because localities seem more likely to protect the family. Home and family were frequently relied on or alluded to in these cases. The early New Jersey cases upheld exclusionary zoning as a means of protecting "the well-being of our most important institution, the home."[40] Those cases saw an intimate connection between the well-being of local residents, the quality of home life, and the character of the surrounding community. Recent decisions continue to recognize the legitimacy of the local desire to limit in-migration in order to secure the "blessings of quiet seclusion and clean air" for suburban householders.[41]

Similarly, for many courts there is a close connection between local control of the public schools and parents' interest in the education of their children. Localist courts frequently refer to residents of school districts not as residents or voters or taxpayers but simply as "parents" engaged in "educating their children."[42]

The hostility evinced by some courts to limiting the ability of richer districts to outspend poorer districts may simply reflect incredulity that there is any constitutional basis for restricting how much parents can do for their children.

The linkage of local government to home and family results in a deferential or protective attitude toward local power. Local governments become an extension of, rather than a threat to, personal freedom; in contrast with states, they may be placed on the private side of the public-private divide. From the courts' perspective, localities control the immediate environment for the protection of the private life of home and family and are not simply deliverers of public services or centers for the development of public life.

This interpretation suggests that the "inherent right of local self-government" is not dead but merely dormant. These courts downplay the createdness of local governments and, instead, take local governments and their powers as givens and not as products of conscious action by the states to structure governmental authority in a particular way. As the New York Court of Appeals explained in denying that the state had any duty to remedy interlocal tax and public service inequalities, "The cited inequalities existing in cities are the product of demographic, economic and political factors intrinsic to the cities themselves and cannot be attributed to legislative action or inaction."[43] That the state chose to delegate public education to units of differing fiscal capacities was not discussed and apparently needed no justification. An important part of localism, then, is the assumption that in a

---

40. *Lionshead Lake*, 89 A.2d at 697.
41. *Livermore*, 135 Cal. Rptr. at 56.
42. *Thompson*, 537 P.2d at 645; *Lujan*, 649

P.2d at 1023; *Walter*, 390 N.E.2d at 820; *Levittown*, 57 N.Y.2d at 46.
43. *Levittown*, 57 N.Y.2d at 41.

system of local governments, inequalities simply happen. The states are not responsible for these inequalities or, it seems, for the system of local governments.

Because these cases generally concerned the efforts of private plaintiffs either to curb localities or to force the states to take a more active role, the power of the states to displace local decisions was usually not at issue, and the inherent right idea was not directly tested. It is thus still good law that there is no inherent right to local self-government and states have plenary power over their political subdivisions. But in the aftermath of these litigations, it is evident that many courts take the existence and power of local governments as both given and highly desirable. Such localism has, in most states, effectively constrained efforts to reduce disparities in the quality of education and to open the suburbs to more low-income residents.

These cases also suggest that the very issue of state versus local power is a false one because of the overinclusiveness of the term "local government." Not all local governments benefit from localism. The larger, older cities, with their concentrations of poor people, high crime rates, crumbling infrastructures, decaying housing, and diminished tax bases, are little advantaged by doctrines affirming local autonomy over school finance and zoning. Cities faced with heavy demands for local public services and with emigration of the middle class are likely to favor greater state support of local public services and regional land-use planning. Local autonomy is of limited use to localities lacking the financial resources to enjoy it.

Middle-class and upper-income suburbs do better under localism. Their primary concerns are for the control of their schools and the protection of their homes. Those powers have been delegated to them by the states and, in general, vouchsafed by the courts. Beyond these concerns, their desire is to be let alone and not be burdened by broader metropolitan problems. These communities may be legally powerless to prevent state legislation from interfering with local autonomy, but they are practically powerful due to the strong and continuing tradition of state abdication to local governments in such matters.

Localism, then, primarily benefits only a subset of local governments, and it does so by enabling them to insulate themselves from responsibility for problems outside their borders. Such a localist allocation of power, which helps one category of localities while harming another, can hardly be wise policy or good law.

State Constitutional Law in Comparative Perspective

By IVO D. DUCHACEK

ABSTRACT: Can the existence and modifications of state constitutions be viewed as being among the nourishing fountains of federalism? A comparative analysis suggests two caveats. While in the United States and Switzerland both the birth and subsequent modification of state constitutions confirm a two-way traffic in federal practices between federal and state governments, in other systems, though labeled "federations," state constitutions rarely reflect political assertions of regional autonomy from below. Instead, subnational constitutions in such federations may only represent a unitary or dictatorial delegation of some administrative powers to territorial subunits, a delegation that can easily be revoked by the central government. On the other hand, due to a federal political tradition, federal practices may flourish in some unions whose territorial components lack indigenous subnational constitutions, as in Canada and Australia.

Ivo D. Duchacek is professor emeritus of political science at the City University of New York and a visiting scholar at the Institute of Governmental Studies, University of California, Berkeley. He is the author of several books in comparative and international politics, including Power Maps: Comparative Politics of Constitutions *(1973);* Nations and Men *(1975 and 1982);* The Territorial Dimension of Politics within, among, and across Nations *(1986); and* Comparative Federalism *(1970 and 1987).*

I N studying various federal systems, can we use the existence and modifications of subnational constitutions as one criterion of federal practice and, possibly, as evidence of a prevailing federal political culture? The answer is, Not exactly.

By "modifications" I mean amendments to or a complete redrafting of a subnational constitution in response to new circumstances and challenges, provided these changes have been initiated and adopted by regional officials and voters, not by the federal center. By "subnational constitutions" I mean the constitutions of federated territorial components, such as states, provinces, cantons, *Länder*, and socialist autonomous republics in the 17 systems that are, or claim to be, federal: the United States, Switzerland, West Germany, Austria, Canada, Australia, India, Malaysia, the United Arab Emirates, Nigeria, Mexico, Venezuela, Argentina, Brazil, the Soviet Union, Yugoslavia, and Czechoslovakia.

By "federal political culture" I mean attitudes, beliefs, values, and behavioral orientations reflecting respect for, and patterns of membership and political participation in, more than one order of government and more than one territorial community, subnational and national. These interlaced orientations toward the institutionalized two-layer, or marbled, political processes include knowledge, judgments, and feelings, which include nationalism—or federal loyalty, *Bundestreue*—coupled with territorial or local loyalty.[1]

MODIFYING STATE CONSTITUTIONS IN THE UNITED STATES

Since 1776 the American states have drafted anew nearly 150 state constitutions and have held over 230 constitutional conventions. Voters in the 50 states have also adopted nearly 5000 state constitutional amendments proposed by their own state political and economic elites, in response to new tasks imposed on all modern states.[2] These new tasks reflect demands and pressures for social welfare, job creation, education, health, culture, and environmental protection. The American state constitutions have proved, on the whole, to be both flexible and important determinants of the quality of the daily lives of their citizens, and this is why they have undergone numerous changes.

In identifying modification of state constitutions as one of the characteristics of American federal political culture, it should be noted that, internally, many states have also redefined their initially centralist positions with respect to local, municipal, and county units of government by granting them home rule. In this way, within their own jurisdictional frameworks, many states have transformed their unitary systems into semifederalized ones.

While the processes of redrafting and amending state constitutions are dominantly concerned with the organizational, fiscal, and social service aspects of state governments, these modifications tend to leave intact the first, all-important constitutional chapter, the declaration of rights, including its archaic wording

---

1. See Ivo D. Duchacek, *The Territorial Dimension of Politics within, among, and across Nations* (Boulder, CO: Westview, 1986), p. 81.

2. Albert L. Sturm, "Development of American State Constitutions," *Publius: The Journal of Federalism*, 12:75-76 (Winter 1982).

and syntax. This respect for eighteenth-century formulations represents perhaps mainly a show of respect for the American political-constitutional tradition and a compliment to the drafting skill of the eighteenth-century statesmen who, in a revolutionary and editorially felicitous fashion, formulated the concept of government limited by inalienable individual rights and liberties. On the part of state constitutional reformers and their publics, there may also be some fear that any tampering with the time-honored guarantees may adversely affect them.

In tune with modern problems and challenges, the newly drafted or amended constitutions have, of course, added many twentieth-century economic, social, and environmental rights to the original eighteenth-century list of individual rights and liberties. The 1972 constitution of Montana, for example, added a right of citizens to have a clean environment; other states have added a so-called right to work.

Immediately following the declaration of rights is an outline of the organizational structure concerning the legislature, state executive, and judiciary, and the separation of their respective powers that expresses and reasserts, conceptually, the collective territorial right of the constituent state to self-government. As Daniel J. Elazar expressed it succinctly, "State constitutions are conceptual, and, at times, very specific statements of who should get what, when and how."[3]

Three observations concerning the amendatory zeal of American states are in order:

1. The high number of redrafted or amended constitutions indicates a healthy

3. Daniel J. Elazar, "Principles and Traditions Underlying American State Constitutions," *Publius: The Journal of Federalism*, 12:17 (Winter 1982).

assertion of state responsibility for responding to new challenges and opportunities. In this sense, constitutional change represents a good measure of the vitality of the American federal political culture.

2. The diligent redrafting and amending of state constitutions are, at least partly, also the consequence of the detailed nature and length of the state constitutions in contrast to the succinctness of the first New England state constitutions, from which the equally succinct federal Constitution drew important inspiration. Such detailed texts are bound to be vulnerable to many even minute changes in the political or economic environment. They simply have had to be updated constantly.

3. The need for frequent additions to, or changes in, state constitutions also reflects the human incapacity to anticipate accurately—and express in detailed legal terms—what will be needed as society changes. The state constitutions, especially, are fundamental blueprints for public action that are closest to the concerns of daily life and the pursuit of happiness.

The point of central importance for comparative speculation is that the American state constitutional responses to change have been largely initiated, adopted, and implemented from below, from their territorial roots, by the state and local governments and their citizens. Whether drawn for the first time in the eighteenth century or only in the twentieth century, the American state constitutions are not preordained spin-offs of some central federal doctrine, as is the case in so many other systems that claim to be federal but whose federal practice and culture are either underdeveloped or outrightly debatable. In the latter type of federal system, the territorial components resemble those units of local or regional administration that any central authority finds useful to create by a revocable unitary delegation of power.

Unitary delegations of powers from the top to the regional bottom—which on paper may sometimes appear close to the federal division of powers and be labeled as such—in the past characterized Argentina's 22 provinces and their relations to the central government; Brazil's 21 states; Venezuela's 20 states; Mexico's 32 states; and pre-Bangladesh, bicommunal federal Pakistan. In the case of three communist constitutions whose language is conspicuously federal—those of the Soviet Union, Yugoslavia, and Czechoslovakia—the practices and spirit have always been tightly centralist, with the partial exception of Yugoslavia.

CANTONAL CONSTITUTIONS IN SWITZERLAND

Can our measuring rod of the vitality of federal political culture—the birth and growth of subnational constitutions from below—be applied to Switzerland and its 26 cantons?[4] It can.

Cantonal constitutions have been considerably modified over the centuries by appropriate revisions from below, including cantonal referenda. Since the 1960s, there has been a new effort to modernize, simplify, and reformulate cantonal constitutions; for example, the cantons of Basel, Nidwalden, and Aargau embarked upon such revisions. The Swiss cantons, too, feel the need to redefine their contemporary relationships toward the federal government and its centralizing tendencies as well as toward their own administrative subdivisions, such as counties, districts, and communes.

In addition, some Swiss cantons have become increasingly concerned with the modern trans-sovereign roles of subnational governments. This is especially so in the case of cantons contiguous with France. These cantons must deal with issues associated with a commuting, foreign labor force and with the rights and taxes of those workers. Transborder economic cooperation and environmental problems, as in Basel, also occupy the attention of cantons. Unlike the U.S. Constitution, the Swiss federal constitution grants the cantons a limited right of paradiplomacy.[5] The newly created canton of Jura, for example, began to interpret its paradiplomatic autonomy as including the right to conclude compacts—though not treaties—with foreign provinces, such as Quebec, and sovereign states, for example, Seychelles.

In Switzerland, too, modern social, economic, and environmental rights are on the cantonal constitutional agenda. In contrast to the traditional rights and liberties that impose limits on government, modern general-welfare rights impose on cantonal governments more initiative, responsibility, planning, and

---

4. The 26 cantons consist of 23 cantons, 3 of which were split by cantonal decision into two half-cantons.

5. Article 9 of the Swiss Constitution states, "Exceptionally, the cantons retain the right to conclude agreement with foreign states on matters of public economy, neighborship, and police relations, provided such agreement contain nothing contrary to the Confederation or the rights of other cantons." Article 10 distinguishes between cantonal international relations with neighboring subnational units and sovereign states: "Official intercourse between cantons and governments of foreign states or their representatives takes place through the agency of the Federal Council [that is, the Swiss National Executive and its Department of Foreign Affairs]; (2) with respect to matters enumerated in Article 9, the cantons may however correspond directly with subordinate authorities and officials of foreign states."

action; yet simultaneously, of course, these new welfare rights also require an increased protection of individual citizens against bureaucratic excesses. The cantons tend to solve, in the traditional European way, the dilemma of more government with more protection against the government, by establishing administrative courts, unfamiliar to the U.S. judicial system. The role of European administrative courts is precisely to protect individuals against administrative abuses.

Another important subnational issue, absent from the American scene, is the cantonal redefinition of the church-state relationship. In numerous Swiss cantons, the state and church are not separated. As in the United States, there is also a lively controversy as to the best way to redraft cantonal constitutions, including such issues as the role of the general public before constitutional referenda, the role of constitutional experts in a constitutional council or convention, and the roles of the cantonal legislatures, whose members had been initially elected to implement, not to change, a given constitution.

In all these attempts, the constitutional reformers aim also at replacing nineteenth-century constitutional legalese with modern, easy-to-read language. In this framework, the 1977 constitution of Jura is particularly praised for its succinct, carefully edited, and truly modern wording.[6] This search for modern wording contrasts with the respectful American attitudes toward the eighteenth-century language of bills of rights.

SUBNATIONAL CONSTITUTIONS IN WEST GERMANY AND AUSTRIA

The 10 West German states (*Länder*)—plus West Berlin, in a special category—and 9 Austrian *Bundesländer* all have their own constitutions. In federal Germany, all subnational constitutions and, in Austria, some of the constitutions have predated the federal charter.[7]

In West Germany, even without knowing about the existence of its 11 subnational components and their constitutions, one can readily observe the federal practice and federal political culture.

The West German *Länder*, for example, are quite visible and influential on the federal level through their state representatives in the federal chamber, the Bundesrat. Unlike U.S. senators, members of the Bundesrat are not individually elected by the voters in their respective state constituencies but are appointed by the *Land* governments to represent them in the second chamber. Instead of the American principle of equal representation of unequal states, the representation of the German *Länder* is weighted according to size and importance, although not in exact proportion. The largest states are entitled to five representatives, the medium states to four, and the three smallest ones—Saarland and the two city-states of Hamburg and Bremen—to three. The *Länder* are represented in the Bundesrat by ministerial delegations composed of high officials who vote as a bloc. Their

6. Hanspeter Tschaeni, "Constitutional Change in Swiss Cantons: An Assessment of a Recent Phenomenon," *Publius: The Journal of Federalism*, 12:113 (Winter 1982), presents an excellent analysis of Swiss subnational constitutions and their recent changes.

7. Most Austrian provinces predated the creation of the federal republic, which was founded in 1918 and reestablished in 1945. There are three exceptions: the Austrian province of Burgenland, which belonged to the Hungarian segment of the Hapsburg empire before World War I; Vorarlberg, which separated from Tyrol; and Vienna, which was separated from Lower Austria and became the ninth Austrian city-*Land*.

inputs into the legislative processes—and into amendment of the federal constitution, for which a two-thirds majority of *Land* votes is required—are significant, even though the popularly elected House (Bundestag) is politically decisive, especially as a federal cabinet maker. The *Länder* implement federal laws, an administrative task that adds to their powers but also calls for supervision by the federal center and causes, therefore, some central intrusion into local affairs. In Austria, the power is tilted toward Vienna even more clearly.

All *Land* constitutions in West Germany, and the resulting *Land* practices, vary somewhat, especially in fixing the relationship between the state legislature and the state executive and in electoral processes. The *Länder* run their own governments and internal affairs quite autonomously. As a result, there are differences in political and economic goals among the *Länder*, reflecting the various ideologies and programs of state parties and their subnational coalitions, as between the Socialists and the Greens in some *Länder*.

Unlike some American states and Swiss cantons, there are some detectable leftovers of foreign occupation and its political influence after World War II. Among the 10 West German *Länder*, only 3 have true historical antecedents: the Free State of Bavaria and the two formerly Hanseatic port cities of Hamburg and Bremen, now each a city-state whose premier-governor (*Minister-President*) is called mayor or lord-mayor (*Burgermeister* or *Erster Burgermeister*). The boundaries of the other seven nonhistorical *Länder* were drawn after 1945 to coincide with the great powers' occupational zones, imposed on West Germany by the United States, the United Kingdom, and France. The *Land* constitutions were drafted before the adoption of the West German Basic Law, or

Federal Constitution, in 1949. The imprint of the occupying and administering Allies influenced the organization of local government and even, in some cases, the determination of regional goals. In the Constitution of Hesse, for example, the American authorities vetoed an article allowing a *Land* takeover of local industries.

However conceived and then born with foreign assistance, the West German *Länder* and their boundaries are now a generally accepted fact of German political and federal life. Changes in *Land* electoral processes have been adopted without serious controversy. As John H. Herz has expressed it: "The 'cake of custom' by now has endowed the ten *Länder* structure with some kind of general recognition."[8] A special committee appointed twenty years ago to reform and reorganize the ten-*Länder* structure into only five more or less equally large units to be provided with new constitutions failed to produce results.

In general, in partial contrast to the United States and Switzerland, neither in West Germany, despite the somewhat artificial beginnings of its subnational constitutional law, nor in Austria does there seem to be any significant insistence on a need to begin a general process of amending subnational constitutions. With the passage of time, however, amendatory zeal may take hold within the territorial components of both federal Germany and federal Austria.

LIMITS OF A
SPECULATIVE COMPARISON

When we attempt to apply the measuring rod of the existence and modifi-

8. John H. Herz, "The Government of Germany," in *Major Foreign Powers*, ed. Gwendolen M. Carter and John H. Herz (New York: Harcourt Brace Jovanovich, 1972), p. 472.

cation of subnational constitutions to other federal scenes, we encounter three problems.

The first is posed by countries that claim to be federal and endow their federated components with detailed constitutions. These constitutions, however, are centrally drafted to mirror either a foreign model or some central doctrine of federalism; they are not outgrowths of a provincial tradition of self-rule. This circumstance applies to a large extent to the Latin American federations—Argentina, Brazil, Mexico, and Venezuela—which, in institutional segments, imitated the American federal and presidential system rather than the unitary, Westminster cabinet model.

The second problem is posed by communist federations, which combine elaborate constitutional federal rhetoric with the undivided power of one-party dictatorship.

The third problem is the existence of federations, such as Canada and Australia, whose federal political practice and culture are beyond any doubt, yet whose territorial components have not enacted their own constitutions, in the sense that their organic laws do not correspond to our definition of a constitution.

Federal India with its 23 states is another example of a federal union whose national constitution details central, state, and concurrent powers—which may preempt many state jurisdictional domains—in its Seventh Schedule. India represents a somewhat less eloquent example of a federation consisting of constitutionless territorial components because the central government's frequent breaches of democracy and federalism by means of emergency proclamations, and the ensuing federal takeovers of state administration, pose some questions about the existence of both pluralism and federalism.

Venezuela's 20 states have no constitutions either. While the federal constitution is committed to both democracy and federalism, noncentralism and state autonomy remain weak, even after the overthrow of the dictatorship in 1958. The federal constitution of Nigeria contains articles concerning the self-government of federated states, which do not now have their own constitutions—they once had them—but the number of military coups d'état, followed by various tightly centralized controls, raise serious doubts about Nigeria's practice of federalism. The United Arab Emirates is a federation in name only; in fact, it is a quasi confederacy of monarchs whose territorial components—emirates—have never experienced constitutionalism nor can expect to do so in the foreseeable future. A similar observation applies to federal Malaysia, consisting of states administered by hereditary rulers.

SUBNATIONAL CONSTITUTIONS AND QUESTIONABLE FEDERALISM

The territorial components of three of the U.S.-inspired federal systems in Latin America—Mexico, Argentina, and Brazil—have their own constitutions. While two of these federations—Argentina and Brazil—were under military dictatorship and therefore did not practice democratic pluralism, one could hardly have spoken of federalism in these two countries. It seems still premature to say whether the two countries, now on their way to democracy, will in due time add to their political practices democracy's territorial twin, federalism.

Democracy can prosper without federalism, as France and the Scandinavian countries demonstrate, but federalism needs democracy. A meaningful territorial political pluralism is inherently contrary to the authoritarian or totalitarian concentration of all political and economic power at a central point, which organizationally and ideologically cannot transfer any significant portion of that central power to any other organized group, whether ideological, functional, or territorial. Federalism is but a territorial expression of the core creed of democracy, which requires that public power be limited by both individual and collective-functional or territorial rights.

As to the United Mexican States, all 31 or 32 states have their own constitutions.[9] The dominant one-party system—with its state and local branches—tends to distort Mexican federalism. Even though the state constitutions seem to guarantee the states a relatively high potential for territorial autonomy, it is ordinarily the trust of the central party headquarters in Mexico City and of the president's aides that represents the essential precondition for the exercise of state powers. Although the governors, formerly appointed by the president, are now locally elected, their exercise of power and ability to stay in power depend more on the satisfaction with their performance at the federal top than on genuine local support. In the case of Mexico's recent movement toward greater local autonomy, especially in its northern states, a question could be asked whether, in this special case, the road to democratic pluralism might eventually pass through territorial federalism whereas, so often in the past, we have assumed that pluralism is a precondition for true federalism.

COMMUNIST FEDERATIONS AND SUBNATIONAL CONSTITUTIONS

The Soviet Union, Yugoslavia, and Czechoslovakia are socialist dictatorships that claim to be federal. The Soviet Union and Yugoslavia have endowed their component territorial republics with elaborate constitutions. Czechoslovakia has only promised to do so eventually. In both the Soviet Union and Yugoslavia, the constitutional texts are designed to resemble a territorial division of power in order to express the multiethnic composition of each nation.

The Soviet federal constitution of 1977 prescribes, as did the Stalin Constitution of 1936, separate constitutions for its 15 Union republics, which are called "sovereign" in Article 76. These republics are granted the right of secession, in Article 72, and the right to "enter into relations" with other nations, in Article 80. The texts of the state constitutions follow the prescribed party pattern, although they refer, of course, to the name of particular ethnic territories—Russian, Ukrainian, Belorussian, Kazakh, Uzbek, Georgian, Latvian, Kirghiz, and so forth—in their otherwise rather uniform texts.

The Soviet Constitution, in Article 85, also prescribes subnational constitutions for its 19 autonomous republics, established within the boundaries of 4 of the 15 Union republics. In addition, there are, within the boundaries of the various Union republics and autonomous republics, territorial units with a still lower degree of self-rule—autonomous regions and national, or ethnic, districts—which derive, constitutionally,

9. Baja California was subdivided into California Norte and California Sur. The Mexican state constitutions proclaim full adherence to the federal Bill of Rights. Some add other rights. For example, the Constitution of Chihuahua adds the right to cultivate land for each inhabitant of the state. Article 38 prohibits detention of citizens on the eve of elections, except in *flagrante delicto*.

their power from the state constitutions of the Union republics within whose territories they find themselves. Nevertheless, even these units have the right to be directly represented in the Soviet of Nationalities, that is, the federal chamber of the Supreme Soviet. Yet on account of the absolute dominance of the Communist Party throughout the Soviet polity, the various territorial components do not enjoy any degree of political autonomy. Meetings of the Soviet of Nationalities fulfill only a symbolic function; their contributions to the political and legislative processes are nil.

Furthermore, the last article of the Constitution, Article 174, stipulates that the whole Constitution of the USSR may be amended by a majority of not less than two-thirds of the total number of deputies in each of its chambers. In this way, the federal feature of the whole country could be either substantially altered or eliminated. After World War II, for example, the status of the Karelo-Finnish Republic—the Soviet Union was initially divided into 16 Union republics—was scaled down to that of an autonomous republic. During World War II, several ethnic autonomous territories—for example, Ingush and the Tatar Republic—were wiped out not only constitutionally but also physically for alleged disloyalty. The existence and possible modifications of the 31 subnational constitutions of the Soviet Union, therefore, do not tell us anything about federalism.

Yugoslavia, with its six constituent socialist republics and two autonomous regions—Vojvodina and Kosovo, both in the territory of the Serbian Republic—represents a variation of the Soviet multiethnic federal formula. The Yugoslav system recognizes the ethnoterritorial components as constituent parts of the federation. In contrast to the Soviet Union, the constitutions of the federal components have provided a framework for the subnational elites to channel direct pressures from below to the top—though, of course, within a single ruling-party system. These pressures and the resulting negotiations or compromises have, however, forced upon the authoritarian regime distinguishable elements of federal practices at the very top of the structure.

The final result is controversial. Some observers view federal Yugoslavia as simply another socialist dictatorship, though highly sensitized to various ethnic self-assertions and even centrifugal trends, particularly in Croatia and Albanian Kosovo. Other analysts argue that multiethnic federalism without democracy within the component units but with some degree of consociational decision making at the top is federal democracy sui generis. Still others take the autonomy of the component republics and their party organizations seriously and view Yugoslavia as a confederal league of territorial socialist dictators who maintain their union by constant negotiations, as do sovereign states, but keep themselves in power in their respective territorial domains by one-party, nondemocratic controls.

The Czechoslovak Socialist Federation, consisting of the Czech Socialist and Slovak Socialist republics, was established by a new constitution promulgated on 1 January 1969. The biethnic Czech-Slovak federal union is dominated by a single, tightly centralized Communist Party. The Slovak territory, formerly neglected politically and economically, in terms of development, by the industrialized Czech lands—Bohemia and Moravia—now seems to enjoy a limited self-rule as well as relatively healthy industrial development and a feeling of self-confidence. As in all dictatorial regimes, these features of quasi-federal balancing seem to result from negotiated intraparty—consociational—agreements rather than from the formal federal provisions of the new constitution. For some twenty years, for example, the Czech and Slovak Communist leaders have not implemented their initial promise to revise the first federal constitution after a trial period and provide the two component republics with their own constitutions.[10]

FEDERATIONS WITHOUT SUBNATIONAL CONSTITUTIONS

In examining federations without subnational constitutions, very much naturally depends on our definition of what is and is not a constitution.

This article views a constitution as a collection of principles and rules that define the constituent people and identify the sources, purposes, uses, and restraints of public power, usually in the form of a bill of rights and liberties. Most constitutions also contain a preamble—the nonlegal, declaratory, but politically important portion of a constitution that often glorifies the territorial community's past achievements and identifies its commitment to an ideologically defined future. As a manifesto of nationalism or subnational territorial pride, the pre-amble addresses itself to the collective memories and emotions of the constituent people rather than only to the legislators and constitutional lawyers. With its preamble and bill of rights, a constitution is more than an organizational chart, more than a "power map."[11]

Canada, Australia, India, and Nigeria claim that they are federal but do not endow their constituent states or provinces with locally initiated and enacted constitutions. For their territorial jurisdiction, the Indian states rely on appropriate federal articles in the national constitution. Similarly, the de jure status of Nigeria's 19 states is determined by federal articles in the national constitution, although their de facto status is determined by the power of the central government.

Canada, with its ten provinces, and Australia, with its six states, engage in federal practices in combination with pluralistic democracy without any major interruption by military coups or proclamations of states of emergency. One relatively short-lived Canadian exception was during the Quebec agitation for secession during the 1960s. Canada's and Australia's respective commitment to unity and diversity, certainly also conditioned by the immense size of these two countries, is firmly rooted in the conscience and political practice of both the federation and its component parts. Yet territorial constituent units have no subnational constitutions in the sense articulated earlier, no state bills of rights and liberties, and no preambles proclaiming common values and territorial pride. In Canada, even the occasionally rebellious francophone province of Que-

10. The Czechoslovak federal constitution was adopted by the Parliament on 27 Oct. 1969, following the Soviet occupation of the country in Aug. 1969. In an official commentary accompanying its digest, the constitution was described as provisional, which, following sufficient experience with the 1969 constitution, would be replaced by a new federal constitution and two subnational constitutions for the two constituent republics, the Czech lands and Slovakia. This was promised to happen in two years, that is, in 1971.

11. Ivo D. Duchacek, *Power Maps: Comparative Politics of Constitutions* (Santa Barbara, CA: ABC-Clio, 1973).

bec—which in the 1960s and early 1970s aimed at sovereignty in a confederal framework, *souveraineté/association*, and whose distinctiveness was finally recognized by the other nine provinces and Ottawa in the so-called Meech Lake Agreement of 30 April 1987—has not devoted much time or energy to provincial constitution making.

The general lack of Canadian and Australian interest in subnational constitutions may well reflect the political-legal tradition inherited from their former mother country, the United Kingdom, and its Westminster cabinet system, which makes the House of Commons the fundamental fountain of public power. There, in the Commons, resides the supreme law of the land, subliminally shaped by tradition and some solemn documents of a distant past. When it comes to Canadian and Australian federalism, implemented without the benefit of subnational constitutions, one may perhaps paraphrase Rousseau and suggest that the state constitutions of Canadian provinces and Australian states are being "not graven on tablets or brass but on the hearts of the provincial citizens" and federal political elites.

The so-called constitution acts, which the Canadian provinces and Australian states did enact, are instruments of management of the Westminster cabinet system. For example, British Columbia's Constitution Act of 1979 dryly describes the various aspects of the functions of the lieutenant governor, Executive Council, and Legislative Assembly and describes their method of election, their qualification and disqualification, and so forth but contains no list of purposes and values underlying the governmental institutions and processes. Article 2 subjects the Constitution Act clearly to the federal Constitution—the British North American Act of 1867—and "amending Acts as applicable to this Province and to the order of Her late Majesty Queen Victoria in Council for the union of this Province with the Dominion of Canada." Even the most down-to-earth preamble to the Constitution of Nebraska of roughly the same period, 1875, is more laden with emotion: "We, the people, grateful to Almighty God for our freedom, do ordain and establish the following declaration of rights and frame of government, as the Constitution of the State of Nebraska."

Yet, even though subnational constitutions are absent in Canada and Australia, any observer of their respective political scenes would certainly agree that a federal political culture is both well and vigorous in both countries.

CONCLUSION

The existence and modifications of subnational constitutions represent a useful though only auxiliary criterion of federal political culture and practice. Many other questions have to be asked and answered before subnational constitutions can be analyzed as nourishing fountains of federalism. One of the central questions is, Are the existence of, adherence to, and modifications of state constitutions the result of political demands and action from below, or is their existence only a regional ramification of some central, ideologically motivated doctrine of federalism?

Such a more or less revocable spin-off from the center to the provinces, however well received and accepted by the territorial community and anchored in a formal constitutional document, may simply mirror the predilection on the part of central leaders for institutional neatness and completeness. A particular caveat, therefore, should be applied to political systems dominated by military juntas or by one-party directorates that claim adherence to federalism but are incapable of dividing power, either functionally or territorially.

On the other hand, we have noted federal systems in which federal practice and federal culture flourish but in which the federated territorial components lack subnational constitutions, as in Canada, Australia, and, with some qualifications, India. In and of itself, therefore, the existence of subnational constitutions is not a necessary or sufficient condition for a federal political culture. Only in the United States and Switzerland do both the birth and subsequent modifications of state constitutions seem to offer a significant confirmation of federal political culture and a two-way traffic in federal practices between the federal and state governments.

Book Department

INTERNATIONAL RELATIONS AND POLITICS

BLUMENTHAL, HENRY. *Illusion and Reality in Franco-American Diplomacy, 1914-1945.* Pp. xi, 358. Baton Rouge: Louisiana State University Press, 1986. $32.50.

The span from 1914 to 1945 witnessed a remarkable shift in the respective positions of France and the United States in the world arena. That period saw America's rise to economic and military preponderance, as well as its transformation from a debtor to the world's foremost creditor nation. Safe behind two oceans, the United States clung to its traditional policy of nonentanglement with outside powers, despite its global industrial and commercial involvements. During that period, America's foreign policy was motivated chiefly by its economic interests: it sought above all to foster world prosperity and simultaneously promote U.S. accessibility to foreign markets. Though hard hit by the economic crisis of the 1930s, the nation retained its buoyant faith in an exceptional destiny. France, on the other hand, tumbled during that period from the rank of a major European state to an almost total eclipse from power. A leading exporter of capital on the eve of World War I, France became a debtor country in its aftermath. France's self-confidence and its *élan vital* were broken by the staggering losses that it suffered in that war. Fear of a resurgent Germany dominated its foreign policy throughout these years. While the United States spurned binding commitments to other nations, France worked feverishly during the interwar period to build a system of alliances that would strengthen its power and contain Germany. In the book under review, Henry Blumenthal traces the diplomatic relations between these two unequal countries in a rapidly changing world environment.

In view of the wide divergence of American and French interests and the vast difference in the two countries' respective situations, it is small wonder that their diplomatic relations were far from harmonious from the Paris Peace Conference of 1919 to the end of World War II. Except for a brief period between the Mellon-Bérenger Accord of 1926, which settled France's war debt to the United States, and the Kellogg-Briand Pact of 1928, which outlawed offensive war, the two powers worked at cross-purposes between 1919 and 1945, despite their joint commitment to universal peace, human freedom, and the rule of law. The United States strove for the elimination of Europe's perennial conflicts through an economic revival of the Old World, by which it meant primarily a restoration of Germany. But the precondition for a European renewal was Franco-German political, commercial, and industrial cooperation, which the United States opposed as contrary to its own trading interests. France, on the other hand, sought in the early 1920s to obtain an American and British security guarantee against another German invasion, while simultaneously resisting the Anglo-Saxon economic predominance on the continent. Illusionism marked the diplomacies of both countries during the interwar years. American opinion did not realize that the nation could not serve its global economic concerns by standing aloof from the rest of the world politically and militarily. France, for its part, did not see that its persistent hope of reinvigorating its transatlantic tie was bound to founder on the shoals of America's isolationism and neutralism. Blumenthal is a trustworthy guide through the thickets of these Franco-American differences in the period that began with the legendary duel between Woodrow Wilson and Georges Clemenceau in 1919 and that ended in 1941-44 in the rancorous strife that opposed Franklin D. Roosevelt to Charles de Gaulle.

PAUL ROSENFELD

Rutgers University
Newark
New Jersey

HANSON, ERIC O. *The Catholic Church in World Politics.* Pp. x, 485. Princeton, NJ: Princeton University Press, 1987. $24.95.

In Poland, the Philippines, Haiti, Lithuania, the Ukraine, Nicaragua, El Salvador, and the United States—to take but the obvious examples—events have answered Stalin's derisory question about the "Pope's divisions." The Pope's divisions exist. They shape history as catalysts for revolutionary change, mediate between states at the brink of war, and serve as a de facto opposition party when totalitarians legally proscribe

political dissent. Sorting through the complexities of Catholicism's modern entry into world politics is surely a worthwhile exercise. That is what Eric Hanson proposed to do; and that, unhappily, is not what he has given us.

The Catholic Church in World Politics covers an immense amount of ground, but Hanson's depth rarely matches his breadth. In addition, for a book—the analytic credibility of which rests in part on its factual accuracy—it is disturbingly full of errors, of which the following are a mere sampler: there is no Trident base at Greenham Common; Walter—not William—Sullivan was the bishop of Richmond investigated by the Vatican, and Archbishop John May, not Archbishop James Hickey, was the investigator; Sister Dorothy Kozel, not Hazel, was murdered in El Salvador; and how in the world was it that Japanese Prime Minister Yoshida was "baptized a Catholic after his death," Catholics not being Mormons?

Hanson's book is even more marred by ideological bias. Leaders of the Roman Curia are involved in "machinations"; abortion and governmental funding for religious schools are "conservative issues"; Cardinal Joseph Ratzinger is "threatening" to the achievements of Vatican II; the Vatican newspaper, *L'osservatore romano* "approximates *Pravda* or the *People's Daily* more closely than it does the *New York Times* or *Le Monde.*" On the other hand, Cardinal Bernardin and Archbishops Roach, Quinn, Hickey, May, and Weakland constitute "the dynamic new leadership of American Catholicism," and to be "deeply committed to peace" is to be a member of the pacifist organization Pax Christi.

These tendentious ecclesiastical judgments are of a piece with Hanson's description of the Red Guards' reign of terror as a "youthful attempt to remake Chinese civilization" and with his reduction of the choices in Eastern Europe as being between the parchment barriers of the Helsinki Accords and a "NATO crusade to free" the countries of the Warsaw Pact. Adam Michnik, Vaclav Havel, and George Konrad, please call the University of Santa Clara and ask for Professor Hanson.

The Catholic Church in World Politics takes up a topic of crucial importance for the Church and for international public life. But we need analysis here, not cheerleading for one camp in the current Catholic debate over war and peace, security and freedom. Hanson's book gives us far more of the latter than his topic deserves.

GEORGE WEIGEL
James Madison Foundation
Washington, D.C.

HIGONNET, MARGARET RANDOLPH et al., eds. *Behind the Lines: Gender and the Two World Wars*. Pp. viii, 310. New Haven, CT: Yale University Press, 1987. $22.50.

ELSHTAIN, JEAN BETHKE. *Women and War*. Pp. xvi, 288. New York: Basic Books, 1987. $19.95.

These two dense but rewarding volumes examine relationships between women, gender, and war. The collection of essays *Behind the Lines: Gender and the Two World Wars* is misleadingly titled: women were not always "behind the lines," nor did the debate over gender only take place there; much of the volume concerns women more than gender; only the best essays examine homosexuality and homoeroticism, powerful wartime phenomena and symbolic weapons in contests over gender; and although world war engulfed Asia, only Western attitudes and experiences are examined.

But these essays powerfully demonstrate how much the world wars provided battlegrounds not only for nations but for the sexes. The most provocative—lengthy, paired essays by Sandra Gilbert and Susan Gubar—explore highly charged territory. They suggest how World War I, when the mass slaughter of men coincided with rising feminism, unleashed among women an intense but guilt-ridden sense of triumph over men, complete with dreams of "a revisionary worldwide Herland, a utopia arisen from the ashes of apocalypse." It also unleashed a powerful misogynist reaction, shared by some women but shaped by men's fury over their carnage, their emasculation, their apparent eclipse by women. Played out against that background and drawing women far deeper into the carnage, World War II saw women's aspirations far more guarded and male assertion of dominance more sustained, successful, and sometimes vicious.

Indeed, a certain bleak tone about war's capacity to reorder gender relations recurs in this volume: "Women have been victimized, as a group, throughout history," we are reminded on the last page. In that regard, there is, unsurprisingly, tension among the many contributors, not to mention variations in quality and in the resort to faddish jargon—"discourse" to irritating excess.

But such reservations testify largely to the volume's provocative power and the uncharted nature of the territory it enters. In passing, it also raises an ahistorical question—"whether women are essentially or naturally peace-loving"—which is one of several that Jean Elshtain addresses. She does not pretend to offer a final answer to that question. Given prose at times more confusing than subtle, those answers that she does offer are sometimes unclear.

But she does challenge conventional notions. More consistently than the contributors to *Behind the Lines*, she recognizes the appeals of war to women. It may be, as the press release on the book states, that "war has always created history's greatest gender gap, casting men as 'Just Warriors' [and] women as 'Beautiful Souls.'" But Elshtain's argument is more subtle than that: it is less war than "representations" of it that perpetuate the gap. "Because women are *exterior* to war, men *interior*," their representations do often differ. She hopes, however, that "history's gender gap" is now narrowing, as male and female writers on the Vietnam war have joined in constructing "a story of universal victimization."

She may too quickly read too much transformative power into the remembrances of one lesser war: after the Great War, powerful stories of "universal victimization" neither closed the gender gap nor arrested the drift back to war. But she assembles other arguments—too complex for summary here—as well to hold out hope that "the traditional, and dangerous, narrative of war and peace"—variously ahistorical, arid, and apocalyptic—may be rewritten. Less pretentiously and more probingly than most such books, this one offers illuminating commentary—not just on what we think about war, but on the ways we think and express it.

MICHAEL S. SHERRY
Northwestern University
Evanston
Illinois

PARK, WILLIAM. *Defending the West: A History of NATO.* Pp. x, 242. Boulder, CO: Westview, 1986. $38.50.

RALLO, JOSEPH C. *Defending Europe in the 1990s: The New Divide of High Technology.* Pp. xxix, 136. New York: St. Martin's Press, 1986. $29.95.

Given that there is no shortage of books on the North Atlantic Treaty Organization (NATO), one almost wonders what could be profitably said in yet another book on the subject. Yet both books under review here are well worth reading, although for different reasons.

Park's book is a condensed history of NATO that identifies influential factors in the creation and maintenance of the alliance. He notes, for example, how U.S. public opinion, the Korean War, and the failure of the European Defense Community all affected the structure and goals of NATO. He also suggests that NATO has become the victim of its own policies—the rapid demobilization of the post-World War II years and the failure of the Lisbon conventional

force goals made NATO reliance on U.S. nuclear weapons a given. He suggests that the Americans may be more responsible for the schisms that have marred alliance relationships, noting that the Americans were the first to view theater nuclear weapons as a substitute for conventional force—and their forces at that, because in the early 1950s European defense spending was at historically high peacetime levels. Flexible response was adopted after Washington itself came under the range of Soviet missiles.

Park is at his best in explaining the reasons for the growing disagreement within NATO on nuclear policy, particularly as the doctrine shifted toward limited nuclear options in the 1970s. As war fighting as a concept moved to emphasize conventional forces, the internal difficulties for NATO increased, given that both the credibility of the doctrine and the cost of conventional modernization were contentious and often provoked by the United States. It is at this point that Rallo steps in. His book suggests that a European union could partly replace the role now played by the United States. Given that Rallo's book is problem oriented, he might have started with an introduction to NATO's problems. Indeed, there is an excellent presentation of them in the concluding chapter, and the interested reader might start there before tackling the rest of the book.

Rallo's theoretical preference is "complex interdependence," and this shapes much of what follows—the juncture of NATO's military and economic nature. Rallo notes that the American military and economic dominance of Western Europe immediately after World War II declined at the economic level as Europe recovered and the United States became encumbered by economic problems. The military dimension suffered as well, as transatlantic fissures opened over intermediate nuclear forces, arms control, and more recently a whole spate of Reagan-induced pressures.

In the meantime, Western Europe developed the institutions that would pull the region closer in economic terms, and Rallo suggests that such institutional frameworks could be expanded to provide for the advanced military technology market now supplied largely by the United States. Even in the face of some rather disappointing efforts at the European Common Market level to develop high technology in the information and aviation areas, Rallo finds some measure of hope in the growing cooperation on security matters among at least some NATO members, as evidenced in the Milan Summit of 1985 and in the efforts at a European Fighter Plane. Rallo might note, though, that these efforts point not to a European union providing NATO with high-technology weapons, but rather a consortium dominated by Western Europe's two or three most powerful members, which could well create its own set of problems.

Both these books are well written and documented and make important contributions to the existing literature on NATO.

DAVID S. SORENSON

Denison University
Granville
Ohio

AFRICA, ASIA, AND
LATIN AMERICA

BARNHART, MICHAEL A. *Japan Prepares for Total War: The Search for Economic Security, 1919-1941.* Pp. 290. Ithaca, NY: Cornell University Press, 1987. $29.95.

McINTOSH, MALCOLM. *Japan Re-Armed.* Pp. xv, 169. New York: St. Martin's Press, 1986. $27.50.

These two relatively brief books add nicely to our knowledge of Japanese foreign policy in both the period before the Pacific war, addressed by Barnhart, and the period after the Occupation, addressed by McIntosh. Of the two, Barnhart is the more scholarly, utilizing both Japanese and American archival material to break new ground in the already well-plowed field of study of the causes of the Pacific war. McIntosh has little by way of primary source material, but he gives a good general summary of Japan's main concerns, with special attention to the concept of comprehensive security and its application in the 1980s.

A review of Barnhart's study may best begin with mention of the revisionist work of James Crowley, published in book form by Princeton University Press in 1966 under the title *Japan's Quest for Autonomy.* In an era in which most Western studies, and indeed Japanese studies also, were condemnatory of Japan's pre-Pacific-war expansionism, Crowley was trying to be understanding of Japanese needs and aspirations. Although there was a lot of blatant militarism to be considered, Crowley found national security and the "quest for an autonomous national defense" to have been primary and at least semi-justifiable motivating factors. Barnhart follows the same theme, but, probing more deeply into factionalism in the Japanese military and the various plans and programs it produced, he "puts the black hat back on" Japan, to borrow the expression he used in summarizing his findings at the Shumpei Okamoto Memorial forum held at Temple University in April 1987.

Indeed, Barnhart finds Navy competition for materials allocation to have been primarily responsible for the escalation that brought on the challenges to Britain and the United States in Southeast Asia and Pearl Harbor. Meanwhile, the Army kept the China war going to justify its claims to an ever-increasing share of the national budget. Ironically, it was the total-war—against the whole Western world, but later—faction that counseled postponement of these military involvements, to allow time for maximizing Japan's war potential. Barnhart calls these "caretakers of the quest for autarky."

At any rate, it is not a pretty picture that Barnhart draws, and it would seem, indeed, to justify his argument that U.S. State Department China specialist Stanley K. Hornbeck was right in judging Japan to have been on the warpath without equivocation and in advising Secretary of State Hull and FDR not to rely on Japan's phony diplomacy. Barnhart takes this Hornbeck-was-right position in his contribution to the volume of essays *Pearl Harbor Reexamined: Was the Pacific War Inevitable?* (forthcoming), of which I am coeditor.

Certainly Barnhart produces evidence of the madness of the Japanese military in its search for autarky. One must—or at least should, in my opinion—however, continue to ask whether there was no better leadership potential in prewar Japan than the types he discusses. The McIntosh volume, which is a study in peace research undertaken at the School of Peace Studies at Bradford University, England, certainly suggests that from the record of postwar Japan, at least, such must have been the case. Although he calls the former Prime Minister Yasuhiro Nakasone a "nationalist hawk," he finds Japan's "allergy to nuclear weapons" to be both popular and practical and its devotion to the peace constitution, which by Article 18 forbids conscription as "involuntary servitude," to be strong, despite Nakasone's willingness to compromise it. Nevertheless, there is some ambivalence in McIntosh's analysis in that he sees the United States as promoting a "militarized Pacific," in which he hopes Japan will play a role as "peacemaker between the superpowers." He does not, however, foresee or propose any solution to two major Japanese problems: the northern islands question versus the USSR, and the oil supply problem. Clearly, Japan is vulnerable on both of these.

HILARY CONROY
University of Pennsylvania
Philadelphia

BURNS, E. BRADFORD. *At War in Nicaragua: The Reagan Doctrine and the Politics of Nostalgia.* Pp. xi, 211. New York:

Harper & Row, 1987. $14.95. Paperbound, $6.95.

VANDERLAAN, MARY B. *Revolution and Foreign Policy in Nicaragua.* Pp. xiii, 404. Boulder, CO: Westview, 1986. Paperbound, $29.95.

These two books join the long parade of scholarly works critical of the Reagan administration's policy toward Central America and, specifically, Nicaragua. Both authors view the Sandinista revolution as a legitimate exercise in nationalistic self-determination, representative of a general trend among Latin American states to distance themselves from U.S. hegemony. Both authors, moreover, see U.S. policy as badly flawed and counterproductive and U.S. leaders blind to the socioeconomic realities of developing nations in the late twentieth century. But the manner in which Burns and Vanderlaan state their cases is different to the extreme, and the two books complement each other quite nicely.

Burns's book—really a series of interrelated essays rather than a coherent monograph—is written in a breezy style that at times suggests superficiality. His argument is persuasively drawn, however, and centers on the notion that the Reagan administration, searching for the nostalgic days when a Pax Americana reigned in Latin America, has become obsessed with Nicaragua, because the Sandinistas have created a revolutionary state that defies the quest of the United States for what Burns calls global unilateralism. The obsession with Nicaragua leads to actions that violate international law, anger and frustrate other Latin American nations, and strain relations with allies in the North Atlantic Treaty Organization. All of these consequences are justified by casting the Sandinistas as Marxist-Leninist pawns in the global struggle against communism. Burns also makes much of the president's rhetorical warfare against Nicaragua, reminding us of his frequent misstatements of fact, ignorance of history, and soaring hyperbole. In reality, Nicaragua pursues an independent, nonaligned foreign policy, recognizes the need for a close economic relationship with the United States, and is less dependent on the Soviet Union than the Reagan administration would like us to believe.

By contrast, Vanderlaan's book is written in a style that can only be described as ponderous. It leaves no detail undescribed in its careful and thorough examination of Nicaraguan foreign policy. Because U.S. foreign policy is identified as a principal determinant of Nicaraguan policy, it, too, is given exhaustive treatment. Writing from a Nicaraguan point of view—in contrast to Burns—Vanderlaan describes the objectives of Sandinista foreign policy as centered in nonalignment, independence, and collaboration with Third World liberation movements. Despite years of U.S. hostility, the Sandinistas have succeeded in establishing a "fluid and dynamic" record, albeit focused on national survival, in which they have stressed their independence from U.S. dominance. Survival is all the more important to the Sandinistas because, as Vanderlaan emphasizes, they see their revolution as a model for other Third World nations and movements, such as the Palestine Liberation Organization, seeking independence.

Both authors scorn the contra war, citing its ineptness, corruption, and lack of sympathy within Nicaragua, but both point out that U.S. economic warfare has created substantial problems for the Sandinistas, although not to the point, certainly, of bringing the revolution to its knees. Although neither Burns nor Vanderlaan makes specific policy recommendations, both have good things to say about the Contadora process, and Burns, in particular, suggests that a more enlightened U.S. administration might help fund inwardly oriented economic development programs based on agricultural self-sufficiency and local industry.

Both books are lightly footnoted and based on newspaper sources and the accumulation of secondary literature on Central America published since 1980. Vanderlaan also interviewed anonymous U.S. and Nicaraguan officials during visits to Central America

in 1982, 1983, and 1985. Unfortunately, her book is flawed by some egregious spelling mistakes and other poor copyediting that undermine somewhat the credibility of her argument. On the whole, though, both of these books are good pieces of work and are useful contributions to the body of writing on contemporary Central America.

JOHN E. FINDLING
Indiana University Southeast
New Albany

HAHN, WALTER F., ed. *Central America and the Reagan Doctrine.* Pp. xvi, 318. Lanham, MD: University Press of America, 1987. Paperbound, $13.00.

Central America is receiving these days the attention it fully deserves, but, as typical of our information age, the plethora of judgments requires winnowing. A satisfying indicator of the exercise of such choice is the judicious compendium of articles Walter Hahn has prepared from *Strategic Review,* spanning the years 1982 to 1986. Too often articles and even books have appeared written by people of prior belief who, after a few weeks of selective sojourns, give their expert opinions. Here, however, is a collection of thoughtful and realistic insights into Soviet and Cuban objectives.

In a strategic sense, Central America and its Caribbean environs are the backdoor of the United States. Historically, it has not needed guarding and, to American discredit, thus has been tolerated, if not neglected, in its manifold development struggles. Our democracy seems only to respond to large fires, and even here the public is not fully aroused to the stakes. As portrayed, the Soviet Union seeks to develop an axis with Cuba and Central America that will prove a thorny opponent to this country. American plans of rapid and free sea access for troops and supplies, including oil, could be frustrated until America is forced to recognize as *faits accomplis* any possible Soviet capstone aggression in Europe and the Persian Gulf.

In the section focused on Nicaragua, Nestor Sanchez, among others, describes the record of the Marxist-Leninist, or Communist, Sandinistas: the large stream of military supplies from Cuba and the Soviets; the Nicaraguan military buildup overawing Central America; the thousands of Soviet and Cuban military and economic advisers; the Communist control of the nine comandante directorates, and President Ortega's "fraternal" and "enthusiastic" congratulations to a new chairman of the Soviet Union's presidium.

The Reagan doctrine, as explained by William Bode, endorses the Nicaraguan resistance as comprising freedom fighters, even if some are Somocistas, and identifies Cuba and the Soviet Union as responsible for subversive aggression. It asserts "American rights under international law to use force unilaterally in self defense." This response, as in the national interest, is the American stance replacing a vanished Monroe Doctrine.

In retrospect, I may reflect on the irony of the term "Sandinista," which, in an adaptation of communism to locale, took the name of a nationalist American opponent, who was also strongly anti-Communist. Further, one notes the clumsy American efforts at aiding Nicaraguan resistance, confined to less than 100 unarmed contra field advisers, to scourged resources, and to accompanying stark budgets. Tragically for the United States, home-side administration antics have contributed to the public mind-set this has created.

ROY M. MELBOURNE
Chapel Hill
North Carolina

JOSEPHIDES, LISETTE. *The Production of Inequality: Gender and Exchange among the Kewa*. Pp. x, 242. New York: Methuen, 1985. $35.00.

MOORE, HENRIETTA L. *Space, Text and Gender: An Anthropological Study of the Marakwet of Kenya*. Pp. xiv, 213. New York: Cambridge University Press, 1986. No price.

These books have a number of features in common. They are both by women; both are said to be revised versions of Ph.D. dissertations and bear the stamp of British social anthropology, the first produced at University College, London, and the second at Cambridge University; each focuses on a primitive tribal society with a particular emphasis on gender marking; each works within the currently popular amalgam of British and French Marxian *cum* post- or, depending on one's perspective, neo-, structuralism.

They differ in that, first, one is located in the Highlands of New Guinea and the other in East Africa. Second, Josephides is concerned with production and exchange as these relate to "the production of inequality" in what more naive observers might perceive as an egalitarian society while Moore has the avowedly theoretical purpose of discussing "the relationship between symbolic forms and the social and economic conditions within which those forms are produced, maintained and ultimately transformed." Third, one is very good and the other is not.

Josephides writes with clarity and constraint, presenting material that will be of interest to those from a variety of disciplines and, for example, working in the area of inequality, elitism, gender, or governing—especially relative to the role of big men. She is concerned with exploring relations of inequality in a small-scale society that lacks hereditary offices and explicitly values egalitarian relationships among men whose world-view, sociocultural identity, and orientation present the dominant ideology for males and females alike. All males own their own means of production—that is, land and control over their own labor—but warfare and exchange "together [define] and [reproduce] the group"; thus warriors and big men hold the group together politically. Despite the fact that villagers have recently become incorporated into a wider cash economy, gift exchange—particularly of pigs—is the activity that colors and cements all bonds with others. Such exchanges are symbolic representations of actual social transactions that are the everyday stuff of Kewa existence whether between husband and wife, parents and children, big men and followers/competitors, village and village. Though not always answering them to my satisfaction, Josephides addresses such provocative questions as, Why do big men seek to become big men—individuals who, almost daily, must legitimate their power over others through strenuous efforts geared to the production of material goods as well as nonmaterial goods, all the while at risk of the collapse of their status as movers and shakers? Or, again, given the egalitarian ethos, why does it apply only to males—and why do women actively participate in the perpetuation of their own inequality vis-à-vis that of males? Finally, what is a big man, how is his status achieved, and what does the status mean in its sociocultural context?

Reading about the Kewa leaders, one is constantly reminded of the big men in our society—those gray eminences with no formal political status but great political power, such as Armand Hammer; the politican now deemed statesman because no longer in office, such as Tip O'Neill, who is still a kingmaker despite posing in beach garb in ads for American Express credit cards. One wonders if Jane Fonda's retreat from political activism to help build her husband's career through the fat of the land is much different from that of the Kewa women whose labor is co-opted by their husbands in order that the latter may give pig feasts to gain followers and power. As Josephides points out, the building up of renown and prestige creates a "symbolic capital" the assets of which are primarily social recognition. "The mere exhibition of this capital, once created, can call up material wealth" in a process that the French anthropologist Pierre Bourdieu has summed up as "'capital [going] to capital.'" The parallels between the New Guinea political processes and those in our own Western society—as well as elsewhere!—are endless; the exercise is insightful. I highly commend it.

The Moore study is not so rewarding, though it is not without some merit to those interested in spatial arrangements as representations of power relations. Moore seems to believe that if one says the same thing over and over, with slight variations in the wording, the reader will be convinced of its truth value. This could be excused in a dissertation but not in a published presentation. Not so easily overlooked is its pretentiousness. For example, in a nine-page introduction, we are treated, in true dissertation style, to a "survey of the literature"—some three dozen names and theories are flashed past us under subheadings such as "The Structural/Semiotic Approach," "Contextuality," "'Reflection Theory,'" "Social Change," and "Social Actors." Then we are treated to a rather ponderous text, conjoined with 47 figures—for example, the location of Sibou village, genealogies of *Kapchemosi* households, the cardinal points of the house, the position of animal dung in relation to the gender association of the houses, compounds with square houses, interiors of two modern round houses—and 30 black and white plates—for example, a store, a modern store, a square house, mending a calabash, pounding maize—and the calling up, almost as incantations, of the "models," "theories," and "paradigms" of most of the currently fashionable, mandatory big men, such as Geertz, Foucault, Eco, Ricoeur, E. Said, Lacan, and so on and so on.

In her preface (p. xi) Moore states:

It is now axiomatic that spatial relations represent and reproduce social relations and it is the view that relations of likeness exist between social distinctions and spatial boundaries that links the study of gender to the study of space.... My focus is on the organization of household space in an attempt to understand one particular form of cultural representation, how it is produced and how it changes. My broader aim is to discuss the relationship between symbolic forms and the social and economic conditions within which those forms are produced, maintained and ultimately transformed.... I hope that the book sheds some light on the more general problems of understanding cultural representation.

Save, perhaps, for a small group of like-minded anthropologists, immersed in the literature of this genre, I would say she does not succeed.

M. ESTELLIE SMITH
State University of New York
Oswego

KALIA, RAVI. *Chandigarh: In Search of an Identity.* Pp. xiii, 201. Carbondale: Southern Illinois University Press, 1987. $22.50.

AHMED, SHARIF UDDIN. *Dacca: A Study in Urban History and Development.* Pp. xii, 266. London: University of London, School of Oriental and African Studies, 1986. $27.00.

These two monographic studies of vastly differing cities in India and Bangladesh are both of excellent quality and make welcome additions to the scanty list of South Asian urban histories. Each author deals with details of people, places, and events rather than theorizing. Yet each offers conclusions with general meaning for our understanding of the processes of modernization and urban development theory. Kalia holds up Chandigarh as a bad example of European urban design, superimposed by central authority in the twentieth century after independence, that failed to take account of Indian conditions and has yet to become adjusted to the regional sociopolitical context. Ahmed traces the slow evolutionary responses of East Bengali elites under unchallenged British control during the nineteenth century to changing economic and social conditions, resulting in organic growth more suited to the physical and institutional constraints of life in the region.

Kalia tells the story of the planning and development of the new capital of Indian Punjab from the beginning of 1948, when Jawaharlal Nehru chose the site, subsequently named the architects, and repeatedly intervened as conflicts inevitably arose between

the foreign experts and the local staff. Complete control of Chandigarh by the central government became necessary in 1966 when the previously consolidated Punjab state was partitioned between Sikh and Hindu majority areas, leaving Chandigarh as a centrally administered area used by both states for their respective governmental functions—a status that continues today.

The design of Chandigarh is rooted in Western experience, specifically in the ideas of the French-Swiss architect Le Corbusier, not in local realities. The master plan established single-purpose land-use zones that are not compatible with Indian mixed-use practices. The main streets have limited access and are oversized to accommodate high-speed motorized traffic but are not suited to mixtures of pedestrians, livestock, bicycles, and light motorized vehicles. High physical standards established for single-family dwellings do not allow for the customary compact grouping of dwelling places and convenient shopping. Even the least costly housing built for low-paid government workers proved beyond the means of many of the city's inhabitants. Unplanned or semiplanned settlements are now accepted as permanent features on the fringes of the planned sectors because the city must include spaces to be occupied by low-income workers in construction or services and petty trade, who are essential for the people in the higher ranks of government and elite business and professional classes. Chandigarh exemplifies the mistaken assumption that creation of a modern urban environment will cause modernizing effects on the masses of people in India or in any less developed region or country.

Ahmed's history of Dacca describes the evolution of the former Mughal provincial capital from its deep decline following the British conquest of Bengal through its revival as the regional center of commerce and sociopolitical development prior to 1900. It became East Bengal's focus of transport by waterways and railways, its center of business and regional civil administration, and the principal seat of English education and professional services outside Calcutta. The population began to grow after the 1850s with concurrent problems of sanitation and disease. Ahmed enters into a lengthy account of the measures undertaken by municipal authority to improve water supply and waste disposal in order to improve the conditions of public health and reduce the death rate. He provides a fascinating narrative of the interplay of British officers and local leaders in municipal affairs and the successful establishment of a limited form of representative government. But old Dacca's Muslim elite failed to respond as rapidly as the upper Hindu castes to the changes brought by British rule. Thus Ahmed's study shows how the public life of nineteenth-century Dacca was a microcosm of an early stage in the modernization of India under British rule.

JOHN E. BRUSH

Rutgers University
New Brunswick
New Jersey

KHALAF, SAMIR. *Lebanon's Predicament.* Pp. xiv, 328. New York: Columbia University Press, 1987. $30.00.

In "On the Demoralization of Public Life," one of the essays that make up this insightful book, the author introduces the topic with a quotation from Yeats:

Things fall apart; the centre cannot hold
Mere anarchy is loosed upon the world
—"The Second Coming"

There is more, but somehow the observations of an Irish poet on the state of the world in his time apply with peculiar force to contemporary Lebanon. In the same way, Samir Khalaf, sociologist by profession but one uniquely qualified to observe the trauma of more than a decade of violence in his native land by virtue of personal involvement, has provided here an assessment of the historical antecedents and the present disintegration of the Lebanese nation that should stand as the

definitive work on the subject for some time to come.

Lebanon's "predicament," as Khalaf explains it, stems from the fact that the same forces that have enabled Lebanese society to survive at the subnational level have remained major obstacles to nation building and the establishment of a civic consciousness and national identity. He develops this theme in a series of essays. An introductory essay deals with Lebanon as a case study of a society in transition—toward modernization—in which strong patrimonial institutions, extended family associations, and confessional religious communities have hampered the establishment of broad national consensus groups or general agreement on what is best for Lebanon as a whole. Then, in lucid prose, Khalaf describes the historical patterns of Lebanese conflict, particularly in the nineteenth century, when the foundations of civil war were laid down. Subsequent essays deal with the deeply rooted patronage system in Lebanon, the social structure of Parliament, and the role of families in industrial development and social relations. Such social patterns as kinship, patron-client loyalty and mutual obligations, the zu'ama rivalries and confessionalism have been described elsewhere but seldom with such cogency and relevance to the upheaval in Lebanon today.

Two other essays deal with family planning—one of the very few success stories in Lebanese intercommunal progress—and urban planning, another shining example of the absence of civic commitment in the country.

The last two essays, "On the Demoralization of Public Life" and "Ras Beirut in Jeopardy," are very different from the rest. No longer is Khalaf a dispassionate observer of the Lebanese catastrophe; he is a fully engaged participant. As he points out, the decade and more of civil war has dismembered Lebanese society, rendering it incapable of civility and obsessed with violence. All Lebanese suffer, all are equal in their vulnerability. Violence and terror are "everywhere and nowhere; they cannot be identified or linked to a concrete cause. Today's allies are tomorrow's enemies." The result is anomie, total rejection of the norms of social behavior. The real tragedy of Lebanon is thus a moral one. Even if all external and other dislocating elements—Palestinians, the superpowers, Arab rivalries, Israeli forces—were withdrawn, Lebanese society would remain fragmented without a moral commitment to higher civic and national over parochial values.

The final essay is a poignant memoir of Ras-Beirut, the seaside suburb of the Lebanese capital located around the American University of Beirut. Beginning as a garbage dump, it grew under the inspiration of the University into a lively center of literature, the arts, politics, and culture, something unique in the Arab world. But the widening Lebanese conflict has finally washed over Ras-Beirut and its distinguished university. What Khalaf finds emerging in Lebanese society is a monolithic archetype, Islamic in form, hostile to coexistence with any other group. His conclusion, with which I would reluctantly agree, is that only a miracle can save Lebanon from itself and engender a new and workable secular society there.

WILLIAM SPENCER

Gainesville
Florida

ROZMAN, GILBERT. *The Chinese Debate about Soviet Socialism, 1978-1985.* Pp. xi, 396. Princeton, NJ: Princeton University Press, 1987. No price.

Between 1949 and the mid-1980s, Sino-Soviet relations blossomed, declined, and then gradually improved. Foreign policy and ideological differences accounted for most of these seismic changes, but the changing perceptions of each other that Soviet and Chinese intellectuals held also reflected these great fluctuations.

Gilbert Rozman's review of some classified journals and books by Chinese specialists on the Soviet Union published during 1978-85 traces how Chinese perceptions changed after 1978 and reminds us of the importance of taking very seriously what specialists in socialist states say about each other.

Sino-Soviet relations soured after 1957 when Mao led other party ideologues in strongly criticizing the Soviet leadership for rejecting Stalin, initiating policies allegedly reversing the course of socialism, and treating other socialist states as their clients rather than their equals. Chinese criticism of the Soviet Union continued until the Chinese Communist Party line shifted dramatically in the fall of 1978, emphasizing the "forces of production" and downgrading the importance of "class struggle."

Thereafter, Chinese Soviet specialists began to more positively evaluate Soviet socialism and economic performance and the achievements of Soviet leaders. Rozman summarizes what leading Chinese Soviet experts have written since 1978, first narrating how Chinese perceptions of the Soviet Union rapidly changed, then stating what these writings had to say about social strata like the peasantry, workers, intelligentsia, and officials.

Rozman believes that the post-1978 reforms and the new climate of intellectual openness encouraged experts on the Soviet Union to pose new questions: what kind of socialist system had evolved after 1917? Why did certain policy errors like the collectivization of agriculture occur? Would Bukharin's model for building socialism have been superior to that developed by Stalin? Why did the Soviet economy encounter serious difficulties in the 1960s and 1970s? Chinese experts argued that many policy mistakes occurred because the Soviet leadership had no precedents to teach them how to build socialism and that the "cult of personality" also limited debate about policy options. These same experts, however, praised Soviet education and socialist culture for their freedom from the baleful influences of "bourgeois liberalism" and "spiritual pollution"—intellectual currents that have lately divided the Chinese Communist leadership over how quickly to pursue reforms.

Chinese experts still criticized Soviet foreign policy, claiming that its goals seemed to demand that other socialist states coexist with the Soviet Union as dependents, not peers. Since 1983, though, Chinese writings about the Soviet Union have become even more favorable and positive; in the USSR, too, China experts have refrained from severe criticism of Chinese reforms, and have even had mild praise for their achievements. Whether these new mutual perceptions will promote a détente like that of the 1950s is an issue Rozman does not explore, but his findings suggest that such a relationship is unlikely because Beijing's leaders prefer that China remain equidistant from both of the superpowers.

Although Rozman's extremely useful and informative volume could have been condensed and less repetitive, it is still the first of its kind to explore in such depth and detail how one Marxist-Leninist socialist society perceives another.

RAMON MYERS

Hoover Institution on War,
    Revolution and Peace
Stanford
California

EUROPE

CONQUEST, ROBERT. *The Harvest of Sorrow: Soviet Collectivization and the Terror-Famine.* Pp. 412. New York: Oxford University Press, 1986. $19.95.

This is a vivid analytic narrative, based on primary evidence and informed commentary, telling a tragic tale. Robert Conquest is a prolific historian, scholar, and committed critic of the Soviet system. To our previous understanding of the brutality and costs of agricultural collectivization for the USSR as a whole, Conquest's account adds a large body of detail on the deliberate campaign to starve rural Ukrainians.

After sketching the historical background,

Conquest describes in part 2 the national drive to "liquidate the kulaks as a class" during the years 1929-32. Special chapters touch on the impact in Soviet Central Asia and on churches. Part 3 deals in detail with the forced extraction of grain and the deliberate withholding of supplies in 1932-33 that led to famine in the Ukraine, the Kuban, and the lower Don-Volga area, where Ukrainians were concentrated. Short chapters touch on the fate of children, the number of deaths, and the way the West responded. An epilogue reflects on long-run consequences.

The book has a solid scholarly basis. Conquest draws on selected official statements, frequent items in *Pravda*, a variety of Soviet publications, standard Western authorities—Jasny, Davies, Lewin, among others—and on several post-Stalin Soviet scholars—including Moshkov, Danilov, and Nemakov—as well as on Ukrainian commentators and survivors. Footnote references are meticulous, though the truncated bibliography and index make them awkward to use.

This study makes at least three important contributions. It documents Stalin's viciousness toward peasants in general and the Ukrainians in particular. It offers a vivid reminder of the human costs associated with the way agriculture was reorganized in the USSR, and it does so by updating established analyses and adding recent material to provide an intense account of a major tragedy. Demography is not Conquest's forte; others, like Barbara Anderson and Brian Silver, are clarifying the impact of these events on population numbers. Nevertheless, this book is a fine place to begin the study of Soviet collectivization.

HOLLAND HUNTER

Haverford College
Pennsylvania

DEVLIN, JUDITH. *The Superstitious Mind: French Peasants and the Supernatural in the Nineteenth Century.* Pp. xii, 316. New

Haven, CT: Yale University Press, 1987. $30.00.

Superstition is often viewed as the scientific system of the masses. Judith Devlin disagrees, contending that it is better understood in social and psychological terms. To some degree, superstition did explain nature, but this function was not paramount to the peasants. Rather, superstition was more important as a rationale to help survive the rigors and disappointments of daily life. One reason was the prevalence of popular, as opposed to orthodox, religion. There had been an erosion of traditional beliefs in the eighteenth century, due to the Enlightenment, industrialization, and the French Revolution. Indeed, even the faithful sometimes went to church out of habit rather than devotion. Holy Mother Church went along by encouraging popular ideas. It stressed, for example, the sensational terrors of hell rather than the ethereal pleasures of heaven, and it emphasized the human—and sometimes petty—nature of the saints rather than their spirituality.

Apparitions and monsters loomed large in this superstitious mind-set. Ghosts were tormented souls who had not settled their debts with God; in seeking relief, they came back to earth and haunted the places where they had lived. Other superstitions were rooted in reality. The fear of werewolves drew on the real danger of wolves and the forest, on man's fear of nature's wildest things and a hostile environment. For this was a society susceptible to disaster, one that needed to explain and rationalize catastrophes. The connection between superstition and reality can be seen in witchcraft. Peasants often felt victimized, and witchcraft helped them settle what they thought were injustices. Hence Devlin sees necromancy not as science explaining the insoluble but as a means of expressing and overcoming disorienting feelings and of satisfying dreams. It was an emotional and social expression of the not always stoic peasant, a release of frustrations, and a way to transfer personal inadequacy and failure. Devlin argues convincingly that

French peasants did not—indeed, did not seek to—understand the natural world by any means. Rather, they were beset by anxieties and sought to rationalize their being.

Devlin is less convincing in arguing that twentieth-century urban modernism is akin to nineteenth-century rural superstition. Certainly, superstition and irrationality persist; witness racism and anti-Semitism. But they have an entirely different hue, and draw, correctly or otherwise, on scientific, technological, and industrial bases with which traditional societies, by definition, were unaware. Devlin has not, as she implies, discovered a subculture of the masses, and this book is somewhat less innovative than she suggests. Rather, it is well in the mainstream of the new social history, and one of its topics, witchcraft, has been a fertile field of study for three generations. Nonetheless, this does not detract from the quality of an often provocative and always interesting book. It will be useful to historians of popular culture and French rural life, and it is a good read, filled with enough anecdotal material to supply several lectures.

ROBERT S. GOTTFRIED
Rutgers University
New Brunswick
New Jersey

ELWITT, SANFORD. *The Third Republic Defended: Bourgeois Reform in France, 1880-1914.* Pp. xvi, 304. Baton Rouge: Louisiana State University Press, 1986. No price.

CONVERSE, PHILIP E. and ROY PIERCE. *Political Representation in France.* Pp. xiii, 996. Cambridge, MA: Harvard University Press, 1986. $49.50.

If methods, overtly stated goals, perspective, style, and format are considered, it would be difficult to imagine two more different books. What links them, aside from the patience and erudition of their authors, is their subject matter. They deal with the two most successful regimes in modern French history, the Third and Fifth republics, and at some level they both seek to explain the strength and endurance of those regimes.

Elwitt is a historian and very frank about his approach, which is resolutely Marxist. The aim of his industrious research, which has uncovered an intriguing group of little-known individuals whose political and economic activities were interwoven in complex ways and were influential in their day, is to show that "social reform became a vehicle to further the association and collaboration of labor and capital and became a weapon against socialism." Much of this reform was generated from above, indicating an awareness that "paternalism ensured employers against disorder as much as it ensured workers against the worst miseries of their existence."

Elwitt produces a great deal of evidence demonstrating that many of the reformers understood "the superiority of indirect over direct instruments of control." His cast of characters, Emile Cheysson among others, devoted enormous intelligence and energy to strengthening the industrial system just as it was falling into place and to stabilizing the class structure of the moderate bourgeois republic, which had been established under such inauspicious circumstances following the disastrous defeat of 1870.

These reformers—and as much as he dislikes most of them, Elwitt does accept the sincerity of their reformist impulses—tended not to follow the normal political routes of running for the Chamber of Deputies and eventually serving as cabinet ministers, though they were often closely associated with the political elites of the nation. They were instead teachers, lecturers, propagandists, ideologues of several stripes including the great advocate of manual training programs, Gustave Salicis—whose name I am sure was unknown even to the most erudite scholars of the Third Republic until Elwitt delivered him from historical obscurity—supporters of imperialist adventuring like Joseph Chailley-Bert, philanthropists,

museum curators, and businessmen. Cheysson actually spent three years as managing director of the steel complex of Le Creusot, owned by the Schneider family. Through a variety of endeavors, these reformers attempted to "replace the tensions of class antagonism with the bonds of class collaboration."

One does not have to accept all of Elwitt's arguments or his conclusions to agree that he has found some fascinating material and that his treatment, passionately biased as it is, casts new light on how the Third Republic managed to survive so many crises, including the Dreyfus affair, and so many enemies on the Left and the Right until it was brought down by an external foe.

Converse and Pierce are political scientists, and their massive study, based on more than two decades of research, draws heavily upon questionnaires distributed in 1967 and 1968. Converse and Pierce focus on elections held during the first decade of the Fifth Republic. The great divide of May 1968 is crossed and part 3 of their study deals with the system in crisis. The reasons for the regime's surprisingly successful crossing of that hurdle are not discussed in depth. Converse and Pierce are primarily concerned with the implantation and consolidation of the more presidential system of the Fifth Republic, which means concentrating on de Gaulle's terms in office (1958-69). The Pompidou and Giscard d'Estaing years, not to mention the socialist victory of 1981, would merit a sequel.

The research for this work is truly voluminous, and the book is well written, is superbly organized, and has excellent tables. Converse and Pierce's fundamental goal is to search for the "underlying springs of electoral behavior." They have made important strides toward accomplishing that goal. Unlike Elwitt, they are determined to be value neutral, betraying no detectable political preferences. They are as careful and dispassionate in their statements about Communist candidates as they are for Gaullists. Perhaps a skilled semiotician could read between or under the lines and unearth some hidden agendas, but I at least can discover no more than an occasional neatly balanced aside such as "American congressmen . . . act in a manner consistent with perceptions that are inaccurate, while French deputies behave in a way inconsistent with perceptions which we believe to be closer to reality."

The sections of historical review are very useful, and the work is filled with intriguing details, such as the reluctance of French parents to speak of politics in the presence of their children. The discussion of the impact of religion on French voting patterns is excellent, while the presentation of the two characteristics of the parliamentary elite is less impressive, tending to belabor the obvious.

The conceptual key to Converse and Pierce's work is based on a model devised by Miller and Stokes derived from their studies of the U.S. Congress, and it seems to work quite well for France. Historians can learn much from this approach, and it would be enlightening for both disciplines if Converse and Pierce would exchange roles with Elwitt. Elwitt would surely discern many of the ways in which the seemingly scientific tables presented by Converse and Pierce are ideologically tainted and would probe deeply into the question they admit to have only touched upon, namely, who is represented. While Converse and Pierce obviously cannot interview candidates for the Chamber of Deputies of the Third Republic, there may be enough electoral data extant for them to perform some interesting analyses, which might show that some of Elwitt's denunciations are ill founded and that the decade of the 1880s marked the beginning of a true democratic tradition in France. It is perhaps not inconsequential that after 1880 it again became legal to celebrate Bastille Day!

DAVID L. SCHALK
Vassar College
Poughkeepsie
New York

FRANZOI, BARBARA. *At the Very Least She Pays the Rent: Women and German Industrialization, 1871-1914.* Pp. xii, 206. Westport, CT: Greenwood, 1985. $29.95.

Barbara Franzoi states the purpose—and contribution—of her book, *At the Very Least She Pays the Rent: Women and German Industrialization, 1871-1914,* as follows:

This study is an effort to make German working women visible—in their nation's economic and social history and, by so doing, to expand possibilities for comparative analysis of the impact of industrialization (p. 13).

The dominant theme is the adaptive strengths and strategies women generated as they engaged a system in economic transition (p. 185).

She starts with the convergence of capitalism, patriarchy, and Bismarckian state socialism that created a sexual division of labor in Imperial Germany. Women's work was 50 percent less remunerative, on the average, than men's, less steady, and segregated.

Franzoi is interested in the questions, "How did working women respond to industrialization?" "Why were they relatively acquiescent in the face of exploitative conditions?"

She finds that the two major analyses of industrialization's impacts on women do not have sufficient explanatory power. Conservative historiography analytically merges women with the family, while orthodox Marxism merges women's work with men's, hence, factory work. So she uses an empathetic approach and eclectic sources—from census data to diaries—to reconstruct the reasons why German women made the employment choices they did, given their limited options and the contexts of their lives.

German women did the best they could, says Franzoi, to integrate paid employment with their interests in child care and the collective survival and well-being of their families. That is why "they did not confront the system but, rather, negotiated its limited possibilities to suit their needs." Thus the concentration of women in home-based labor— food, clothing, and tobacco processing— served not only the interests of capitalists and the state but of working mothers.

The reader comes away with an appreciation of these sisters' ingenuity, common sense, and courage, as well as new insight into German working women's relative disinterest in factory work, labor unions, and protective legislation.

Franzoi accomplishes her purpose by creating a book as richly textured as the phenomenon she studies. She combines an impressive use of German primary sources with a writing style that is anything but Teutonic. Clear and accessible, her narrative takes the reader into the work and home lives of her subjects. Especially successful in this regard is her discussion of women's sexuality, birth control, and family life, as well as nine memorable photographs of home workers, circa 1905-10. The footnotes, bibliography, and index are well organized.

By looking objectively and creatively at the lives of German working women between Bismarck and World War I, Barbara Franzoi makes a solid contribution to historiography, German studies, and women's studies.

JOY HUNTLEY

Ohio University
Athens

FYRTH, JIM. *The Signal Was Spain: The Spanish Aid Movement in Britain, 1936-39.* Pp. xi, 344. New York: St. Martin's Press, 1987. $32.50.

This exercise in what Fyrth regards as historical justice is designed to show how far the movement in Britain to aid the Spanish Republicans between 1936 and 1939 was "an outstanding example of international solidarity." It counteracts the effects of the cold war and of the painful recollection of British policies to appease fascist regimes that have inhibited historians from recognizing the extent of antifascist and antiwar movements among all classes. Fyrth wants to emphasize that the reaction in Britain against Franco was not merely an intellectual fashion; he condemns the myth that a lot of worthy and

innocent people were manipulated by the Communist Party. His theme is that the relationships between the Labour movement, the Aid Spain organizations, and the Communist Party were more complex than a more orthodox treatment of the subject suggests.

The book began as a labor of love. It was undertaken to complete the work of Tony McLean, whose untimely death in 1982 removed the opportunity he had created to write a record of the British medical personnel in Spain during the Civil War. McLean's material on the Spanish Medical Aid Committee still plays a dominant role in shaping the book; chapter 10, on the medical advances made as a result of treating the wounded at that time, is a characteristic product of these origins. The simple device of triage—sorting, classifying the wounded into different categories—effected a major transformation of medical treatment.

Yet Jim Fyrth decided that he could not deal with the medical contributions without first considering the Aid Spain movement as a whole. The result is an account of events that combines "the response in Spain"—chapters 4 to 13—with "the response in Britain"—chapters 14 to 18. The Spanish section is based on interviews, diaries, and letters; the British, on local history sources. The most original parts of the book are those that chronicle local activity, particularly in the reception of Basque children evacuated from Spain in 1937 and in the endeavor of such organizations as the British Youth Foodship Committee. For instance, Fyrth has used the records of the Eastleigh and District Local History Society as well as those of the Communist and Labour Party.

The division of the material makes it easier for the reader to get a feel for the medical experience in Spain than to appreciate the degree of solidarity on the ground in Britain among those prepared to help the Republican cause. The complexity of the relationships within the Aid Spain movement are not immediately apparent. The difficulties of the National Joint Committee for Spanish

Relief, an organization frequently mentioned, are not properly explained. Perhaps the most interesting conclusion, which requires another book for Fyrth to substantiate, is that the core of people organizing the Aid Spain movement constituted a cadre that developed sufficient organizational skills to change the outlook of the British people during World War II. The British government in 1937 was the most determined exponent of the doctrine that it should not intervene in Spain; the British people were clearly less convinced. But it is never easy to show the relationship between foreign policy and popular feeling if there is little evidence of response in government.

J. M. LEE
University of Bristol
England

UNITED STATES

BALL, HOWARD. *Justice Downwind: America's Atomic Testing Program in the 1950's.* Pp. xviii, 280. New York: Oxford University Press, 1986. $21.95.

SCHUCK, PETER H. *Agent Orange on Trial: Mass Toxic Disasters in the Courts.* Pp. ix, 347. Cambridge, MA: Harvard University Press, Belknap Press, 1986. $25.00.

Two landmark legal cases ended at trial-court level during the same week of May 1984. A New York federal district court judge on 7 May announced settlement of the Agent Orange case just before trial was to begin. Across the continent three days later, a Utah federal district court judge handed down his judgment in the Allen case, 17 months after the trial concluded. Both cases arose from events long past. Both became class actions that involved large numbers of plaintiffs who sought compensation for injuries of ill-defined cause they claimed to have suffered in large government-sponsored programs. Thus both helped define a new class of personal injury, mass toxic disaster.

Though couched in the language of tort, both were as much attempts to redress perceived social wrongs as to win damages for personal injury. Consequently, both raised serious political as well as legal questions still far from resolved. Both cases remain, as of this writing, under appeal.

The first case began in Vietnam, where American troops were exposed to a chemical defoliant, Agent Orange, contaminated with traces of highly toxic dioxin. Controversy still surrounds the health effects of Agent Orange—or of trace dioxin—but ailing veterans in 1978 sued the manufacturers who supplied Agent Orange to the U.S. government. Describing the course of this complex and novel case is Peter H. Schuck's central goal in *Agent Orange on Trial.* Schuck is Simeon E. Baldwin Professor of Law at Yale Law School and has written extensively on the interaction of law and politics in American society. *Agent Orange on Trial* is a strong book, fully documented. In addition to the records of Agent Orange litigation and relevant legal literature, he relies heavily on his interviews with most key participants.

The book is divided into three unequal parts. The first offers a brief but very informative introduction to the issues and the case. Parts 2 and 3 are more problematic. A long and detailed narrative that occupies three-fourths of the book, part 2 may fascinate readers with the complex interplay of legal issue, personality, and accident, but it may more often frustrate their efforts to keep plot and characters straight. The problem of part 3, which briefly discusses the case's political and legal implications, is the weight of a highly technical analysis. Scholars may well benefit from such details and analysis, but nonexperts are likely to find a careful reading of part 1 and a quick look at part 3 sufficient to their needs.

National defense and environmental insult also underlay the second case, derived from the U.S. atmospheric nuclear weapons test program at the Nevada Test Site during the 1950s. Radioactive fallout dusted thousands of people downwind from the test site, in Nevada, northern Arizona, and southern

Utah. Inconclusive scientific studies during the 1960s and 1970s suggested that even such relatively small exposures as so-called downwinders received might have significantly increased their chances of developing leukemia or other forms of cancer. In 1979 they filed suit against the government. That case and its background are the major subjects of Howard Ball's *Justice Downwind.*

Ball is a political scientist at the University of Utah. Like Schuck, he has written about law and politics, and his book, too, is well documented. He makes good use of court records and congressional hearings; he also quotes local newspapers effectively to highlight changing public attitudes. Ultimately, however, he relies on published scholarly sources for the backbone of his story. My qualms about some of Ball's judgments are decidedly minor in view of his accomplishment. His work joins the small company of recent historical studies of radiation hazards that treat the evidence responsibly and deserve to be taken seriously by scholars. Carefully written, well organized, and persuasive, *Justice Downwind* is also one of the few books on its subject that I would recommend to nonexperts.

Although Schuck scarcely mentions the radiation cases, and Ball discusses mass toxic disaster and tort litigation only briefly, the two books nonetheless complement each other nicely. This is unusual, if my experience is any guide, but a pleasure when it occurs. Both books achieve a remarkable level of accuracy and fair-mindedness in dealing with complex and controversial subjects. Each is a good book, but together they are even better in offering thoughtful readers an admirably clear view of one of the central problems of modern society.

BARTON C. HACKER
Oregon State University
Corvallis

BURK, ROBERT F. *Dwight D. Eisenhower: Hero and Politician.* Pp. xii, 207. Boston: G. K. Hall, Twayne, 1986. $24.95.

CONKIN, PAUL K. *Big Daddy from the Pedernales: Lyndon Baines Johnson.* Pp. xii, 324. Boston: G. K. Hall, Twayne, 1986. $24.95.

These are the first volumes in Twayne's Twentieth-Century American Biography Series under the general editorship of John Milton Cooper, Jr., of the University of Wisconsin. The dust jackets explain that the series comprises "one-volume interpretive biographies of the central figures of this century who have changed the way we live and think."

Although Dwight Eisenhower and Lyndon Johnson assuredly deserve to be included in a biographical series about leading Americans of this century, it may be arguable that they truly changed the way we live and think. Both, after all, were essentially traditionalists, with roots in the frontier. Both reflected a cold-war mentality in their desire to check the spread of communism. Both sought to nurture prosperity—their own as well as the nation's. They did differ in their views of government's role in American life, with LBJ, a New Deal acolyte, favoring a more paternalistic one. At least in the short run, Johnson, a legislative magician, did effect some societal changes, notably in the civil rights area. And he might have changed America still more through his Great Society program, but even its myriad legislation, as Conkin points out, was conventional in design and intent. In the end, of course, Johnson was broken and driven from the presidency by the great miscalculation in Vietnam whose antecedents stretched back to Eisenhower.

Eisenhower, a rebellious cadet at West Point, came to stand squarely for preserving the status quo. Burk, who teaches history at Muskingum College, calls him an adaptive hero who mainly attempted "to preserve individual avenues of success within powerful national bureaucracies." Eisenhower was also adaptive in the way he overcame an aversion to politics and learned to play the game as a young army officer faced with limited advancement opportunities in the period between the two world wars. Some luck as well as ambition led him to mentors such as generals Pershing, MacArthur, Marshall, and the less well known Fox Conner. Later, adapting to the managerial techniques of modern government, he became "the manager of the modern American national security state."

Eisenhower was born in Denison, Texas, in 1890—which marked, according to Frederick Jackson Turner, the end of the American frontier—and lived until 1969, when America achieved a major milestone on the space frontier by landing men on the moon. The feat was accomplished by the National Aeronautics and Space Administration, created during Eisenhower's second term under legislation sponsored by Senate Majority leader Lyndon Johnson.

Born in the Texas hill country in 1908, LBJ later was referred to as the last frontier president. Ironically, while Eisenhower abhorred political wheeler-dealers such as Johnson, the latter was deferential to the Eisenhower administration and often shaped winning coalitions for its legislation. According to Conkin, a Vanderbilt University historian, Johnson's mastery of the Senate was achieved partly by viewing his peers as members of his extended family. This familial metaphor is central to Conkin's depiction of LBJ as a big daddy, a man with Texas-sized insecurities due to his hill country origins who sought security in the satisfaction derived from dispensing favors and doing good deeds. But when his goals were thwarted or his accomplishments were unappreciated, he became depressed and periodically withdrew to the familiar surroundings of the hill country. Primarily a practitioner of intellectual history, Conkin is content here with straightforward description. The main exception is his use of policy analysis in a splendid chapter evaluating the Great Society.

Conkin's *Johnson*, like Burk's *Eisenhower*, is an excellent one-volume introduction to its subject; both are distinguished as much by their brevity and evenhandedness as by their comprehensiveness. The books include illustrations and indexes.

DONALD L. SMITH

Pennsylvania State University
University Park

CLIFFORD, J. GARRY and SAMUEL R. SPENCER, Jr. *The First Peacetime Draft.* Pp. xv, 320. Lawrence: University Press of Kansas, 1986. $29.95.

It was the summer of 1940. The winds of war from Europe had spread to the United States. Churchill needed help. Few Americans trusted the unloved dictator of Germany, but a number felt that the large bodies of water that were the Atlantic and Pacific would form a fortress to keep the United States out of war. It was an ambivalent time, when numerous and differing ideological voices jockeyed for position to determine the position of the United States in a war "over there." It was at this time that a small group of businessmen and intelligentsia formed a committee to initiate the first peacetime draft. Forty years in the making, it was originated by Grenville Clark and monitored by Arthur Schlesinger, Jr.

Clifford and Spencer provide exciting reading. Their scholarly account of the beginnings of the selective service describe the hesitations, and the second-guessing, of New Deal politicos who feared that America would be unprepared for war. This is not a musty textbook history, for Clifford and Spencer provide the necessary dramaturgical setting for the onset of an authoritarian measure in a limited republic.

June through August of 1940 were dog days along the Potomac. Congress went into an extended session to pass the Burke-Wadsworth Bill authorizing the selective service. Thousands marched on Washington. Congressmen were cornered by constituents and activists. People sweated and institutions rumbled. A hesitant president with an eye on a third term finally endorsed the bill. With the passage, klieg lights brightened as the world watched Roosevelt draw the first lottery number: 158.

There is much more. Clifford and Spencer had access to numerous original sources, manuscripts, and expert testimony. Their research of secondary sources is voluminous. Their approach is a centrist-consensus history of the two major private market parties struggling to prepare for an uncertain war in uncertain time.

Readers of social history, political sociology, and American history will come to feel that this book must be read.

One will also discover the character of Grenville Clark, a man of peace, who for a short time in his life felt that war was unavoidable and that Hitler could not be believed.

Clifford, professor of political science at the University of Connecticut, and Spencer, president emeritus of Davidson College, provide another portion of the mosaic of World War II. Both scholarship and high-profile interests are brought together for the reader. Their book is well written and invites the reader to return to another era troubled by war and the role that should be played by the citizen soldier.

JOEL C. SNELL

Kirkwood Community College
Cedar Rapids
Iowa

DOWNS, GEORGE W. and PATRICK D. LARKEY. *The Search for Government Efficiency: From Hubris to Helplessness.* Pp. viii, 273. Philadelphia: Temple University Press, 1986. $27.95.

Like Rodney Dangerfield, the federal government gets no respect. Stereotypes of red tape, inefficiency, and overspending keep reappearing in the popular media.

Recently, two books have appeared to provide the basis for a little respect. The first, *The Case for Bureaucracy: A Public Administration Polemic*, by Charles T. Goodsell (2d ed., [Chatham, NY: Chatham House Publishers, 1985]), points out that our bureaucracy is really pretty good, even when compared with our own private sector and especially when compared with other countries. Goodsell counseled that "we deemphasize grandiose nostrums and concentrate on particularized suggestions for improvement and refinement."

The Search for Government Efficiency: From Hubris to Helplessness takes up this theme by examining various grandiose schemes and nostrums advocated in the past

for reform in government in the name of efficiency. Downs and Larkey challenge the widely held view that the private sector is more efficient and effective than the public sector. Noting that in the delivery of certain services, private firms may be more efficient than government, overall there is nothing to demonstrate greater efficiency for corporate life.

This is not to say that all is well in the public sector. There is much room for improvement. But the various broad-based schemes that have been advanced such as decision and benefit-cost analysis, program-planning-budgeting systems, management by objectives, and zero-based budgeting have all proven failures. As the subtitle of the book notes, these high hopes—hubris—of the reformers, many of whom have been drawn from corporate life, have been replaced by a sense of helplessness as one scheme after the other has proven ineffective.

The major explanations of these failures focus on the very political nature of government decried by the reformers, the lack of a sound longitudinal data base, an unwillingness to spend the money necessary to implement many of the reforms, and the short-term political horizons of many who must oversee the process.

Downs and Larkey advocate a less comprehensive approach, one that adds the value of efficiency to the other values of government. Using the Government Accounting Office as a model, they suggest the creation of Government Efficiency Agencies to work on specific reforms related to individual departments and agencies.

All in all, this is a book well worth reading, both for its analysis of past reforms, including the suggestions of the Grace Commission, and for its suggestions for the future.

EDWARD BAUM

Ohio University
Athens

FAIRCLOUGH, ADAM. *To Redeem the Soul of America: The Southern Christian*

Leadership Conference and Martin Luther King, Jr. Pp. x, 504. Athens: University of Georgia Press, 1987. $35.00. Paperbound, $17.95.

ANDERSON, ALAN B. and GEORGE W. PICKERING. *Confronting the Color Line: The Broken Promise of the Civil Rights Movement in Chicago.* Pp. xii, 515. Athens: University of Georgia Press, 1987. $40.00. Paperbound, $17.95.

These books add to the growing library of studies of the civil rights movement. After some two decades, that movement is now coming under close scrutiny, usually by people who participated in it or who were moved by it. As a result, our understanding of this social upheaval that made profound and lasting changes in America is deepening. Among the key issues that need to be examined are not only what changed and why and how, but also what did not change and why and what lessons can be learned about what the civil rights movement failed to accomplish. As we face the future of racial conflict in America, the latter is the more important question, and both of these books shed light upon it.

Adam Fairclough's *To Reform the Soul of America* has a broad focus. His book is a history of the Southern Christian Leadership Conference (SCLC). Fairclough takes us inside the SCLC and gives us a picture of conflicts between its various members, of its fund-raising apparatus and difficulties, of the tactical and strategic considerations that were involved in its campaigns. Along the way, Fairclough enters some of the debates that are ongoing in the study of this movement: were tactics chosen with the aim of provoking the police? The answer—largely. How effective were the demonstrations in forcing government action? Very. To what extent was the church central in shaping and leading the movement? Only partially—the movement also largely adapted the church to its own purposes.

Because Fairclough largely identifies the SCLC as being the organization of Martin Luther King, Jr.—"SCLC was created *for* him but not *by* him"—he does not spend much time discussing the other independent leaders with whom it was constructed. Joseph Lowery, C. K. Steele, even Fred Shuttlesworth do not receive much attention. That the SCLC was based at least partially on movements independent of the Montgomery bus boycott is not really reflected in this book.

Most of the first part of the book is a standard account of the Southern civil rights movement, with the addition of much organizational detail. It is in the latter part, which brings us into the Chicago campaign, the Northern urban riots of the later 1960s, and black power, that Fairclough provides his most interesting material. As King turned from the struggle against state-sponsored segregation to the more complicated discrimination that characterized the North—and, with the success of the civil rights movement, was coming to characterize the South—he perceived that the old civil rights coalition could not hold together for the new battles that were required.

Fairclough contends that King was radicalized as the movement developed and sees this developing radicalism as having taken two directions at once: toward black power and toward a critique of America. Fairclough sees the black-power trend exemplified by King's support for the campaign of Carl Stokes for the mayoralty of Cleveland. That campaign was part of a strategy for blacks to use their votes to take political control of the cities that whites were abandoning. The class critique led King to seek a new coalition of poor and working-class whites and blacks. King's left turn during these years has been documented before but Fairclough provides more detail than most. The second part of the book is rich in material that will be of interest to both scholars and students as well as to the general reader.

Confronting the Color Line by Alan B. Anderson and George W. Pickering focuses on a key aspect of these later years of the civil rights movement. It is a detailed history of the Chicago campaign and an analysis of its failure and of the implications of that failure for American society.

Anderson and Pickering argue that segregated housing and schools had been consciously and intentionally created by the Chicago Real Estate Board and by Chicago mayors. These structures forced blacks to pay more than whites for the same housing and allowed the school board to shift funds away from black schools to white schools, a task that was made easy by segregated housing patterns and by the neighborhood school system. The housing and school structures were then insulated by the ideology of the Civic Credo. The Credo saw educational policy as the object of professionals and not open to politics—"politics" meaning the input of parents who were unhappy with the disposition of funds and with school policy in general. Because the Chicago solution influenced many other cities, Anderson and Pickering argue it was of particular importance.

When at first the Chicago movement, and later King, tried to challenge this structure of discrimination, they were met with an ideology, a structure of power and sophisticated tactics that made success far more difficult to attain than in Southern campaigns. This much is well known and has been stated before, but Anderson and Pickering bring such a wealth of new material and insight as to make it a new story. They provide us with information concerning the maneuverings of the Chicago Board of Education, the school superintendent, the mayor, the actions of white ethnics and their impact on politics, as well as the internal conflicts and considerations of the Coordinating Council of Community Organizations and the SCLC. They consider the impact of black and white rioting and how each was treated by the press, politicians, and the black movement leaders.

They attempt to understand American racism in theory and to provide some guidelines for diminishing racial hostilities. They discuss several analyses of American racism: Tocqueville's racist realism, in which whites would never accept blacks as equals, DuBois's call for blacks to demand equality, Myrdal's "American dilemma," the liberal view of gradual legal change, and what they call the Civic Credo. They find all these models inadequate and argue that the color line itself is the structural basis for the racist realism ideology.

This sophisticated book argues that the struggle against racism has run into what may be a dead end. American society may not be open to liberal racial change. They propose a way out through a program for a new coalition.

So far, they agree with the King that Fairclough portrays. But with their move from scholarship to politics, they, like King, confront the problem of human agency: which whites will join with blacks and for what purposes? They argue that both blacks and whites share an interest in diminishing the violence that the color line has produced, as well as in the need for full employment, and that, within this framework, problems of racial discrimination could be worked out. Here they part with King's last effort to resolve this problem. King's solution—organizing the poor and working people—was more radical than theirs.

One must wonder, given the current state of affairs, if everyone has a common concern with full employment. It seems obvious that there are powerful interests that oppose it. Irrespective of this issue, this book is an important contribution to the scholarly study of this period and is especially important in understanding the latter days of the movement.

JACK BLOOM

Indiana University Northwest
Gary

FURTWANGLER, ALBERT. *American Silhouettes: Rhetorical Identities of the Founders.* Pp. viii, 168. New Haven, CT: Yale University Press, 1987. $17.50.

With respect to a year, 1987, of many words about the U.S. Constitution, Albert Furtwangler's brief *American Silhouettes* is an engaging and readable book with an original slant. The aim of the book is "to trace the identities projected by Franklin, Adams, Washington, Jefferson, and John Marshall" by looking for moments in their lives in which gestures and statements combine to reveal how these men may have thought about themselves as public, history-making figures. In these moments, or "silhouettes," Furtwangler sees the public personas emerge in events often minor or obscure but in ways that reveal major complexities within the men and the history in which they were engaged.

The book is a series of short essays, each one of which could act as an introduction to a long volume on the man's public character. For example, Benjamin Franklin early in his life establishes his voice—"the joco-serious, light-but-penetrating, knowing-but-unknown being"—under the pen name of Silence Dogood, who teases and moderates the citizenry of Boston then embroiled in political and religious contentions over smallpox vaccination. With nice intellectual tact, Furtwangler suggests the identification George Washington may have felt with the hero of Joseph Addison's tragedy Cato, which was performed at Valley Forge, "the civilian patriot turned temporary general, holding together a composite army against overwhelming odds."

John Adams, "imagining himself . . . in a grand court of law where a final demonstrative case can be made and affirmed," is an image revealing the consummate lawyer who became a revolutionary as a way to affirm constitutionalism. And Thomas Jefferson, viewed with a more critical eye than the other founders, is seen at a dinner party championing Bacon, Newton, and Locke as the greatest men of history; Alexander Hamilton opted for Caesar. Jefferson's confidence in science and progress is to Furtwangler both naive and liberating, a point he illustrates in an odd but intriguing juxtaposition of Jefferson with William Blake.

Furtwangler loves ferreting out ambiguities to complicate and enrich our understanding of these men as major public figures. One of the best essays is on the writing of Washington's Farewell Address, and it illustrates the many strengths and occasional weaknesses of this book. In sorting out the contributions of Madison and Hamilton, Furtwangler describes Washington's various plans for retirement, the legacy of his 1783 resignation letter to the army, the relationship between Hamilton and Madison in The Federalist writings, the growing strain between these men on the issue of presidential power, and the final break over the Neutrality Proclamation of 1793. Yet Furtwangler circles around the Farewell Address itself, assuming apparently that we know its final form and content by heart as he no doubt does. He leaves us with a much richer sense of the many layers of meaning embedded in a document that is itself only glanced at. If the Farewell Address is nearly poetry, as Furtwangler claims, it would have been good to have heard it sung.

Furtwangler's emphasis on process rather than product in each of the essays leads to his stance—not really a conclusion, I think he would say—that to understand the Founding Fathers we need to see their work as fluid, in motion, unfinished—not only the result of long-ago struggles and conflicts but still embodying those impulses for us today. In this sense, Furtwangler's rhetorical analysis recaptures the vitality of their lives and writings.

TOM SCANLAN
University of Minnesota
St. Paul

HODGES, JAMES A. New Deal Labor Policy and the Southern Cotton Textile Industry, 1933-1941. Pp. xii, 252. Knoxville: University of Tennessee Press, 1986. No price.

Focusing on the Southern cotton textile industry, James Hodges measures the "extent of continuity and change" in New Deal labor policy. Unlike workers in the Northern steel and automotive industries, Southern textile workers remained largely nonunionized during the 1930s and 1940s. The failure to organize "a significant permanent union" in the Southern textile belt, Hodges asserts, illustrates the limits of the Roosevelt administration's labor policy. Many factors contributed to this failure—mill owners' skillful use of paternalism, Southern communities' traditional antipathy for organized labor, the South's racially charged political environment, and, perhaps most important, the passivity and complacency of the mill workers themselves.

Given these factors and the strong partnership between management and the federal government during the 1930s, it is not surprising that unionism did not flourish in Southern cotton textiles. During the early New Deal, mill owners manipulated the National Recovery Act, first for economic recovery and then for personal financial gain. Under General Hugh Johnson, the act degenerated into "mind-numbing business-dominated bureaucratic boards and empty hopes," and federal officials displayed "only the most jumbled and often contradictory attitudes toward unions and collective bargaining." Hodges describes President Franklin D. Roosevelt as the guardian of corporate interests and industrial revitalization, seldom dealing aggressively with labor problems unless they threatened economic recovery or his political hegemony. Moreover, Hodges argues, FDR occasionally played the demagogue in labor disputes, as shown by his blaming the 1934 general textile strike on Socialist Norman Thomas.

Although United Textile Workers (UTW) leaders hailed the 1934 general strike as a great labor victory, Hodges argues that it merely strengthened the resolve and organizational resources of management. Between 1937 and 1939, responding to the promises of the Wagner Act, masses of cotton textile workers joined the Congress of Industrial Organizations' Textile Workers Organizing Committee. The committee, like the UTW, failed to achieve a lasting union presence in the Southern textile belt. Unfortunately, under guidelines of the National Labor Relations Board, collective bargaining was dependent on the existence of an active, well-organized union. Mill owners shrewdly used the bureaucratic guidelines of the National Labor Relations Board as delaying tactics against collective bargaining and unionism in the mills. By 1941, achievements of "the New Deal labor revolution" were "painfully basic"—the eight-hour day, the 40-hour week, and the minimum wage. The threat of unionism at best accelerated the change from paternalism to modern management techniques, thereby improving the lives of some mill owners. Hodges sadly concludes that cotton textile unionism, because of the size of the work force, had the potential to create a base for unionizing other Southern industries and thus establishing a New Deal political coalition as powerful as the one in the North.

This work is a solid contribution to our knowledge of FDR's labor policy and Southern labor history since 1933. Hodges gives in-depth treatment to mill village society and culture, mill technology, and production methods. He includes an incisive epilogue summarizing developments in the Southern textile region since World War II. Of particular note is his comparison of the movie *Norma Rae* with the true story of Crystal Lee Jordan, an employee at the J. P. Stevens Towel Mill in North Carolina.

The Southern labor history specialist will find this work of great value. The general reader, however, may grow weary of the tedious analyses of the various labor boards and commissions. The abundance of names in this work also may present some difficulties for the lay reader and the specialist. For example, Francis Gorman, a UTW organizer, first appears on page 55, but is not fully identified until page 104. Fuller biographical treatments also would be helpful for mill owners like Donald Comer and William D. Anderson. These minor deficiencies, however, do not detract significantly from the overall value of this fine work.

DAVID E. ALSOBROOK
Jimmy Carter Library
Atlanta
Georgia

LARRABEE, ERIC. *Commander in Chief: Franklin Delano Roosevelt, His Lieutenants and Their War.* Pp. viii, 723. New York: Harper & Row, 1987. $25.00.

This long book on the way in which the United States waged World War II delivers more than what is promised by its title and formal organization. Eric Larrabee presents biographical studies of the president and nine of his principal generals and admirals during the war. In reality, however, the book ranges beyond discussions of the men listed as the subject for each chapter. Larrabee treats grand strategy, military tactics, and diplomacy as well as the leadership of the men in charge.

Here is self-consciously old-fashioned, blood-and-trumpets military history, Larrabee proudly proclaims. He has been industrious in reading the secondary works on the war, and he has made some use of original source material. The result is a story that has been told before, but one that Larrabee has brought to life with good writing and an eye for the telling vignette.

The tale has much contemporary relevance for the organization of the modern American presidency. Larrabee rightly claims that Roosevelt as wartime leader took more interest in military matters than any predecessor other than Abraham Lincoln. His attention to detail and grasp of grand strategy contrasts sharply and painfully with that of successors who left operations to subordinates. Larrabee is partial to FDR and rightly rejects the old charges that he ran the war in a chaotic and insouciant fashion. Yet Larrabee is hardly the first to have restored Roosevelt's reputation as diplomat and strategist.

While there is much to admire in *Commander in Chief*, the old-fashioned biographical approach is unsettling. Covering nine different commanders, who often collaborated with one another, the book is sometimes repetitive. Larrabee has also made some unusual choices for inclusion, notably U.S. Marine Major General Archer Vandergrift, commander of American forces at Guadal-

canal. He is probably there as the one representative of the Marines, but he adds fifty pages to an already long book.

What is missing most from *Commander in Chief*, of course, is the rest of the armed forces and society. FDR and his lieutenants issued orders to about 13 million other men and women. The whole country knew there was a war on. These people make only token appearances in *Commander in Chief*. They are important subjects, but for another, even longer book.

ROBERT D. SCHULZINGER
University of Colorado
Boulder

LINK, ARTHUR S. et al., eds. *The Papers of Woodrow Wilson.* Vol. 54, *1919.* Pp. xxiv, 579. Princeton, NJ: Princeton University Press, 1986. $50.00.

LINK, ARTHUR S. et al., eds. *The Papers of Woodrow Wilson.* Vol. 55, *1919.* Pp. xxii, 570. Princeton, NJ: Princeton University Press, 1986. $52.50.

It gives some sense of how formidable these volumes are, spanning more than a thousand pages, that they deal only with the period between 11 January and 16 March 1919 of the Paris Peace Conference. A comparison suggests itself with the Congress of Vienna (1814-15), following Napoleon's downfall, featuring Metternich, Czar Alexander I, Frederick William III of Prussia, and Talleyrand, among numerous others of power and brilliancy. The Congress mainly concerned Europe but was momentous not only for all its nations but those beyond. The two volumes under review comprise papers that are collected from the standpoint of President Wilson but that move in all directions, involving the great men of the time. These men affect the decades following them even more than did the earlier proud assembly in Vienna.

With petitioners of all kinds asking for aid in Poland, Palestine, Czechoslovakia, and as far away as China, there were many issues to fill these pages. But two issues stood forth: the fate of Germany and that of revolutionary Russia. Here Wilson's fair-mindedness and will toward democracy found new eloquence and argument favoring the establishment of a League of Nations. Its Covenant could not be distorted, he declared. It balanced interests. It allowed for judicious considerations:

Armed force is in the background in this program, but it *is* in the background, and if the moral force of the world will not suffice, the physical force of the world shall. But that is the last resort, because this is intended as a constitution of peace, not as a league of war.

All well intended, and an appeal to reason. But behind these and other words were ominous circumstances that time would unfold. Wilson believed that "an overwhelming majority of the American people is in favor of the League of Nations." He was furious with senators led by Henry Cabot Lodge who opposed U.S. involvement in the League; the journalist Ray Stannard Baker observed that Wilson, despite his public image as a calm and honest broker, was a good hater. But such different senators as Lodge and Robert M. LaFollette represented formidable constituencies. And Wilson himself had his Colonel E. M. House, who worked behind closed doors, as when he held "a most successful meeting in my [Paris] rooms between the President, General Smuts, Lord Robert Cecil, and myself." House believed that "a new order was being inaugurated" and that most matters being discussed in Paris were "simply a question of boundaries and what not." That "what not," however, concerned millions of people, many holding to passionate convictions.

Wilson's moral authority holds its place in history. But he did think the Russian question was mostly a matter of food, and so he failed to weigh adequately the determination of the Bolshevik leaders. Where the Congress of Vienna had taken in defeated France as a partner in restabilizing Europe, Wilson's colleagues at the Paris Peace Con-

ference stripped Germany of its colonies and worked detail by detail to control the potential of its naval and land forces. Clemenceau wanted first and foremost a disarmed Germany, and Winston Churchill an anti-Bolshevik crusade. The "long and weary discussions" that preceded the establishment of the League of Nations would end as wearisome rather than inspiring.

As always with the volumes of *The Papers of Woodrow Wilson*, the volumes under review here mingle such matters with others involving varied partisans and novel nuggets of fact. General Booth of the Salvation Army pleads for the hungry of Germany and Austria. Paderewski, Chaim Weizmann, and the Armenian Boghos Nubar urge their several causes. Douglas Fairbanks installs a motion picture machine in the White House, from which Wilson anticipates much amusement and use. William C. Bullitt is more hopeful of Bolshevik-U.S. relations then than he will be later. Most serious for domestic prospects is a memorandum from Wilson's long-time aide Joseph P. Tumulty. It notes that the Great War's end is disorganizing plans and conditions for peacetime industry. It is influencing inflation and threatening unemployment. There is a need, Tumulty emphasizes, for a program that will diminish the first shock of conversion to peacetime conditions. He offers suggestions for a committee that could meet to consider the problem and make recommendations.

LOUIS FILLER

The Belfry
Ovid
Michigan

MOSHER, FREDERICK C., W. D. CLINTON, and DANIEL G. LANG. *Presidential Transitions and Foreign Affairs*. Pp. xvii, 281. Baton Rouge: Louisiana State University Press, 1986. $19.95.

CAMPBELL, COLIN. *Managing the Presidency: Carter, Reagan, and the Search for Executive Harmony*. Pp. xx, 310. Pittsburgh, PA: University of Pittsburgh Press, 1987. No price.

These two books are vastly different in scope and overall approach and yet could well be read in tandem. For in both the authors' learning and attention to detail guarantee both books' paramount position as valuable works of reference for scholars who study the American presidency.

It is evident from a reading of these books that Americans often have tended to view government as inherently illegitimate. We give it power only grudgingly and then object to its exercise. If we say we want leaders, we undercut them by refusing to be followers. This obduracy has a certain charm, but is it a luxury we can afford in a world less amenable to our influence? In *Presidential Transitions*, Mosher, Clinton, and Lang illustrate how high the stakes are in presidential transitions not only for us but also for the rest of the world; they cite Canadian Prime Minister Lester Pearson's comment that foreign citizens should be allowed to vote in U.S. presidential elections. Our links, our competitions, our antagonisms with the more than 170 nations of the world reach to almost every subject of potential negotiation and confrontation—economic, social, linguistic, scientific, military, environmental—almost without end.

In studying transitions, Mosher, Clinton, and Lang refer to a period when the candidates and incumbents plan to transfer authority from preelection through the budget period of the first year of the new presidency. Their emphasis is on the most dangerous area of presidential transition: foreign affairs.

The book is divided into two parts. Part 1 discusses the five interparty transitions since World War II utilizing examples and generalizations. The introductory chapter analyzes the transitions in comparative context. Chapter 2 discusses the constraints and calendar limits imposed on our government. Chapter 3 gives special emphasis to efforts to systematize transition practices since World

War II. Chapter 4 discusses the difficulties of communication between outgoing and incoming administrations. Organization, budget, and personnel are developed in chapters 5 and 6.

Part 2 begins with a brief prologue followed by five chapters, each devoted to the interparty transitions since World War II. These include the transitions from Truman to Eisenhower; Eisenhower to Kennedy; and from Johnson to Nixon, which, incidentally, was the smoothest and most effective, primarily due to the two men's knowledge of government as well as to Johnson's strenuous effort to prepare his successor. A point made in the book is that Nixon knew and understood the Washington career establishment and brought into his administration many people with foreign affairs experience, his forte! Also included are the transitions from Ford to Carter and Carter to Reagan, which, Mosher, Clinton, and Lang indicate, was one of the most difficult transitions. The leaders' differing ideologies and the recent weakening of the American party consensus in foreign affairs were major reasons.

The book closes with a few observations and recommendations on the Janus-like institution of transition. The stress is on a suggestion for harmony between incoming political appointees and career governmental personnel.

In this exemplary book, Mosher, Clinton, and Lang once again illustrate that it is in the nature of good scholarship that the obvious, once exposed to rigorous examination, seems inevitable.

Colin Campbell's book attempts to redress the imbalance in the studies of the U.S. presidency, which Campbell suggests focus too often on the personality of the president. With erudition and provocative insight, Campbell delves into the mechanics of governing and the president's relationship with advisers and the machinery of office.

In his invaluable quarry of detail, Campbell draws upon 192 in-depth interviews with senior members of the White House Office, the Executive Office of the President, and the Department of the Treasury during the

Carter and Reagan administrations. He examines fully the organization and executive management of the Reagan and Carter White Houses and contrasts them to those of Franklin Roosevelt, Truman, Eisenhower, Kennedy, Johnson, and Ford.

And he finally contrasts Ronald Reagan's political competence and success with Jimmy Carter's fascination with bureaucratic intricacies and concludes that the successful management of the presidency requires a balance between these two styles.

Through eight chapters, Campbell pursues his central thesis by studying the president, executive harmony, and state apparatus; and the presidents and their staff and cabinets. He contrasts Carter's spoke-in-the-wheels philosophy with Roosevelt's style of using personal charm to move his subordinates. Eisenhower utilized a heavily structured, more impersonal cabinet system, while Kennedy virtually ignored cabinet structures. Finally, we view the modes, strategies, and cyclical forces of Carter and Reagan.

One key chapter, titled "Structures and Three Bureaucratic Cultures," allows us to benefit from Campbell's skill in tabulation. Using the terms "politicos" to refer to appointees who have gained their positions by functioning within political campaigns, Campbell compares their orientation, education, and characteristics with a group called "amphibians," who include career government officials and those claiming to have an expertise within a substantive policy field. The conclusion is that the Reagan appointees are better prepared for the team approach to leadership.

Yet, despite Campbell's dedicated attempt to avoid the persona in studying the presidency, it is evident that each president is unique. Clearly, the person must be taken into account. In this day, the public sector manager—the president—must not only arrange his or her staff and cabinet but must also lead by communication and persuasion. In contrast with the private sector manager, the president must be a negotiator who understands the constraints of shared power.

This important scholarly and balanced book interweaves the light and shadow of progress and imbalance of the U.S. presidency so assiduously that Campbell has, in some sense, petrified the office, preserving it, like amber, with all its impurities.

GERALD L. SBARBORO

Chicago
Illinois

NELSON, JOHN R., Jr. *Liberty and Property: Political Economy and Policymaking in the New Nation, 1789-1812.* Pp. xv, 221. Baltimore, MD: Johns Hopkins University Press, 1987. $25.00.

This is a major study of the political economy of the Federalists and the Jeffersonians. It presents a new, cohesive synthesis that should attract wide attention.

Here liberty is grounded in property, especially as represented in the thought of David Hume. The focus is on American manufactures, beginning with Alexander Hamilton's Society for Establishing Useful Manufactures (SEUM). But Nelson's provocative thesis argues that Hamilton's real interest was in "the merchants, who invested in the SEUM and had access to bank loans, not the manufacturers." Hamilton's Report on Manufactures was chiefly a means of "advancing the SEUM," and his primary concern was a stabilization program in which his fiscal policy was supported by British imports. The Jay Treaty virtually abandoned an independent merchant marine and "sacrificed domestic manufacturing." Nelson writes that "one major thesis of this essay is that Hamilton was not an advocate of American manufacturing."

In this analysis, Jefferson, Madison, and Gallatin reacted primarily against the speculative side of Hamilton's policies, which brought "the corrupt enrichment of the few," differing little on issues of property or federal economic powers. For the Republican triumvirate, economic stability required economic independence. Following recent scholarship, Nelson notes Republican interest in manufactures, Republican merchants, Republican mechanics, and the Republican pursuit of a market economy. Albert Gallatin, who "owned a manufactory," surpassed Hamilton in his political economy, while Hamilton was "timid and mundane" as he subordinated American economic policy to Great Britain. In sum, the Republican triumvirate's political economy was a "more comprehensive and effective expression of liberal economic nationalism" than that of Hamilton.

Nelson challenges traditional views repeatedly and with vigor. "It is of monumental importance," he writes, "to recognize that Jefferson's foreign policy mandated the development of domestic manufactures and that Hamilton's did not." He refers to the "legend" of Hamilton's economic nationalism, arguing that Hamilton would have maintained an agrarian America while the Republican triumvirate moved toward economic independence. Jefferson won the election of 1800 because he carried the cities where the "manufacturer-mechanic vote went Republican." And to believe that Republicans adopted Federalist policies after 1800, writes Nelson, is to misunderstand Hamilton's policies.

In Nelson's concluding assertion that political economy was the basis for "the structure of policymaking" in the early national period, there is little room for the complex interaction of personalities or chance. But his scholarship is impressive and he has given a persuasive revision of long-held views about the policies of the Federalists and Republicans in the founding of the new nation.

RONALD E. SHAW
Miami University
Oxford
Ohio

O'BRIEN, DAVID M. *Storm Center: The Supreme Court in American Politics.* Pp. 384. New York: Norton, 1986. $18.95.

Storm Center examines the evolution and role of the Supreme Court in the contemporary American political system. As such, it provides a broad overview of the politics of the Supreme Court and is quite timely given those changes that will inevitably occur in the Court in the not too distant future. As the title implies, O'Brien believes that the Court long ago ceased to become, in Hamilton's words, "the least dangerous branch," and today serves as the decisive arena in which political conflict is played out, though he does not view the Court's power as becoming overweening. The abortion issue, which is well analyzed, symbolizes for O'Brien the Court's increasingly assertive role in American politics.

Although several works, both popular and scholarly, have emerged in recent years, *Storm Center* is one of the few that should be of interest not only to the lay person but to American and judicial politics specialists as well. This work benefits from a richness of detail, although the anecdotal character of some sections may prove tiresome to specialists. Nonetheless, O'Brien does succeed in peeling away part of the mystery surrounding Supreme Court decision making.

Chapters 2 through 5 provide an excellent introduction to judicial process and politics. While saying little that is new, O'Brien does evaluate the problems any president faces in choosing individuals who will support his or her own political and judicial views on the bench. O'Brien then proceeds to a fascinating discussion of the Court's developing institutional identity over the nearly 200 years of its existence, even suggesting that the move to its current home has served to enhance its position as well as to structure working relations between the justices.

Much of the rest of the work is devoted to examining the process of deciding cases and writing opinions. O'Brien's discussion of the bargaining process between justices is especially illuminating. He also expresses concern over the increasing individualism of the justices, as typified by the growth of separate and concurring opinions in this century, and the possible impact this may have on the institution of the Court.

O'Brien concludes with a cursory glance at the relationship of the Court and its decisions to other institutions and public opinion, as well as the implementation of its decisions. It is not unfair to suggest, however, that each of these areas is worthy of separate chapters. Nonetheless, *Storm Center* is a solid, scholarly, albeit essentially descriptive, piece of work that fulfills its goal of providing a broad overview of the importance of the Supreme Court to the American political process.

EWEL ELLIOTT

University of Oklahoma

Norman

ORMAN, JOHN. *Comparing Presidential Behavior: Carter, Reagan and the Macho Presidential Style.* Pp. viii, 190. Westport, CT: Greenwood, 1987. $35.00.

SCHORR, ALVIN L. *Common Decency: Domestic Policies after Reagan.* Pp. x, 246. New Haven, CT: Yale University Press, 1986. $20.00.

Both these books are efforts to assess and look beyond the years of the Reagan administration. As such, they may be regarded as part of a small ripple that will become a tidal wave when the ex-governor of California and the ex-grade-B movie star assumes the dignified status of an ex-president. The Reagan administration has been such a sharp departure from the Republican and Democratic presidencies since Franklin Roosevelt that it seems likely that an academic industry will arise devoted to seeking explanations of its significance and its implications for the future.

John Orman's book is a surprising effort to revive the tattered reputation of President Jimmy Carter by demonstrating that Carter's failure was one of style, not substance. Carter failed to live up to the "macho presidential style" that, Orman believes, has been preferred by the press and the general public, in spite of the inappropriateness of

this blunt, chauvinistic approach to democracy's most powerful office. Orman contends that each American president "more or less embodied the seven components of the macho presidential style and the myth of masculinity." These macho presidents must be competitive in politics and life; sports-minded and athletic; decisive and never wavering; unemotional; strong and aggressive; powerful; and "real men." I guess this style includes Millard Fillmore and Benjamin Harrison, as no exception is made for them. Only Carter with his "androgynous style of leadership" escapes the taint of macho style, but for his unaggressiveness the press portrayed him and his vice-president as wimps.

Much has been written by James Barber and others about presidential style, character, and personality. Unfortunately, scholars are not agreed on the proper classifications to apply to recent presidents. Orman does attempt to provide empirical methods for evaluating both the Carter and the Reagan administrations. Some of these are useful, such as his comparison of the use of presidential advisers, but much of the book is more impressionistic, as when Carter's unjust and negative treatment by the press is seen as an explanation for his unpopularity. Orman tries to show how the press has promoted the macho myth, but the fate of Reagan after Irangate suggests that neither the public nor the press will forgive any president, no matter how macho his pose, if he is perceived to have lied to the people or deceived the Congress and the press. In fact, every recent presidency seems to have suffered from disappointed popular expectations for candor from political leaders.

As a result of his analysis, Orman predicts that the 1988 election will probably favor a macho candidate such as a former football quarterback or a former pro-basketball star. It seems more likely, however, that Americans will seek a leader who appears to be pure and innocent, in reaction to the excesses of Watergate and its echoes in Irangate—episodes that, while deplorable, would not have been so damaging to the careers of politicians in other democratic nations. Still, Orman deserves credit for listing the many positive achievements of Jimmy Carter and noting the exaggerated and sometimes dubious attainments of Ronald Reagan.

Alvin L. Schorr is professor of family welfare at the School of Applied Social Sciences of Case Western Reserve University. A well-known administrator as well as a teacher, Schorr lays out a super-liberal reformist program for the post-Reagan era that will bring a warm smile to those who had feared that liberal reformism had been discredited. Not so, says Schorr. Instead, Schorr points toward a new set of domestic policies devoted to fairer income distribution, greater protections for women and children, and major improvements in health and housing. This enlarged welfare state is seen as a positive good but one that is far more rational and well-conceived than that which Reagan sought to dismantle. Like other welfare statists, Schorr assumes that government alone must solve difficult social problems—a questionable thesis.

Schorr believes that a coming collapse of the values of the Reagan administration could result in either sharpened class conflicts or the rise of a nationalistic corporate state with excessive central planning. He warns liberals that new answers to pressing social needs will require a fresh approach to human want and the sense of social deprivation. Schorr proposes a new social philosophy based upon a drive for community resting upon a fairer distribution of social goods. The new welfare state must have full employment and a more egalitarian division of income. Unfortunately, we are not told quite how this would be accomplished.

Still, Schorr does provide a number of stimulating ideas about social insurance, health care, housing, and taxation. Some of the solutions proposed are mildly radical in terms of the political spectrum of contemporary America. Schorr's tax treatment of pension plans and retirement funds is very thoughtful, as is his detailed analysis of housing and the health care system. His notion of a refundable tax credit as a means of assisting poor families is inventive and

deserves much closer examination. Schorr's concern with the special needs of poor women and children also deserves serious consideration.

But the prospect of "deep reform," as Schorr calls it, seems remote in modern America. Which candidate out of the vast array of would-be presidents—aside from Jesse Jackson—shares in any small way the vision of an enlarged and fairer welfare state? The voting public does not seem to be in a mood for new experiments in welfare programs. Moreover, the budget constraints that Schorr tends to ignore are real enough to discourage any large-scale program for years to come. Perhaps Ronald Reagan did overemphasize the productive powers released by a freer, less-regulated economy. Perhaps the tax reforms of the supply-siders overaided the rich. But until the anguish of a severe recession returns to haunt the nation, the issues raised by Schorr will not even be on the political agenda—though a more decent society is a vague wish of most Americans.

JAY A. SIGLER

Rutgers University
Camden
New Jersey

PARKER, GLENN R. *Homeward Bound: Explaining Changes in Congressional Behavior.* Pp. xxi, 207. Pittsburgh, PA: University of Pittsburgh Press, 1986. $22.95.

We might pause in celebration of constitutional origins to consider recent congressional scholarship, cogently summarized and extended in this little volume, because it demonstrates the remarkable resilience of the framers' creation. Congress, the centerpiece, has adjusted to contemporary member needs, political balances, and voter limitations. Washington legislators seek career stability and autonomy to pursue policy and career advancement. Their constituents, surveys tell us, expect nonpartisan service, and vote on personal qualities of incumbents rather than partisanship, ideology, policy position, or group identification.

Lacking the framers' wisdom, yet with all their petty vices and ambitions, most members, removed in time, space, and experience from their constituents, nevertheless retain their confidence and, despite twentieth-century complexities, arguably represent them effectively in bill making, casework, and oversight. They achieve this in spite of their constituents' lacking the knowledge to monitor their efforts. Parker fathoms this paradox of an institution in low repute, but filled with trusted, hard-working, easily reelected members.

Expanding on Richard Fenno's "attentive homestyle," Parker shows how, by frequent district visits and use of official perquisites, constituent trust is cultivated. Casework, days in session, roll calls, bills, and hearings relentlessly increase, but members still manage more days in their districts than they did thirty years ago.

Parker fashions literally dozens of recent studies into a persuasive analysis of possible causes and consequences of dramatically increased commitment to district displays of attentiveness, credit claiming, and self-serving explanations of Washington activities. House incumbent reelection has become virtually certain; subservience to White House, committee, and party leaders reduced; and thus member freedom expanded. In the latest election, after October publication, fully 98 percent of House incumbents won, and 85 percent with 60 percent of the vote or better—both records. Similarly, despite losses by seven Reagan Republicans, 75 percent of the Senate incumbents were returned—to match a 40-year average. Districts change hands only with death, retirement, reapportionment, or, occasionally, where a member's Washington or national activities are seen to interfere with district service.

In Parker's book, tabulations of member travel vouchers (1960-80) make attentiveness operational, but reelection rates and margins and other researchers' interviews and district observations are also reviewed. Unlike other studies of district behavior, this one is longitudinal and bicameral, assessing interrelationships among historical circumstances; individual strategies, styles, and career cycles; institutional developments; and constituent attitudes. While the treatment is methodologically sophisticated—panel, cohort, and time series—conclusions ultimately rest on the reliability of the vouchers. Embedded in other studies and election data, they ring true.

It would seem that Democratic congressional leaders in the 1960s increased district-serving perquisites and facilitated business—Tuesday-Thursday sessions and recesses—for reelected Democratic incumbents in marginal districts, especially the big classes of 1958 and 1964. This just might be more important than partisan identification, gerrymandering, fund-raising, computer technology, or consensus building in perpetuating the Democratic congressional majority in the face of Republicans in the White House. But as a consequence of these centrifugal forces, party discipline, programmatic unity, and Southern conservative domination were lost. Under normal conditions, Democrats could not recapture the presidency. These connections with district serving remain to be fully explored.

FREDERICK J. ROBERTS
Illinois State University
Normal

REID, JOHN PHILLIP. *Constitutional History of the American Revolution: The Authority of Rights.* Pp. ix, 374. Madison: University of Wisconsin Press, 1986. $25.00.

This is a fitting book for celebrating the bicentennial of the U.S. Constitution, because it presents the legal and historical background that guided the Founding Fathers in formulating the American frame of government. Reid, a professor of law at

New York University and a legal historian par excellence, analyzes with great precision the constitutional debate between American Whigs and their British counterparts over the abridgement of colonial rights by the British parliament prior to the American Revolution.

A seminal work exhibiting superb erudition, this study elucidates in prodigious detail the grievances of the American colonialists from the era of the Stamp Act to the issuance of the Declaration of Independence. Topical as well as chronological, it traces the course of disputation over constitutional theory and the legality of specific acts enacted by the parliament in London with regard to the acceptable parameters and propriety of British imperial rule. In analyzing the arguments made by the leading political figures of the time, as well as the rhetorical propaganda of pamphleteers, Reid distinguishes between inflated discourse and legal fact as to the validity of their respective positions.

It is Reid's basic thesis that when the colonialists arrayed arguments to dispute the abrogation of certain fundamental colonial rights, the American position regarding these alleged intolerable acts was based on the old, and by then outmoded, conception of the British constitution. By custom and inheritance it traditionally had proscribed limits on sovereignty. British leaders, however, justified their legislative actions on a new perception that regarded parliamentary sovereignty as absolute. Thus American appeals to the authority of natural law, their version of the social compact theory, and their assumption of the transference of fundamental English rights to the 13 colonies were rejected in terms of what then constituted contemporary British legal thought. American polemicists could state grievances, but they could not translate theory into acceptable procedural practices that would limit parliament's absolute rule over the colonies. Due to the acceptance of different premises, what to the Americans was patently unconstitutional was to the British perfectly legal.

Historians and political scientists, whether in the fields of legal, constitutional, or colonial studies, will find this work both provocative and valuable. Its compact style and many perceptive insights are fascinating and make for thoughtful reading. Massive research, persuasive evidence, and judicious logic will force readers to reexamine old interpretations about the prime cause of the American Revolution.

EDWARD L. SCHAPSMEIER
Illinois State University
Normal

ROGIN, MICHAEL. *Ronald Reagan, the Movie and Other Episodes in Political Demonology.* Pp. xx, 366. Berkeley: University of California Press, 1987. $25.00.

By focusing on the demon images that give form to anxieties, Michael Rogin offers a provocative analysis of American political culture. He makes a case that the paranoid style is not a phenomenon of the fringes but rather part of the mainstream. It is, he argues, an integral part of the American political experience. While the particulars of his argument may be disputed and some will balk at the psychoanalytic interpretation of American fears and anxieties, overall Rogin makes a persuasive case.

The book has shortcomings; it is a collection of essays built around a common theme rather than an integrated and comprehensive account of political demonology. Its publication nevertheless is a significant event in American intellectual life. Among other tasks, Rogin undertakes a critique of American historiography. His comments are so incisive that I was left disappointed that he did not pursue the analysis further. He has important things to say about the American experience and how we interpret it.

The demonological perspective in analysis has both strengths and weaknesses. It makes vivid the symbolic dimension of politics, and it lends itself well, Rogin shows, to the consideration of a variety of materials from movies to leadership biography. It enables Rogin to treat what he calls the interpenetration of society and psyche, to relate a political worldview to private troubles and anxieties. Yet Rogin is not entirely clear about how symbolic politics operates. For example, the link between the personal fears and anxieties of leadership figures and mass response is not specified. There are occasional references to mass resonance, but the matter is not pursued. Moreover, some of the analytic terms employed—"anxiety about boundary breakdown," "desire for merger," "simple reversal," and "twinning"—seem subject to fairly free interpretation. Even so, the evidence that Rogin presents makes a strong case that personal anxieties are expressed in the public arena. The reader, however, is left without any guidance as to what makes some leaders more susceptible to demonic images than others. If the demonological urge lies in the psyche of some leaders, how is that connected to their capacity to become leaders? And why do other leaders have an eye for redemptive possibilities in American traditions, as Rogin indicates, "without making devils of their foes"? While Rogin perhaps raises more questions than he answers, that is often the case in worthwhile books. This study of political demonology is deserving of attention both for what it tells us and for the further inquiry it invites.

CLARENCE N. STONE
University of Maryland
College Park

SCHLESINGER, ARTHUR M., Jr. *The Cycles of American History*. Pp. xiv, 498. Boston: Houghton Mifflin, 1986. $22.95.

Blurbs on jackets are invariably inflated commendations, but I accept Harrison E. Salisbury at his word: "Thank God for Arthur Schlesinger to remind us that this nation was founded by principled . . . men who knew they were carrying out one of man's greatest experiments in society . . . and

fulfilled their obligations with genius." The heart of the book, of course, is chapter 2, "The Cycles of American Politics." Here Schlesinger reiterates and updates his famous father's 1949 essay on 11 alternations "between periods of concern for the rights of the few and periods of concern for the wrongs of the many." The younger Schlesinger, now 69, fascinatingly embellishes such periodization with his own views and those of Ralph Waldo Emerson, Henry Adams, Albert O. Hirschman, V. O. Key, and other observers of "The Cycles."

The profoundness of this book is that this most eminent of liberal historians presents in one volume an eclectic montage of his views of twentieth-century American history, constantly rooting such contemplations in the rich context of America's observers, such as Jefferson, Emerson, Henry Clay, John Hay, and Cyrus Vance. Some observers he cannot abide and refutes them with scholarly wit—as for example, cold-war revisionist William Appleman Williams.

Surely any reviewer of this book would want to offer an array of choice nuggets. A few examples may give a sense of the book's coverage. Schlesinger notes that "history walks on a knife edge"—thus parents now learn from children. Still, history helps explain where we are. And surely we know that ideology is a formula for hypocrisy; that "prudential judgment must have priority over simple moral verdicts"—such as Ronald Reagan's; that "humane rights" can be only one of several competing interests in the world; that a true geopolitical interpretation, unlike that of William Appleman Williams, distinguishes economic necessities of the state from profit interests of private owners; that cold-war revisionists err in seeing the USSR as a traditional national state; that American affirmative action is rooted in Jefferson's desire for internal improvements; that competent presidents one day will neutralize the weaknesses of present political parties; that our separation of powers will hopefully ward off the "Imperial Presidency"; that "the vanity of historians is to suppose that they understand better than the people who were there what the shouting was about," a not unkindly reference, in part, to my view of Herbert Hoover.

Schlesinger, usually the optimist, closes on a somber note:

Humanity has never needed great leadership more urgently than it does in the nuclear age. For the infinitely powerful engines humans have recently invented are moving beyond their strength and wisdom to control. And leadership has never more urgently needed the collaboration and criticism of an ardent and informed people. We can avert the impending catastrophe only when leaders listen to followers as carefully as followers listen to leaders—which is why democratic leadership holds out the best hope.

MARTIN L. FAUSOLD
State University of New York
Geneseo

THOMPSON, JOHN. *Closing the Frontier: Radical Response in Oklahoma, 1889-1923*. Pp. xiii, 262. Norman: University of Oklahoma Press, 1986. $18.95.

As an expanding industrialism penetrated the American West in the late nineteenth century, many of the inhabitants of this vast area, particularly the small farmers, rose up in desperation, forming radical economic and political organizations to forestall the consequences of industrial dominance. John Thompson analyzes the experience of frontier Oklahoma, one of the centers of revolt.

Even as settlers entered Oklahoma territory, they found themselves harassed by the outriders of corporate capitalism: railroads, banks, and absentee landlords. Because of the frontier's malleable, unstructured environment, these pioneers felt they could fight back and fashion anticapitalist alternatives in their emerging society. They supported numerous causes, especially populism and socialism, which sought to give the people control over the economy. Populism flourished in Oklahoma and was followed by a

Socialist Party, which had the nation's strongest state organization. Although rarely dominant, these dissidents proved a potent force, keeping the area in turmoil until the 1920s. Then the frontier era ended. Gone was the pioneer setting that could nourish impossible dreams. The state was absorbed into the larger modern industrial America. The radicals gave up, admitting there would be no alternative to a capitalist Oklahoma.

Such is Thompson's story, one ably and persuasively presented. Contained within it is also the most sophisticated account yet of Oklahoma's radicals. They were a mixed group—Yankee wheat growers, cotton tenant farmers out of the South, plus some miners and other laborers. They had different backgrounds, problems, and approaches. They did not always agree with each other. Yet hard times and a perceived enemy in capitalism did ultimately unify them in common cause on the essential issues. One of the special strengths of this work is that Thompson is able to keep the reader clear about the general thrust of the radical movement while delineating lucidly the diversity that existed within the ranks.

Closing the Frontier is a distinctively impressive case study of Western radicalism. Although focusing on Oklahoma, it is replete with insights that should be of invaluable assistance to those trying to comprehend the turbulence of the entire region. Space limitations preclude much elaboration here of Thompson's findings, but two of his contentions are of such significance they must be mentioned.

Many have seen the radicals' ideology as suspect, masking a basic desire for quick economic relief. But Thompson argues that Oklahomans sincerely wanted to reshape the fundamental economic order.

The frontier process once was stressed as a generating factor in the discontent of the plains and prairies. In recent years, such an interpretation has been downgraded or ignored. Thompson, however, reclaims the frontier's importance, asserting that it was crucial in encouraging the Oklahoma insurgents to believe they could accomplish their anticapitalist goals.

If Thompson is correct about the role of the frontier and the depth of ideological conviction in Oklahoma, then what he has to say has important implications for evaluating the dynamics of radicalism elsewhere in the American West.

CLARKE L. WILHELM

Denison University
Granville
Ohio

WRIGHT, ESMOND. *Franklin of Philadelphia.* Pp. xvii, 404. Cambridge, MA: Harvard University Press, Belknap Press, 1986. $25.00.

In *Franklin of Philadelphia*, Esmond Wright presents a remarkably fresh retelling of Benjamin Franklin's life. Wright covers the entire range of Franklin's multifaceted career, and, if certain episodes call out for more detail, it is due to the richness of the subject rather than the oversight of the author.

Franklin, whether as Poor Richard or as minister plenipotentiary in France, always exhibited an exaggerated concern with his reputation and public image. Wright takes his cue from this trait and skillfully compares Franklin's motives and deeds with contemporary opinion and historical judgment. In American myth, there have always been two Franklins: the avuncular observer of human folly, ready to offer good-natured humor on the pompous ways of others, and a far less attractive image of the calculating self-promoter, unable to recognize any broad vision of history or higher purpose to human society. While refusing to confirm either of these stereotypes, Wright demonstrates how Franklin's contemporaries were apt to see him in these terms. Wright also admits that this most public of eighteenth-century figures remained elusive to contemporaries as well as to the historian. In spite of these acknowl-

edgments, Wright offers the most entertaining and enlightening view of Franklin available.

Wright is most revealing when he discusses Franklin's involvement with the British Empire. More than the younger members of the founding generation, Franklin was closely involved with the imperial administration as a royal officeholder and colonial agent in London. Franklin's role in the campaign to replace the Penn proprietary with a royal administration also contributed to his faith in the Empire long after other Americans had begun to think of a future separate from Great Britain. Although Franklin's opposition to the Stamp Act was stronger than Wright suggests, he was willing to consider a ministerial post as late as 1768. Until late in the imperial conflict, Franklin believed in a community of interests between the mother country and the rapidly expanding American colonies. Yet, as Wright makes clear, Franklin's belief in the Empire was based on an expectation of American development that fundamentally differed from the goals of Whitehall. When the final crisis developed in 1774, Franklin had no doubts about which side he would support.

Franklin's apparent delay in embracing the patriot cause was the result of his concentration on the practical demands of his role as colonial agent rather than any desire to protect his own livelihood. Wright suggests that Franklin's tendency to focus on the pragmatic and the utilitarian also explains his success as a diplomatic negotiator in France as well as his failure to glimpse any of the tension that would soon result in that nation's revolution.

Wright is less convincing when he strays from Franklin's life to offer comments on the American Revolution or generalizations about American character. Still, this splendidly written book has something to offer both the specialist and anyone looking for an introduction to the man who defined America for eighteenth-century Europeans.

BRUCE A. RAGSDALE

U.S. House of Representatives
Washington, D.C.

SOCIOLOGY

BELL, J. BOWYER. *To Play the Game: An Analysis of Sports.* Pp. viii, 187. New Brunswick, NJ: Transaction Books, 1987. No price.

RUCK, ROB. *Sandlot Seasons: Sport in Black Pittsburgh.* Pp. xiii, 238, Champaign: University of Illinois Press, 1987. $21.95.

These texts represent statements by two historians on the role of sport in America. Bell's *To Play the Game* is an analytical essay that asserts that sports reflect America as well as being crucial to the formation of central values and behaviors. According to Bell, sport is a distinct social institution, not peripheral to life but a major aspect of reality. One can know any society by knowing its games. Ruck's *Sandlot Seasons* is actually an illustration of how sport can be central to a community, namely, the black population of Pittsburgh from 1900 to 1945. Sport compensated for the grim life of black Americans. It gave them a sense of competence, it enhanced self-esteem, and sport provided a vehicle to demonstrate prowess in political struggles with whites. Thus sport is serious, not mere play, for both Bell and Ruck. This fact is well known, but few, particularly scholars, are willing to admit its truth.

The nature of a society's games is crucial to the understanding of that society and its major events. According to Bell, the extent of the development of a society can be determined by analyzing game levels. There are seven: primitive, tribal, communal, polistic, imperial, mass, and decadent. These represent evolutionary stages where the structure of games changes from spontaneous to constrained, from local to extranational, from amateur to professional, from nonmonetary to commercial, and from self-enhancement to structural compensation. In this evolution, sport moves from a vehicle of expression to one of societal control of the population. Bell illustrates this evolution with a discussion of the history of American baseball and football. Games are also characterized by an attraction based on a ratio of awe and anxiety. This distinction is not entirely clear in Bell's analysis, but it does suggest that allure is based on the risk and the skill games demand as well as on the envy we have for the participants. This is not a useful analytic tool and seems to detract from Bell's argument for the importance of game structure in understanding social organization. Gamesters, as Bell calls persons who control games, can adjust the structure of games—change the awe-anxiety appeal—by manipulating money, violence, time, variety, ritual, arena, and other components. Finally, what matters for Bell is "not that one wins or loses or even how one plays the game but, rather, how the game is made"—an interesting insight.

Rob Ruck's history of sport in the black community of Pittsburgh illustrates Bell's evolution of the structure of sport. The sandlot represents the early primitive and tribal stages while seasons illustrate the stages in which black sport has broadened its allure and visibility beyond Pittsburgh's boundaries to national and international arenas. The integration of American sport was the event that vaulted black games out of the self-contained, spontaneous sandlot variety to the commercialized, mass-appeal version. The dispersion of black games and talent over time also reflected the deconcentration of black political power in Pittsburgh. The Pittsburgh teams were black-operated unlike those in other cities, where whites owned and controlled black athletic teams.

Black sports in Pittsburgh are viewed by Ruck as a source of pride, self-esteem, and community anchorage. They were a compensation for the drudgery of black working life. These assertions seem idealistic particularly because there never has been any research evidence to support the compensation hypothesis. Ruck believes in the compensatory role of sport, but the evidence is not substantial. What is more revealing in *Sandlot Seasons* is racism in America as illustrated by the denial of access to playgrounds and leagues, the rationalization of leisure as represented by the creation of leagues and organizations to control black communities, and the neglect of the obvious ability of blacks like Gus Greenlee and Cum Posey to own, manage, and supervise highly proficient operations such as the Homestead Grays and the Pittsburgh Crawfords, the elite of black sport in America in the 1920s and 1930s. This status of black sport reflects black life in America today: even though blacks are more visible in all settings, including sport, they have less power. This is the tragic outcome of the transformation of black sports. Even though *To Play the Game* is a philosophical essay and *Sandlot Seasons* a historiography, Bell and Ruck are commenting on something similar—the transformation and the reality of sport in America.

JAMES H. FREY
University of Nevada
Las Vegas

FOX, DANIEL M. *Health Policies, Health Politics: The British and American Experience, 1911-1965.* Pp. xi, 234. Princeton, NJ: Princeton University Press, 1986. $25.00.

NAVARRO, VINCENTE. *Crisis, Health, and Medicine: A Social Critique.* Pp. vi, 281. New York: Tavistock, 1986. Paperbound, no price.

Daniel M. Fox's *Health Policies, Health Politics* is a chronological account of proposals for the reorganization of medical services in the United States and Britain from 1911 to 1965. The thesis of the book is that in both Britain and the United States, hierarchies of health care institutions have developed on a regional basis, though in different forms and for somewhat different reasons. Over the period studied, hierarchical regionalism evolved at least partly in response to changing views of the role of medical care, from an emphasis on reducing poverty by improving health to a view of medicine as a

scientific activity best disseminated through hierarchical relations between general practitioners, specialists, and medical teaching and research faculty. Proposals for such hierarchies became policy in Britain under the National Health Service but were implemented only indirectly and informally in the United States.

The book's strength is its meticulous research into scores of publicly and privately considered proposals for reorganization. The care taken over matters of fact is exemplified in Fox's reanalysis of data from the 1930s to refute prevailing historical views about the lack of new hospital bed construction during the Great Depression. Less positively, however, the volume becomes, especially with regard to the earlier years covered, a compilation of the content of the proposals with little analysis of the motivations of the actors or coalitions that produced them and with little discussion of their influences. Though Fox concludes by noting that there is "no correct description of an earlier time," the lack of commentary on motives or effects finally limits his ability to make a convincing case for the importance of hierarchical regionalism in the organization of twentieth-century health care.

Crisis, Health, and Medicine by Vincente Navarro is a collection of seven essays, originally published or presented elsewhere, that offers a radical, Marxist analysis of several topics ranging from worker health and safety to international health policy. The broadest and longest essay, "The Western System of Medicine," counters current liberal establishment explanations of the twin crises in medicine: rising costs, and ineffectiveness in improving the overall health of the population. The main theme is that medical institutions and health policies have been controlled by forces of capital so that the amelioration of health problems and teaching personal responsibility for prevention have been defined as the correct roles for medicine rather than the elimination of the conditions of workplace and environmental health that are actually responsible for much illness and premature death.

Navarro's analysis enables him to offer challenging interpretations of current health policy questions, as well as some cogent observations on critical historical events. Commenting on some of the same events Fox reports, proposals by Dawson in Britain and Flexner in the United States, Navarro's analysis shows the constellation of group interests that motivated coalitions around these proposals and interprets their importance within his radical framework. Navarro, too, identifies a prevailing hierarchy among medical care givers, but he interprets this as a sign of the control within the "house of medicine" and ultimately as evidence of the control of medicine. This analysis is weakened, however, by the absence of evidence to support the claims of abuse of worker health or of the manipulation of the medical establishment. The former, at least, is available and reported by other critics of contemporary medicine.

JULIANNE G. MAHLER
George Mason University
Fairfax
Virginia

GREENHOUSE, CAROL J. *Praying for Justice: Faith, Order, and Community in an American Town.* Pp. 222. Ithaca, NY: Cornell University Press, 1986. $24.95.

This is an ethnographic account of attitudes toward conflict and law in a small Southern town that Carol Greenhouse calls "Hopewell," in the grand tradition of American community studies. Located in Georgia, Hopewell is a white, middle-class, suburban community near Atlanta with a large Southern Baptist population. Anthropologist Greenhouse lived for a while in the town, in the early 1970s, initially to study dispute settlements and to write a legal study, but she soon realized that the more interesting thing to study was the norms and beliefs surrounding disputes. At the center of the normative order was a complex set of injunctions against conflict arising out of the Baptists' ethic of avoidance. Departing from the stereotypical image of the litigious American, against whom they contrast themselves, the Baptists in Hopewell not only avoid legal action but even try to refrain from the mere voicing of interpersonal disputes.

Greenhouse's analysis begins with family and friendships, and the personalism generated in the more intimate realms, and then looks at the diffusion of these values more broadly in the community. She discusses at some length the role of the Southern Baptist faith—as it is understood locally—in shaping people's aversion to discord. Conflict is viewed as something brought about by the unsaved, and whatever interpersonal discord is experienced in social life tends to be dealt with internally, in terms of the believer's relationship with Jesus Christ; thus an ability to get along, to create harmony, to maintain order, is a test of an individual's spiritual maturity. Of interest is Greenhouse's argument that avoidance in interpersonal relationships is the stuff out of which a type of ahistoricism, or the selective reading of history dating from Civil War times, arises in Hopewell. Viewing local historical consciousness as a process of selective memory, she links contemporary avoidance of conflict to the community's unwillingness to confront particular issues and contradictions in the region over two centuries.

Having been born and reared in the South, I found the book a sensitive and insightful portrayal of small-town life in the region. At times, when reading about family customs and church life, I felt transported back to my own younger days. The book is lucid and well written and captures the normative system in a way that is far more engaging than is often the case in such studies. The community is portrayed a bit too much as a closed system for my own taste, and the cultural and religious changes that must be occurring in the Atlanta metropolitan area are played down. Even so, the book will stimulate thinking and research on the role of the local community in shaping norms and values and is of use to those interested in either religion or American culture generally.

WADE CLARK ROOF
University of Massachusetts
Amherst

HERTZ, ROSANNA. *More Equal Than Others: Women and Men in Dual-Career Marriages.* Pp. xi, 245. Berkeley: University of California Press, 1986. $18.95.

Much of the literature on dual careers focuses on the two careers: his and hers. Rosanna Hertz, instead, treats the phenomenon as a three-career marriage: his career, her career, and the career marriage. She focuses not on the careers affected by the relationship but on the relationship itself, specifically on the relationships of corporate couples who are financially privileged. Emphasizing the diverse and continual negotiation processes involved in the career marriage, she helps debunk the myth that dual-career couples have a glamorous life-style that is easily attained and sustained.

Hertz's research, constituted by interviews with each member of 21 dual-career couples, touches on the major issues in combining career and family, from career decisions and obstacles to decisions about having children and choosing child care. Her findings indicate that there is no magic formula for determining the evolution of gender-role responsibilities for women and men in corporate dual-career relationships; these roles are not predictably egalitarian or traditional. Rather, the way in which the relationship becomes more or less egalitarian often depends on individual incomes and the income differential between spouses, the way in which the couple manages its finances—pooled or separate accounts—and the influence of corporate employers on the couple's decision making, especially the lack of corporate support for childbearing and child care. Hertz argues that the women's movement of the 1970s and

1980s is not entirely responsible for the emergence of dual-career couples—via wider opportunities for women in the corporate world—but that the movement was crucial in making possible a revolution in marital roles and procedures by legitimating careers for women. Although corporations and slowly changing societal expectations have done very little to assist dual-career couples in their negotiations, Hertz finds that many of the relationships have endured because of the couple's financially privileged status and the hard work the couples have done on behalf of their third careers.

Although limited in scope, the book effectively addresses the issues that are central in the lives of privileged dual-career couples. Moreover, Hertz does not fall into the trap of claiming universality for her findings. She carefully and thoroughly discusses the specificity of her research in the context of class differences and the existing dual-career literature. The book is clearly organized and contains skillfully excerpted interviews that make it interesting and engaging reading for undergraduates in sociology, women's studies, or interdisciplinary courses focusing on career and personal life. The absence of jargon and assumptions about readers' previous knowledge of the dual-career literature makes it very readable and useful for introductory college courses or even for nonacademic readers.

CHERI SISTEK
Duke University
Durham
North Carolina

LEAVITT, JUDITH WALZER. *Brought to Bed: Child-Bearing in America, 1750-1950.* Pp. ix, 284. New York: Oxford University Press, 1986. $21.95.

In this eight-chapter book, with an epilogue on changes since 1950, Leavitt traces the social, psychological, and medical factors that contributed to major changes in the birthing process in America over a 200-year period. The major changes, which moved at different rates, were the shift from midwife-attended to physician-attended births; from home-delivered to hospital-delivered births; the introduction and growing use of forceps, anesthesia, and aseptic techniques; and the change from female-centered decision making about the birthing process with female support groups to physician-centered decision making without female support groups.

In the first two chapters, Leavitt illustrates the great fears and heavy burdens that women had regarding birthing in early America and well until after 1900. Because the average woman then had five live births, the chance was about one in thirty during her childbearing years that she would die during or soon after childbirth. Today there is only one maternal death per 10,000 births. Understandably, many women feared birth for its pain, its preceding frequent prolonged illness, and its threat to life, and they developed female networks for mutual support during these times. But as upper-class and middle-class women began using physicians as birth attendants, female support networks diminished and women slowly lost control of the birthing process. But this loss of control occurred primarily with the shift to hospital births, and it was not until 1918 that one-half of the births occurred in hospitals.

In the next six chapters, Leavitt deals with (1) the social factors that contributed to variation in the birthing experience; (2) the controversies over the role of gender in the birthing room at different points in time; (3) the issues and movements surrounding the use of anesthesia for pain control; (4) the controversies surrounding the proper aseptic conditions to lower puerperal infections; (5) the medicalization of birthing when it was moved to the hospital; and (6) how women's control of birthing was gradually lost over time in exchange for reducing pain, infection, and the threat of death.

Using diaries, letters, and medical journal accounts, Leavitt provides an excellent historical review of the intersection of medical

developments, social change, and women's views on birthing. While the book has almost excessive illustration of its points and lacks subchapter headings to help organize its topics, it is well written and most informative of changes in birthing in America and the complex ingredients behind those changes.

DUANE F. STROMAN
Juniata College
Huntingdon
Pennsylvania

LINSKY, ARNOLD S. and MURRAY A. STRAUS. *Social Stress in the United States: Links to Regional Patterns in Crime and Illness.* Pp. xii, 174. Dover, MA: Auburn House, 1986. $24.95.

Sometimes books fail because they are poorly conceived and sometimes they fail because they are poorly executed. The book under review is an example of the former. Linsky and Straus propose to build a geography of stress that systematically ranks different states as to how much stress they manifest and what the consequences of that stress are for those who live in a given state. There is much to commend in the endeavor, for the social sciences often fail to ground themselves in the reality of American life. The abstracted empiricism of most social science detracts from the utility and applicability of much research and any move in a more concrete direction is to be applauded. The problem lies in the conceptual strength of the stress paradigm as a structure on which to hang the enterprise. This scaffolding does not support the analysis presented and in many ways detracts from what are impor-- tant and useful analyses of interstate variations in crime and health problems.

What is stress as distinct from the stimuli that cause it and the consequences that follow from it? If stress is a feeling that accompanies the situation of being or feeling overtaxed by one's environment, then how are states stressed? If stress and its behavioral consequences are confused, it is not clear what analytic power is gained through the use of a stress paradigm relating antecedent behavior to consequent problems.

There are five related concepts to be defined and distinguished if the stress paradigm is to be useful: the sources of stress, the appraisal of threat, the experience of stress, the coping mechanisms used to handle stress, and the consequences of stress. Crime, for example, can cause stress, can be a way of coping with stress, or can be a consequence of stress. The proper designation may vary with individuals or situations.

The stress paradigm is inadequate for identifying the influence of social organization on behavior. People with the same motives will behave differently because the normative structure of their groups differs. Surely there are important differences within states as to the social organization through which people interpret the events that affect them.

The stress paradigm lacks the specificity and rigor to drive the analysis in this book. Rather, the analysis drives the theory as findings are coaxed into the stress paradigm. The book ends quietly, identifying some of the limitations of the stress paradigm and suggesting that other approaches might be as productive.

Stress is a lot like pornography, hard to define but easily recognized. Both may best be left to our colleagues outside the social sciences for sensitive analysis and description.

DAN A. LEWIS

Northwestern University
Evanston
Illinois

MORRIS, MICHAEL and JOHN B. WILLIAMSON. *Poverty and Public Policy: An Analysis of Federal Intervention Efforts.* Pp. xii, 236. Westport, CT: Greenwood, 1986. $35.00.

CLAVEL, PIERRE. *The Progressive City: Planning and Participation 1969-1984.* Pp. xviii, 262. New Brunswick, NJ: Rutgers University Press, 1986. $28.00. Paperbound, $10.00.

The common theme of these two books is how to assess the results that have accompanied two policy goals, popular at least since the 1960s, seeking enhanced equity in the fruits of public decision making. The two policy goals are (1) assured participation in shaping particular program objectives by those directly affected by the objectives, and (2) targeted governmental intervention to improve the lot of the poor. These goals are not mutually exclusive, nor are these accounts of experiences involving them the only things written. Their findings, nevertheless, allow for generalizations that could prove useful to citizens, lawmakers, and administrators.

Under the circumstances recounted here, both policy goals have proved controversial from the outset; they still attract proponents as well as harsh critics, and they leave an uncertain legacy to date. Targeted intervention is well known, if only cyclically popular. In its contemporary form, it represents several facets of a broad, historical theme that has enticed political philosophers as diverse as Adam Smith, Karl Marx, and Robert Owen—mitigating poverty. Targeted intervention revolves around direct income strategies such as public assistance and employment insurance; in-kind benefits such as food stamps, child nutrition, medical care, and community health; housing; and social services, mostly grants-in-aid. The authors conclude that direct-income strategies demonstrate some economic impact over the short run. Their more lasting significance, however, is deemed to hinge somewhat on the political importance of the particular constituency served. Social security beneficiaries fare better economically than families with dependent children on welfare, partly because the former command more political clout. The authors conclude that ideology, rather than empirical evidence, fuels most criticism of direct-income strategies, notably the contention that they dissuade the will to work.

In-kind benefits have a significantly positive effect on the economic condition of the poor. It is mainly the failure to enlist participation from those eligible to benefit from these programs that deters their effectiveness. Beneficiaries give these kinds of benefits a high, cash-equivalent value. Viewed from the perspective of fostering self-sufficiency, however, the authors find these kinds of intervention to be less auspicious. Federally aided efforts embrace an assortment of programs intended to attack poverty indirectly. They range from employment, job training, and a minimum wage through work incentives and vocational education. The overall assessment of their impact is deemed to be modest, both because they embrace many people who are really unemployable—due to age or handicaps—which fuels cost-ineffectiveness and because program purposes are too diffuse. Poverty is often only one of a number of objectives addressed. Clearly, direct cash benefits and in-kind assistance, together with an improving national economy, attack poverty's causes and effects best.

In the matter of fostering greater public participation in policymaking, *The Progressive City* examines experiences in five cities in which attempts have been made to enhance the importance of the socially disconnected. The rationale is part Great Society social engineering and part traditional progressive reform in an urban setting. The focus is on planning as a means of strengthening mass participation in public policymaking. The book addresses how that kind of participation has transpired, operationally and structurally, in five municipalities of varying size: Berkeley, Cleveland, Hartford, Santa Monica, and Burlington, Vermont. Results reflect quite mixed outcomes. In this book, planning transcends simple land use; rather, it emphasizes the strategies attending public efforts to offset the consequence of absentee private ownership, unrepresentative city councils and bureaucracies, and other private sector benefits of concentrated economic power. Grass-roots involvement of citizens in public policymaking and various institutional innovations stemming from that involvement are the meat of the book. Desirable partici

pation has a mass, instead of a special interest, basis.

In Berkeley, emphasis lay with ballot initiatives, wider access to public information, a neighborhood-structured form of police organization, an elected rent-control board, and enhanced participation by public employees in their governance. In Cleveland and Hartford, there have been strengthened ties between some city departments and neighborhoods; these took the form of regular, structured consultations. In Cleveland, actual participation by the disconnected was very meager; in both communities, giving permanent design to greater participation to sustain its momentum has proved elusive. Citizen advisory committees having durability and impact seem to have been the principal derivatives of reform efforts in the remaining two cities.

Reform tactics in all cities studied have been analogous—dramatizing issues, supporting and manipulating neighborhood organizations, recasting the strong executive form of organization in various ways, and simultaneously trying to impart a lasting design to nonhierarchical alternatives.

These books provide useful links to some of the cumulative experiences of public policy. The one assesses a large number of programs intended to aid the poor; the other ties together recent municipal experiences with client participation in policymaking as part of an exciting tradition best identified—but not noted—with the farmer committee systems in crop production, now over a half century old, and the more recent effort to decentralize and reorganize public schools in several major metropolitan centers. If *The Progressive City* has a shortcoming, it is its failure to note these ties as fully as they warrant. Clavel treats recounted experiences as truly unique; in a limited sense, they are, but, in a broader sense, they are part and parcel of a participatory form of public decision making about which we know all too little. Clavel misses an important point of ancestry here. For all their focus on policy evaluation, Morris and Williamson, the au thors of *Poverty and Public Policy*, deal hardly at all with the strengths and weaknesses of the art and science of policy evaluation per se, and do not really empirically bring theory and practice together very well.

HARRY W. REYNOLDS, Jr.
University of Nebraska
Omaha

PERRY, RONALD W. and ALVIN H. MUSH-KATEL. *Minority Citizens in Disasters*. Pp. xii, 205. Athens: University of Georgia Press, 1986. $25.00.

This book is written primarily for emergency managers who must deal with disasters, defined as unanticipated events that bring the threat or reality of loss of life to large numbers of people. But this book will also hold some interest for social scientists in that disasters, though uncommon, are recurrent events in human experience, may profoundly affect whole communities and even societies, and evoke human reactions that are deeply grounded in the social structure and culture from which the victims come.

Managing a disaster means, among other things, preparing a community for disaster, warning people once a disaster has occurred, persuading them to comply with the warnings and to follow the suggestions made for their safety, relieving the immediate effects of disaster, and beginning the long-term process of reconstruction. It involves knowing what channels of communication to use, what previous experience people have had with disasters, and how people can be involved in all aspects of disaster relief. All this means that the emergency manager must know a good deal about the type of people and the type of community with which he or she is dealing.

In this study, Perry and Mushkatel are primarily concerned with one element in reaction to behavior during disasters, namely, race and ethnic membership. In order to study this, they have investigated the behavior

of blacks, whites, and Mexican Americans in different types of communities and in relation to different types of disasters. These latter are (1) Abilene, Texas, with a population of 100,000 subjected to a flood; (2) Mt. Vernon, Washington, 13,000 population, where a tank car loaded with propane derailed but did not rupture; and (3) Denver, Colorado, where a derailed tank car did rupture, spewing forth nitric acid and causing several small fires.

Perry and Mushkatel proceed to investigate the behavior of each of the ethnic groups in each of these settings. Among the many findings, some will prove of interest to social scientists. For instance, in many of the aspects of disaster outlined earlier, Mexican Americans seem to rely on their families more than other ethnic groups do. Blacks are more likely to seek public shelter than are whites or Mexican Americans. On the other hand, blacks show less readiness to place reliance on public authorities, especially the police, than do the other groups. Other differences seem to be related more to rural-urban distinctions or population size than to race or ethnicity.

In spite of the small number of communities and types of disaster studied, specialists in race and ethnic relationships should find value in this work. Not only does it provide some solid empirical data in an area marked by a paucity of studies, but it is suggestive of the value of studying behavior under extreme conditions, where the realities of social and cultural life are made manifest.

EUGENE V. SCHNEIDER
Bryn Mawr College
Pennsylvania

ECONOMICS

AGARWAL, BINA. *Cold Hearts and Barren Slopes: The Woodfuel Crisis in the Third World*. Pp. xvi, 209. Riverdale, MD: Riverdale, 1986. No price.

If you were to come across this book in a

bookstore, you would see a book whose eye-catching dust jacket shows a photograph of what appears to be a group of North Africans congregated around a cooking fire. If you were to open the book you would find that its contents are printed on very cheap paper—the book is printed in India by Allied Publishers, New Delhi—and the quality of the numerous photographs appearing in it is that of Indian newspapers. Do not be put off by what you see—read the book. It is excellent.

The book is a study of the crisis of wood-fuel shortages facing a vast proportion of the peoples of the Third World. Wood fuel for hundreds of millions of these people "is the principal, and often, the sole source of inanimate energy." The wood-fuel crisis affects not only the quality of life of these people but is leading in major ways to deforestation, soil erosion, the flooding and silting of rivers and reservoirs, and other detrimental effects on agriculture and the environment.

The study notes that the availability of wood, a renewable resource, is fast becoming increasingly short in supply. Vast wooded areas of the Third World are being denuded and lie barren. According to some estimates, in some Third World countries, in half a century or so, virtually no forests of any consequence will be left. Aside from the aforementioned deleterious effects on the environment, there are climatic ill effects, desertification, the drying up of perennial streams, and increased frequency of serious flooding.

For the individuals in these countries, there are direct effects of deforestation relating especially to the decreasing supply of wood fuel. There is a substantial increase in the expenditure of time and energy, especially by women and children, to gather firewood. For example, in parts of Niger and in the Chamoli hills of India, people are having to spend three to five hours and to travel three to ten kilometers a day collecting firewood. And the story is repeated in numerous parts of Africa, Asia, and even Latin America.

It is noted that in parts of Africa, because of the extra time needed to collect firewood, daughters are now taken out of school to help their already overburdened mothers. A related aspect is the greater time now spent by women in cooking to adapt their cooking methods to conserve fuel. In some areas of Bangladesh and the African Sahel, families have had to reduce the number of cooked meals. In other cases, as in Guatemala, to conserve firewood, there is a shift away from nutritious foods, such as beans, to less nutritious foods requiring less cooking time. Such examples of ill effects on nutrition are to be found in the Sahel, where there has been a shift from millet to rice, and the forgoing of meat supplements, and in the Upper Volta, where there is resistance to the use of soybeans, which require much cooking time relative to the traditional cowpeas. "Necessity is also driving people in some areas to shift to food which can be eaten raw, or to eat partially cooked food (which could be toxic), or to eat cold leftovers (with the danger of food rotting in a tropical climate)," and so on. All this leads to poorer health and greater vulnerability to disease.

Increased deforestation also adversely affects people in other ways. It decreases the income of those forest-dependent people who gather wood for sale, and it direly reduces their supply of fruit, fodder, herbs, and plants for local medicines, turpentine, and resin.

Agarwal notes that because of deforestation there is a shift from firewood to other fuels such as cattle dung and maize stalks. The use of cattle dung as fuel rather than as manure has a high cost in terms of reduced agricultural production.

Bina Agarwal devotes sections of her study to analyzing causes of the wood-fuel crisis and the search for solutions. Chapters of the book are devoted to wood-fuel innovations—wood-burning stoves, for example—diffusion of these innovations, social forestry, and so on, and to the social, economic, and political complex of factors associated with the wood-fuel crisis.

In conclusion, let us note that according to a 1981 Food and Agriculture Organization study cited by Agarwal, in Africa, the Near East, Asia and the Pacific, and Latin America, 1.395 million people were experiencing an acute scarcity or deficit of wood fuel, and by the year 2000 the projected population suffering from this burden would, in all likelihood, more than double to 2.986 billion.

SURINDER K. MEHTA
University of Massachusetts
Amherst

BERGMANN, BARBARA R. *The Economic Emergence of Women.* Pp. 372. New York: Basic Books, 1986. $19.95.

BROWN, CLAIR and JOSEPH A. PECHMAN, eds. *Gender in the Workplace.* Pp. xiv, 316. Washington, DC: Brookings Institution, 1987. $32.95. Paperbound, $12.95.

The Economic Emergence of Women is written in what may roughly approximate traditional academic style and format, complete with 16 pages of citations, 26 tables, 9 figures, more than 11 pages of index, and a bibliography that covers nearly 7 pages, in small type. So far, nothing out of the ordinary for an academician. Bergmann is professor of economics at the University of Maryland. While traditional academic writing concerns itself with precise use of language that is put at the service of analysis that illuminates various sides of an issue, Bergmann appears to be one of a growing number of academicians who have at least partially shucked such constraints. Instead, elements of pop journalism creep into the narrative. While this may result in what some may consider to be a more readable document, clarity and precision frequently suffer. In a discussion of child-support payments, for example, we find the following noninformative sentence: "Currently fewer than a quarter of absent fathers make substantial, steady contributions." Bergmann does not bother to inform the reader of the meaning of "substan-

tial" and "steady," and mixing the two in a single declarative sentence completely mangles the sentence beyond meaning. But the major failing of this work is the failure to clothe a 12-point policy agenda and other goals with their related political and financial realities. To list goals without fully considering real-world resources, needs, and resistances is little more than the creation of a wish list. Wish lists abound at this point of the feminist movement and add little to the present-day knowledge base.

The strength of the book lies with the data that are presented in a variety of tables and figures and in two appendixes. These data range from social data, such as divorce rates over the past century and more, to useful data on women in the workplace over varying time periods; these data are the major contributions of the book.

Gender in the Workplace consists of eight papers that are the outgrowth of a 1984 conference sponsored by the Brookings Institution and the Committee on the Status of Women in the Economics Profession. An 11-page introduction penned by the editors provides a good introduction and overview of what is to follow. Interestingly, each of the papers is followed with brief commentary by two commentators; the commentaries tend to lend emphasis on key points and data and enrich the discussion of the topic. Additionally, 50 tables and 5 figures supplement and blend with the narrative portions of the papers.

The papers are varied in focus. Topics include Clair Brown's examination of consumption patterns as related to income over roughly the past sixty years; the role of gender in the labor market; occupational segregation among bank tellers; how work in the home and by subcontracting affect gender differentiation in the labor market of Mexico City; how females have fared in unions during recent years; how women part-time workers have changed in recent years; child support and welfare; and sex-based employment quotas, based largely on the Swedish experience. The papers are all of excellent quality, and this collection of papers should be of interest to any serious student of how gender functions in the economic sector.

GEORGE R. SHARWELL

University of South Carolina

Columbia

COHEN, STEPHEN S. and JOHN ZYSMAN. *Manufacturing Matters: The Myth of the Post-Industrial Economy.* Pp. xiv, 297. New York: Basic Books, 1987. $19.95.

Manufacturing Matters is undoubtedly a significant contribution to the discussion of the U.S. balance-of-payments problem and, more generally, the U.S. economic malaise. It is a product of the Berkeley Roundtable on International Economy (BRIE), a study group that Cohen and Zysman direct.

The thesis of this book is that manufacturing jobs have been and are being surrendered by this country in the mistaken belief that we will be better off transformed into a service economy. One thread of the argument is that when manufacturing—that is, blue-collar—jobs move offshore, the more skilled, higher-paid service jobs associated with that industry will soon emigrate as well. If we buy steel from Korea, for example, we will soon be hiring Korean metallurgists to tell us how best to use that steel. This idea is reasonable on its face and it is discussed at length.

Another principal point is that we could become more competitive and thus retain manufacturing work by adopting production techniques that the Japanese have developed and that Cohen and Zysman call "programmable automation." This means using robotics not to replace workers along the traditional assembly line but instead to lower the cost of switching from one product to another. This use considerably lowers the cost of variety in the product line, which in turn improves market penetration.

A third basic theme is that "a disaster for the wealth and power of the United States" will not be forestalled by readjustment of exchange rates, by the schoolbook principle of comparative advantage, or by any appeal to the mechanics of free markets. Unless all the nations we deal with play by those laissez-faire rules, then we only assure our own defeat by sticking with them. And the other nations that matter—Japan, Germany, France, and Italy, with places like Korea coming up fast—operate under firm directives aimed at strengthening the country's relative world position. So we had better reform very quickly, Cohen and Zysman say, by making our blue-collar labor force vastly more proficient and productive than it is today. The model for doing that seems to be mainly Japanese.

The book's style is journalistic, not academic, and thereby increases the number of people it will reach, and that is to the good. Most readers will recognize the book's limitations, and that is also good. For example, though they are obviously interested in showing that the service industry cannot supersede manufacturing, Cohen and Zysman find the concept of a service industry elusive or "rubbery." Had they looked not at the industry breakdown of employment—manufacturing, retail, personal services, and so on—but at the parallel breakdown by occupation—managers, clerical, operatives, and so forth—there would be no mystery; operative jobs might move offshore, but perhaps the management jobs would remain in Michigan or California. This small point weakens the authority of the book.

But it reflects more than a statistical gaffe. American technology is management rather than production. Our high-technology solution is to "offshore" production; the verb "offshore" is used repeatedly in the book. U.S. firms produce offshore to sell at home because we cannot be a niche economy. A niche economy produces cheaply at home to sell abroad; Japan has learned that there is an upper limit to the size of a niche economy and is beginning to suffer the consequences. We cannot all be just sellers. The BRIE enterprise sorely needs a global model of producers, payments, and markets.

Much more, though, Cohen, Zysman, and their BRIE colleagues lack a real constituency for their interesting exhortation. The entire book is in the first person plural—"we"—meaning not Cohen and Zysman but "we the American people." This is surely ingenuous; there is no "we" here in the sense of a collective will to be powerful and rich. If one thinks of "we the corporations," one is nearer the truth. Perhaps in Japan there is a national will, but the notion that U.S. corporations wish to so improve the skills and productivity of workers here that they can then employ our workers and pay them well in preference to all the willing substitutes abroad is unrealistic. The famed invisible hand holds a valid passport.

There is a memorable line in *Teahouse of the August Moon* about "Okinawa get-up-and-go." It does not refer to technology but mostly to pulling up one's socks, a community reasserting its ethos and its dignity. *Manufacturing Matters* derives not too distantly from that uplifting allegory of our golden age. But is there anyone left who cares if our socks are drooping?

WALLACE F. SMITH
University of California
Berkeley

FELDMAN, ROBERT ALAN. *Japanese Financial Markets: Deficits, Dilemmas, and Deregulation.* Pp. 245. Cambridge: MIT Press, 1986. $27.50.

Feldman's account of Japanese financial liberalization adds an important perspective to our understanding of Japan's economy. Despite the inherent problem of describing a system in rapid transition, especially to an English-reading audience with a limited inventory of knowledge about Japanese finance, Feldman's book will prove useful to both the general and the technical reader.

There are two focal points of the book. First, Feldman analyzes the catalysts for financial change that are described in a flow-of-funds framework. The emergence of large central government deficits after 1975 and the need to fund these deficits are emphasized as the major catalysts for financial liberalization. The portfolio adjustments required to absorb the huge amount of government debt demanded a financial system with more flexibility than the existing highly regulated and controlled system was capable of providing. Changes in the current account are also singled out as a catalyst for financial liberalization.

The discussion of the liberalization process is informative and in some parts excellent, often providing a historical perspective of current Japanese practices not easily found elsewhere. In this regard, Feldman's discussion of the internationalization of finance and the development of the government bond market is noteworthy. Feldman's most original contribution in this regard is a three-part taxonomy of financial innovations in terms of how an innovation influences feedback between different financial sectors.

The discussion would have been improved, however, if Feldman had devoted attention to the 1983-84 yen-dollar discussions and devoted greater attention to monetary policy issues. While the latter is part of the second focal point of the book, the general reader will find the discussion of monetary policy less satisfactory than the discussion of the changing financial system.

The second focal point of the book is technical. Feldman develops a complex multiequation financial model of the transmission of monetary policy. The model is estimated through 1981 and even though Feldman recognizes the problems of ending the estimation interval in 1981, the model's usefulness lies in understanding past monetary policy. Feldman points out, though, that any model will be of limited usefulness given the rapid change in Japanese finance. The theoretical model is extended to incorporate recent internationalization of Japanese finance; however, no empirical estimates are provided.

Feldman's book adds to our understanding of Japanese finance and thus can be highly recommended. The technical discussion, however, will appeal only to specialists interested in modeling the Japanese financial system.

THOMAS F. CARGILL
University of Nevada
Reno

KEYSSAR, ALEXANDER. *Out of Work: The First Century of Unemployment in Massachusetts.* Pp. xviii, 468. New York: Cambridge University Press, 1986. $49.50. Paperbound, $14.95.

CROUSE, JOAN. *The Homeless Transient in the Great Depression, New York State 1929-1941.* Pp. xii, 319. Albany: State University of New York Press, 1986. $39.50. Paperbound, $14.95.

One of the venerable legends of academe is the very bad condition of workers during the industrial revolution of the nineteenth and early twentieth centuries. This legend has been severely shaken by the discovery of new economic historians that real wages, far from falling or remaining stagnant during the English and American experiences, rose substantially after the Napoleonic Wars. In fact, a rather stunning comparison can be made between long-run real wage growth in the United States during the heyday of laissez-faire, 1870 to 1926, and the 43 years since the end of World War II. Real wages of manufacturing workers actually rose by a higher mean percentage per year when predatory robber barons roamed the land than they did after the onset of the welfare state during the New Deal.

As a consequence, scholarship has turned to other aspects of worker experiences than real wages, and Keyssar's book is a product of this new emphasis. It focuses on unemployment in Massachusetts, a heavily industrialized state, from the early nineteenth century to the Great Depression. His conclusion is that unemployment, far from being a child of the Great Depression, was a serious problem

well before that. All of us can agree and then go on to the really interesting question, How serious was it?

Space is lacking to analyze Keyssar's many grave methodological errors, so I must concentrate on only one. To measure the frequency of unemployment—not a self-evident concept despite his failure to discuss it—he multiplies unemployment rates derivable from state, federal, and union censuses by a factor that equals the year divided by the proportion of the year during which the average worker was unemployed. The product is supposedly the unemployment frequency, measured industry by industry and year by year.

First of all, the statistic in question is not the unemployment frequency but the unemployment rate adjusted to an annual basis. One measure of frequency is instead the reciprocal of his multiplier. The method would be sound when redefined if in fact unemployment had been measured in his sources as the proportion out of work on a given day or month and thus had to be converted to its annual equivalent. But his own appendixes show unequivocally that his data sources measure the number of unemployed as those having any unemployment during the whole year. Therefore, he overstates unemployment by a proportion equal to the factor itself, generating huge overestimates of the unemployment problem. In fact, the correct, unadjusted statistics show unemployment to have been still large. But what proportion was voluntary, consisting of those quitting jobs to search for better ones? We do not know, because all unemployment is implicitly defined by him as involuntary despite both modern and historical evidence. The search for statistically reliable answers must begin anew.

By contrast, Joan Crouse's book on homeless transients during the Great Depression is a competent, well-researched study of the administration of government programs to help the homeless. She emphasizes what is often forgotten, that President Roosevelt was rather conservative in his attitudes toward the relief of unemployment; and she has fascinating descriptions of the many different types of the homeless and the vagabond.

PAUL McGOULDRICK
State University of New York
Binghamton

KOCHAN, THOMAS A., HARRY C. KATZ, and ROBERT B. McKERSIE. *The Transformation of American Industrial Relations.* Pp. viii, 287. New York: Basic Books, 1986. No price.

Kochan, Katz, and McKersie's central premise is that the 1980s represent a period of fundamental transformation in American industrial relations. Historically, labor-management relations have been characterized by periods of stability punctuated by sudden upheavals in the institutions, values, and laws governing the employment relationship. One such upheaval occurred during the New Deal; another is under way in this decade. The current transformation is driven both by changes in the economic environment and by strategic choices made by managers, unions, and government policymakers.

This argument is informed by a wide range of empirical research on contemporary industrial relations, much of it conducted by the authors as part of a five-year study at the Massachusetts Institute of Technology sponsored by the Sloan Foundation and the U.S. Department of Labor.

Theoretically, the book polemicizes industrial relations research that focuses narrowly on collective bargaining or, in the case of nonunion firms, personnel policy. Kochan, Katz, and McKersie argue persuasively that a comprehensive theory of industrial relations must extend beyond this middle tier to the lower and higher tiers of workplace practices and strategic decision making in the firm.

According to Kochan and his coauthors, two distinct and in many respects contradictory industrial relations systems now coexist in the American workplace. The first, which they term the "union" or "New Deal" system, is founded on collective bargaining, job control unionism, and a system of industrial jurisprudence based on grievances and arbitration. Dominant from the late 1930s through the 1960s, this system is now waning as union membership and coverage decline.

Since the 1960s, a second "nonunion" or "human resource management" (HRM) system of industrial relations has competed with increasing success. Key elements of the HRM system include high levels of employee involvement; flexible job design emphasizing variety, challenge, and personal growth; and compensation based on individual skill and firm performance rather than seniority. This system has emerged in both large, innovative, nonunion firms—such as IBM and Delta Airlines—and in the unorganized plants of partially unionized firms.

In the 1980s, growing environmental pressures—mainly increased foreign competition and domestic deregulation—and the success of innovative nonunion HRM practices have combined to generate great pressure for change in unionized settings. In the empirically richest sections of the book, Kochan, Katz, and McKersie carefully document recent changes in the process and structure of collective bargaining, workplace-level experimentation with various employee involvement programs, and increasing involvement by some unions in strategic decision making of the firm.

This ambitious study makes important contributions to the industrial relations literature both theoretically and empirically. Especially useful theoretically are the authors' emphasis on developments above and below the formal collective bargaining or personnel relationship and their appreciation for the dynamic interplay of union and nonunion systems. The summary of research on contemporary innovations in industrial relations in union settings is simply the best currently available.

Inevitably, there are weaknesses. By focusing on innovation, Kochan and his coauthors underestimate the significance of old-line practices and resistance to change in both union and nonunion settings. Indeed, unionized and innovative HRM firms probably employ a minority of American workers; the majority's work experiences remain unexplored. In their enthusiasm for innovation, Kochan, Katz, and McKersie often neglect the negative potential of practices they describe, such as the deliberate manipulation of worker participation programs to thwart or undermine unions.

Overall, however, by combining theoretical sophistication with state-of-the-art empirical research, this study poses the right questions and provides many answers for both students and practitioners of industrial relations in the 1980s.

ANNE T. LAWRENCE
San Jose State University
California

ROSE, PETER S. *The Changing Structure of American Banking.* Pp. xii, 419. New York: Columbia University Press, 1987. $45.00.

This study is basically a summary of the state of banking in the mid-1980s, a short, encyclopedic survey of the evolving nature of the banking industry, its issues and problems, including laws and regulations, internal and external competitive forces, efficiency, and so forth. Chapter by chapter, Rose analyzes issues and arguments, following with a review of the empirical evidence found by investigators. Although the perspective is mainly of a micro character, that is, in terms of what is good for banks, the consequences for the general public are also examined.

Specific topics covered include entry and exit, including bank failures; scale of operations and role of multiproduct lines; growth from within versus growth via mergers; branch banking; holding company opera-

tions; concentration, including methods of measurement; bank performance and difficulties in its measurement; competition from thrifts, money market funds, financial conglomerates, and financial affiliates of industrial and commercial firms; and regulation and deregulation. These and related topics are covered in terms of the dynamics of the market, including technology.

This study should be valuable for financial decision makers and their advisers in the financial services industry, those seeking to enter it, and those on the legislative and regulatory sides. It should also be useful to students of banking. Surveyed are a very large number of empirical findings as well as theoretical analyses. Supporting bibliographies are huge. Users will find that there are few issues with simple answers. Whether it be an issue of large versus small firms, of branch versus holding company operations, of competition between banks and thrifts, or of the virtues of nonbank financial conglomerates, the reader will find evidence supporting both sides with rarely a sure answer.

Given its purposes, this book is admirable, dealing with the whole gamut of issues facing the banking industry and the government. From the reader's point of view, it may, however, have only a short life span. Change of revolutionary proportions has beset the financial services industries in recent years and its pace seems unlikely to diminish. This extraordinary pace, too, probably has significance for the usefulness of some of the empirical material surveyed in this book because many findings are cited from studies covering a long span of years. One must at least question whether the results can realistically be extrapolated to an environment of revolutionary change in markets, technology, and governmental behavior.

ERVIN MILLER
University of Pennsylvania
Philadelphia

OTHER BOOKS

ABEGGLEN, JAMES C. and GEORGE STALK. *Kaisha: The Japanese Corporation.* Pp. 309. New York: Basic Books, 1985. $22.50.

ALEXANDER, JEFFREY C. *Twenty Lectures: Sociological Theory since World War II.* Pp. 393. New York: Columbia University Press, 1987. $35.00.

ALLEN, CALVIN H. *Oman: The Modernization of the Sultanate.* Pp. 154. Boulder, CO: Westview, 1987. $28.00.

ALTMAN, DENNIS. *AIDS in the Mind of America: The Social, Political, and Psychological Impact of a New Epidemic.* Pp. viii, 228. New York: Doubleday, 1987. Paperbound, $8.95.

American Foreign Policy: Current Documents, 1984. Pp. lvi, 1174. Washington, DC: Department of State, 1986. $37.00.

ANWAR, MUHAMMAD. *Race and Politics: Ethnic Minorities and the British Political System.* Pp. x, 182. New York: Tavistock, 1986. No price.

ASHE, GEOFFREY. *The Discovery of King Arthur.* Pp. 224. New York: Henry Holt, 1985. Paperbound, $8.95.

AZAR, EDWARD E. and JOHN W. BURTON. *International Conflict Resolution: Theory and Practice.* Pp. ix, 159. Boulder, CO: Lynne Rienner, 1986. $30.00.

BALASSA, BELA et al. *Toward Renewed Economic Growth in Latin America.* Pp. 205. Washington, DC: Institute for International Economies, 1986. Paperbound, $15.00.

BALDWIN, DAVID A. *Economic Statecraft.* Pp. xiv, 409. Princeton, NJ: Princeton University Press, 1985. $55.00. Paperbound, $12.50.

BALDWIN, ROBERT E. *The Political Economy of U.S. Import Policy.* Pp. xi, 238. Cambridge: MIT Press, 1985. $22.50.

BALL-ROKEACH, SANDRA J. and MURIEL G. CANTOR. *Media, Audience, and Social Structure.* Pp. 400. Newbury Park, CA: Sage, 1986. Paperbound, no price.

BANERJEE, DIPTENDRA, ed. *Marxian Theory and the Third World.* Pp. 322. Newbury Park, CA: Sage, 1986. $29.95.

BAUER, HENRY H. *The Enigma of Loch Ness: Making Sense of a Mystery.* Pp. xiii, 243. Champaign: University of Illinois Press, 1986. $22.95.

BECK, BRENDA E.F. et al., eds. *Folktales of India.* Pp. xxxi, 357. Chicago: University of Chicago Press, 1987. $29.95.

BELL, MARILYN J., ed. *Women as Elders: Images, Visions, and Issues.* Pp. xiv, 90. New York: Haworth, 1986. $19.95.

BENTON, J. EDWIN and DAVID R. MORGAN, eds. *Intergovernmental Relations and Public Policy.* Pp. viii, 224. Westport, CT: Greenwood, 1986. $35.00.

BESCHLOSS, MICHAEL R. *Kennedy and Roosevelt: The Uneasy Alliance.* Pp. 318. New York: Harper & Row, 1986. Paperbound, $8.95.

BESCHLOSS, MICHAEL R. *Mat Day: The U-2 Affair: The Untold Story of the Greatest US-USSR Spy Scandal.* Pp. xx, 494. New York: Harper & Row, 1986. Paperbound, $8.95.

BIANCHI, SUZANNE M. and DAPHNE SPAIN. *American Women in Transition.* Pp. xxii, 286. New York: Russell Sage, 1986. Distributed by Basic Books, New York. $32.95. Paperbound, $14.95.

BLACK, JAN KNIPPERS. *Sentinels of Empire: The United States and Latin American Militarism.* Pp. xix, 240. Westport, CT: Greenwood, 1986. $35.00.

BLYTON, PAUL. *Changes in Working Time: An International Review.* Pp. 184. New York: St. Martin's Press, 1986. $25.00.

BONIOR, DAVID E., STEVEN M. CHAMPLIN, and TIMOTHY S. KOLLY. *The Vietnam Veteran: A History of Neglect.* Pp. xix, 200. New York: Praeger, 1984. $21.95.

BORDA, ORLANDO FALS. *The Challenge of Social Change.* Pp. 134. Newbury Park, CA: Sage, 1985. No price.

BOSWORTH, BARRY P. and ALICE M. RIVLIN. *The Swedish Economy.* Pp. 338. Washington, DC: Brookings Institution, 1987. $32.95. Paperbound, $12.95.

BROWN, ALAN. *Modern Political Philosophy: Theories of the Just Society.* Pp. 215. New York: Viking Penguin, 1986. Paperbound, $6.95.

BROWN, LESTER R. et al. *State of the World: A Worldwatch Institute Report on Progress toward a Sustainable Society.* New York: Norton, 1987. Paperbound, $9.95.

BROWN, MICHAEL BARRATT. *Models in Political Economy: A Guide to the Arguments.* Pp. 281. Boulder, CO: Lynne Rienner, 1986. $27.50. Paperbound, $13.50.

BROWN, SEYOM. *The Causes and Prevention of War.* Pp. 274. New York: St. Martin's Press, 1987. $32.50.

BUKOWCZYK, JOHN J. *And My Children Did Not Know Me: A History of the Polish Americans.* Pp. xiii, 190. Bloomington: Indiana University Press, 1987. $27.50. Paperbound, $8.95.

BURNS, E. BRADFORD. *Eadweard Muybridge in Guatemala, 1875: The Photographer as Social Recorder.* Pp. viii, 136. Berkeley: University of California Press, 1986. $35.00.

BURTLESS, GARY. *Work, Health, and Income among the Elderly.* Pp. 276. Washington, DC: Brookings Institution, 1987. $26.95.

BYRD, ROBERT O. *Decision at Richmond, June 1788: A Documentary Drama of the Constitutional Ratification Convention in Virginia.* Pp. 174. Chicago: World without War, 1986. Paperbound, $14.95.

CARLSON, DON and CRAIG COMSTOCK, eds. *Securing Our Planet: How to Succeed When Threats Are Too Risky and There's Really No Defense.* Pp. 395. Los Angeles: Jeremy P. Tarcher in association with the Ark Communications Institute, 1986. Distributed by St. Martin's Press, New York. $18.95.

CHALLINOR, JOAN R. and ROBERT L. BEISNER, eds. *Arms at Rest: Peacemaking and Peacekeeping in American History.* Pp. xiv, 224. Westport, CT: Greenwood, 1987. $35.00.

CHILDERS, THOMAS, ed. *The Formation of the Nazi Constituency, 1919-1933.* Pp. viii, 263. Totowa, NJ: Barnes & Noble, 1986. $32.50.

CHUNG, HAN-KU. *Interest Representation in Soviet Policymaking: A Case Study of a West Siberian Energy Coalition.* Pp. 192. Boulder, CO: Westview, 1987. Paperbound, $22.00.

COMBS, JERALD A. *American Diplomatic History: Two Centuries of Changing Interpretations.* Pp. xii, 413. Berkeley: University of California Press, 1986. Paperbound, $11.95.

COTTAM, MARTHA L. *Foreign Policy Decision Making: The Influence of Cognition.* Pp. xiii, 262. Boulder, CO: Westview, 1986. Paperbound, $26.50.

COUSINS, NORMAN. *The Pathology of Power.* Pp. 228. New York: Norton, 1987. $15.95.

DAHLBERG, KENNETH A. *New Directions for Agriculture and Agricultural Research: Neglected Dimensions and Emerging Alternatives.* Pp. 436. Totowa, NJ: Rowman & Allanheld, 1986. No price.

DAS, DILIP K. *Migration of Financial Resources to Developing Countries.* Pp. xix, 263. New York: St. Martin's Press, 1986. $29.95.

DAVIS, PERRY. *Public-Private Partnerships: Improving Urban Life.* Pp. 161. New York: Academy of Political Science, 1987. Paperbound, $9.95.

DEMOTT, BOBBY J. *Freemasonry in American Culture and Society.* Pp. 346. Lanham, MD: University Press of America, 1986. $29.50. Paperbound, $16.50.

DENISOFF, R. SERGE. *Tarnished Gold: The Record Industry Revisited.* Pp. xvi, 487. New Brunswick, NJ: Transaction Books, 1986. $29.95. Paperbound, $16.95.

DESARIO, JACK and STUART LANGTON. *Citizen Participation in Public Decision Making.* Pp. 237. Westport, CT: Greenwood, 1987. $35.00.

DOMHOFF, G. WILLIAM and THOMAS R. DYE, eds. *Power Elites and Organiza-*

tions. Pp. 292. Newbury Park, CA: Sage, 1987. No price.

DONOVAN, HEDLEY. *Roosevelt to Reagan: A Reporter's Encounters with Nine Presidents.* Pp. xviii, 344. New York: Harper & Row, Cornelia and Michael Bessie Books, 1987. Paperbound, $8.95.

DRAGAN, J. C. and M. C. DEMETRESCU. *Entropy and Bioeconomics: The New Paradigm of Nicholas Georgescu-Roegen.* Pp. 240. Milan: Nagard, 1986. Paperbound, no price.

DROR, YEHEZKEL. *Policymaking under Adversity.* Pp. 437. New Brunswick, NJ: Transaction Books, 1986. $39.95.

DUFFY, BERNARD K. and HALFORD R. RYAN. *American Orators of the Twentieth Century: Critical Studies and Sources.* Pp. 468. Westport, CT: Greenwood, 1987. $65.00.

EDWARDS, JOHN. *Positive Discrimination: Social Justice and Social Policy.* Pp. 243. New York: Tavistock, 1987. Paperbound, $18.95.

EMERSON, CARYL. *Boris Godunov: Transpositions of a Russian Theme.* Pp. 272. Bloomington: Indiana University Press, 1986. $25.00.

ENGERMAN, STANLEY L. and ROBERT E. GALLMAN. *Long-Term Factors in American Economic Growth.* Pp. 884. Chicago: University of Chicago Press, 1987. $79.95.

ENGLIS, KAREL. *An Essay on Economic Systems.* Pp. 153. New York: Columbia University Press, 1987. $20.00.

ENNEW, JUDITH. *The Sexual Exploitation of Children.* Pp. x, 163. New York: St. Martin's Press, 1986. $25.00.

ERLICH, HAGGAI. *Ethiopia and the Challenge of Independence.* Pp. xii, 265. Boulder, CO: Lynne Rienner, 1986. $32.50.

ETTINGER, ELZBIETA. *Rosa Luxemburg: A Life.* Pp. 286. Boston: Beacon, 1987.

FARAH, TAWFIC E. and YASUMASA KURODA, eds. *Political Socialization in the Arab States.* Pp. xiv, 215. Boulder, CO: Lynne Rienner, 1987. $25.00.

FILLER, LOUIS. *Dictionary of American*

Conservatism. Pp. 380. New York: Philosophical Library, 1987. $29.95.

FORTUESCUE, STEPHEN. *The Communist Party and Soviet Science.* Pp. x, 234. Baltimore, MD: Johns Hopkins University Press, 1987. $28.50.

FOSS, PHILLIP O. *Federal Lands Policy.* Pp. 201. Westport, CT: Greenwood, 1987. $37.95.

FRESIA, GERALD JOHN. *There Comes a Time: A Challenge to the Two Party System.* Pp. 255. New York: Praeger, 1986. $38.95.

GAITONDE, P. D. *The Liberation of Goa: A Participant's View of History.* Pp. 192. New York: St. Martin's Press, 1987. No price.

GALDERISI, PETER F. et al., eds. *The Politics of Realignment: Party Change in the Mountain West.* Pp. xi, 235. Boulder, CO: Westview, 1987. Paperbound, $23.50.

GARRISON, MARK and ABBOTT GLEASON, eds. *Shared Destiny: Fifty Years of Soviet-American Relations.* Pp. xxxii, 167. Boston: Beacon, 1987. Paperbound, $8.95.

GIBNEY, MARK. *Strangers or Friends: Principles for a New Alien Admission Policy.* Pp. xv, 169. Westport, CT: Greenwood, 1986. $29.95.

GLENNON, JOHN P., ed. *Foreign Relations of the United States, 1955-1957.* Vol. 3, *China.* Pp. xxiii, 689. Washington, DC: Government Printing Office, 1986. No price.

GORDON, JOHN W. *The Other Desert War: British Special Forces in North Africa, 1940-1943.* Pp. xix, 241. Westport, CT: Greenwood, 1987. $39.95.

GOTTDIENER, MARK, ed. *Cities in Stress: A New Look at the Urban Crisis.* Pp. 295. Newbury Park, CA: Sage, 1986. $29.95. Paperbound, $14.95.

GRAHAM, HELEN and PAUL PRESTON. *The Popular Front in Europe.* Pp. 171. New York: St. Martin's Press, 1987. $32.50.

GRONOW, JUKKA. *On the Formation of Marxism: Karl Kautsky's Theory of Capitalism, the Marxism of the Second*

International, and Karl Marx's Critique of Political Economy. Pp. 253. Helsinki: Finnish Society of Science and Letters, 1986. Paperbound, no price.

GUNTER, MICHAEL M. *"Pursuing the Just Cause of Their People": A Study of Contemporary Armenian Terrorism.* Pp. viii, 182. Westport, CT: Greenwood, 1986. $29.95.

HAKOVIRTA, HARTO. *Third World Conflicts and Refugeeism: Dimensions, Dynamics, and Trends of the World Refugee Problem.* Pp. 160. Helsinki: Finnish Society of Science and Letters, 1986. Paperbound, no price.

HALEY, P. EDWARD and JACK MERRITT, eds. *Strategic Defense Initiative: Folly or Future?* Pp. ix, 193. Boulder, CO: Westview, 1986. $24.00. Paperbound, $9.95.

HAMLIN, ALAN P. *Ethics, Economics and the State.* Pp. x, 198. New York: St. Martin's Press, 1986. $32.50.

HAMPSHIRE, STUART. *Morality and Conflict.* Pp. vii, 175. Cambridge, MA: Harvard University Press, 1983. $17.50. Paperbound, $9.50.

HARRIS, LILLIAN CRAIG. *Libya: Qadhafi's Revolution and the Modern State.* Pp. 157. Boulder, CO: Westview, 1986. $24.95.

HAWLEY, JAMES P. *Dollars and Borders: U.S. Government Attempts to Restrict Capital Flows, 1960-1980.* Pp. 203. Armonk, NY: M. E. Sharpe, 1987. $29.95.

HAYWARD, JACK. *Out of Slavery.* Pp. 200. Totowa, NJ: Frank Cass, 1985. $29.50.

HELLER, CHARLES E. and WILLIAM A. STOFFT, eds. *America's First Battles, 1776-1965.* Pp. xiii, 416. Lawrence: University Press of Kansas, 1986. $29.95. Paperbound, $14.95.

HESS, STEPHEN. *The Ultimate Insiders: U.S. Senators and National Media.* Washington, DC: Brookings Institution, 1986. $22.95. Paperbound, $8.95.

HILLIER, JIM, ed. *Cahiers du Cinema: The 1960's: New Wave, New Cinema, Reevaluating Hollywood.* Pp. xiv, 363. Cambridge, MA: Harvard University Press, 1987. $25.00.

HIRSCHHORN, LARRY. *Beyond Mechanization.* Pp. ix, 181. Cambridge: MIT Press, 1984. No price.

HOCH, STEVEN L. *Serfdom and Social Control in Russia: Petrovskoe, a Village in Tambov.* Pp. x, 220. Chicago: University of Chicago Press, 1986. $25.00.

HOFFMAN, PIOTR. *Doubt, Time, Violence.* Pp. 139. Chicago: University of Chicago Press, 1986. $25.00.

HOFFMANN, STANLEY. *Janus and Minerva: Essays in the Theory and Practice of International Politics.* Pp. 457. Boulder, CO: Westview, 1987. $39.95.

HOLMES, JOHN W. *The United Nations in Perspective.* Pp. 24. Toronto: Canadian Institute of International Affairs, 1986. Paperbound, $2.00.

HOPE, MARJORIE and JAMES YOUNG. *The Faces of Homelessness.* Lexington, MA: D. C. Heath, Lexington Books, 1986. No price.

HOROWITZ, IRVING LOUIS. *Cuban Communism.* Pp. 736. New Brunswick, NJ: Transaction Books, 1986. Paperbound, $19.95.

HREBENAR, RONALD J. *The Japanese Party System: From One-Party Rule to Coalition Government.* Pp. 330. Boulder, CO: Westview, 1987. $42.50. Paperbound, $19.95.

HUMAN SCIENCES RESEARCH COUNCIL. *The South African Society: Realities and Future Prospects.* Pp. 217. Westport, CT: Greenwood, 1987. $29.95.

HUYSER, ROBERT E. *Mission to Tehran.* Pp. ix, 306. New York: Harper & Row, 1986. $20.95.

INTERNATIONAL CENTRE FOR PARLIAMENTARY DOCUMENTATION OF THE INTER-PARLIAMENTARY UNION. *Parliaments of the World.* Vols. 1 and 2. Pp. xiii, 1422. New York: Facts on File, 1986. $95.00.

ISMAEL, TAREQ Y. *International Relations of the Contemporary Middle East.* Pp. x, 290. Syracuse, NY: Syracuse University Press, 1986. $29.95. Paperbound, $14.95.

JESSOP, BOB. *Nocos Poulantzas: Marxist Theory and Political Strategy.* Pp. xviii, 391. New York: St. Martin's Press, 1985. $39.95. Paperbound, $14.95.

JOHNSON, LOCH K. *The Making of International Agreements.* Pp. xx, 206. New York: New York University Press, 1984. Distributed by Columbia University Press, New York. $30.00.

JOWETT, GARTH S. and VICTORIA O'DONNELL. *Propaganda and Persuasion.* Pp. 244. Newbury Park, CA: Sage, 1986. $25.00. Paperbound, $12.95.

KAHNE, HILDA. *Reconceiving Part-Time Work: New Perspectives for Older Workers and Women.* Pp. xv, 180. Totowa, NJ: Rowman & Allanheld, 1985. $35.00.

KAPLAN, KAREL. *The Short March: The Communist Takeover in Czechoslovakia, 1945-1948.* Pp. xvi, 207. New York: St. Martin's Press, 1987. $29.95.

KAVASS, IGOR, ed. *United States Legislation on Foreign Relations and International Commerce.* Pp. xxii, 316. Buffalo, NY: William S. Hein, 1986. Paperbound, no price.

KHALIFA, AHMAD A. *Adverse Consequences for the Enjoyment of Human Rights of Political, Military, Economic and Other Forms of Assistance Given to the Racist and Colonialist Regime of South Africa.* Pp. 209. New York: United Nations, 1987. Paperbound, no price.

KING, PRESTON. *An African Winter.* Pp. 249. New York: Viking Penguin, 1986. Paperbound, $5.95.

KNEVITT, CHARLES. *Space on Earth: Architecture: People and Buildings.* Pp. 232. London: Thames Methuen, 1985. Paperbound, no price.

KOLINSKY, EVA, ed. *Opposition in Western Europe.* Pp. 400. New York: St. Martin's Press, 1987. $35.00.

KUMAR, SATISH, ed. *Yearbook on India's Foreign Policy, 1983-84.* Pp. 270. Newbury Park, CA: Sage, 1986. $49.95.

LANDE, STEPHEN L. and CRAIG VANGRASSTEK. *The Trade and Tariff Act of 1984: Trade Policy in the Reagan Administration.* Pp. ix, 168. Lexington, MA: D.C. Heath, Lexington Books, 1986. $21.00.

LAUREN, PAUL GORDON. *The China Hands' Legacy: Ethics and Diplomacy.* Pp. 196. Boulder, CO: Westview, 1987. $24.00.

LEVENESS, FRANK P. and JANE P. SWEENEY. *Women Leaders in Contemporary U.S. Politics.* Pp. 164. Boulder, CO: Lynne Rienner, 1987. $25.00. Paperbound, $12.95.

LEWIS, DAN A. and GRETA SALEM. *Fear of Crime: Incivility and the Production of a Social Problem.* Pp. 146. New Brunswick, NJ: Transaction Books, 1986. $19.95.

LICHTHEIM, GEORGE, ed. *Thoughts among the Ruins: Collected Essays on Europe and Beyond.* Pp. xxix, 492. New Brunswick, NJ: Transaction Books, 1986. Paperbound, $24.95.

LINDSAY, BEVERLY, ed. *African Migration and National Development.* Pp. xii, 180. University Park: Pennsylvania State University Press, 1985. $22.50.

LOGUE, CALVIN M. and HOWARD DORGAN. *A New Diversity in Contemporary Southern Rhetoric.* Pp. 268. Baton Rouge: Louisiana State University Press, 1987. $32.50.

LONNER, WALTER J. and JOHN W. BERRY. *Field Methods in Cross-Cultural Research.* Pp. 368. Newbury Park, CA: Sage, 1986. No price.

LOVE, NANCY S. *Marx, Nietzsche, and Modernity.* Pp. 264. New York: Columbia University Press, 1986. $27.50.

MACKIE, THOMAS T. and BRIAN W. HOGWOOD, eds. *Unlocking the Cabinet: Cabinet Structures in Comparative Perspective.* Pp. vi, 185. Newbury Park, CA: Sage, 1986. $40.00. Paperbound, $16.00.

MAHADEVAN, K. *Fertility and Morality: Theory, Methodology and Empirical Issues.* Pp. 351. Newbury Park, CA: Sage, 1986. $29.00.

MARABLE, MANNING. *Black American Politics: From the Washington Marches to Jesse Jackson.* Pp. ix, 366. London:

Verso, 1986. Distributed by Schocken Books, New York. $27.50. Paperbound, $8.95.

MARIEN, MICHAEL and LANE JENNINGS. *What I Have Learned: Thinking about the Future Then and Now.* Pp. 204. Westport, CT: Greenwood, 1987. $29.95.

MARTIN, LINDA G. *The Asean Success Story: Social, Economic, and Political Dimensions.* Pp. 253. Honolulu: University of Hawaii Press, 1987. Paperbound, $15.00.

MARVICK, ELIZABETH WIRTH. *Louis XIII: The Making of a King.* Pp. xx, 278. New Haven, CT: Yale University Press, 1986. $31.50.

MATEJKO, ALEXANDER J. *The Self-Defeating Organization: A Critique of Bureaucracy.* Pp. xxviii, 395. New York: Praeger, 1986. $44.95.

MATTHEWS, ROGER and JOCK YOUNG, eds. *Confronting Crime.* Pp. viii, 231. Newbury Park, CA: Sage, 1986. $32.00. Paperbound, $15.95.

MAY, ERNEST R., ed. *Knowing One's Enemies: Intelligence Assessment before the Two World Wars.* Pp. xii, 561. Princeton, NJ: Princeton University Press, 1986. Paperbound, $14.50.

McCORD, WILLIAM. *Paths to Progress: Bread and Freedom in Developing Societies.* Pp. 352. New York: Norton, 1986. $17.95.

McQUAIL, DENIS and KAREN SIUNE, eds. *New Media Politics: Comparative Perspectives in Western Europe.* Pp. viii, 216. Newbury Park, CA: Sage, 1986. $40.00. Paperbound, $14.95.

MELVIN, PATRICIA MOONEY. *American Community Organizations: A Historical Dictionary.* Pp. 233. Westport, CT: Greenwood, 1986. $45.00.

MERRIAM, EVE, ed. *Growing Up Female in America: Ten Lives.* Pp. 308. Boston: Beacon, 1987. Paperbound, $9.95.

MESA-LAGO, CARMELO. *Cuban Studies.* Vol. 16. Pp. x, 297. Pittsburgh, PA: University of Pittsburgh Press, 1986. $24.95.

MILIVOJEVIC, MARKO. *The Debt Rescheduling Process.* Pp. 240. New York: St. Martin's Press, 1985. $27.50.

MITZMAN, ARTHUR. *Sociology and Estrangement: Three Sociologists of Imperial Germany.* Pp. xxxiv, 375. New Brunswick, NJ: Transaction Books, 1986. Paperbound, $14.95.

MOLLAT, MICHEL. *The Poor in the Middle Ages.* Translated by Arthur Goldhammer. Pp. viii, 336. New Haven, CT: Yale University Press, 1986. $30.00.

MOORE, LYNDA L. *Not as Far as You Think: The Realities of Working Women.* Pp. xii, 201. Lexington, MA: D. C. Heath, Lexington Books, 1986. $15.95.

MORGAN, DAVID. *The Flacks of Washington: Government Information and the Public Agenda.* Pp. xiii, 165. Westport, CT: Greenwood, 1986. $29.95.

MORRIS, BERNARD S. *Communism, Revolution, and American Policy.* Pp. xv, 200. Durham, NC: Duke University Press, 1987. $32.50. Paperbound, $12.95.

NATOLI, MARIE D. *American Prince, American Pauper: The Contemporary Vice Presidency in Perspective.* Pp. xiii, 204. Westport, CT: Greenwood, 1985. $35.00.

NELKIN, DOROTHY. *Selling Science: How the Press Covers Science and Technology.* Pp. 182. New York: W. H. Freeman, 1987. Paperbound, no price.

NETTON, IAN RICHARD, ed. *Arabia and the Gulf: From Traditional Society to Modern States.* Pp. xviii, 259. Totowa, NJ: Barnes & Noble, 1986. $32.50.

O'DONNELL, GUILLERMO, PHILLIPPE C. SCHMITTER, and LAURENCE WHITEHEAD. *Transitions From Authoritarian Rule: Prospects for Democracy.* Pp. 646. Baltimore, MD: Johns Hopkins University Press, 1986. $49.50.

OLSEN, EDWARD A. and STEPHEN JURIKA, Jr., eds. *The Armed Forces in Contemporary Asian Societies.* Pp. viii, 368. Boulder, CO: Westview, 1986. $43.50.

OLSON, WILLIAM C. *The Theory and Practice of International Relations.* Pp.

375. Englewood Cliffs, NJ: Prentice-Hall, 1987. No price.

ORDESHOOK, PETER C. *Game Theory and Political Theory: An Introduction.* Pp. xv, 511. New York: Cambridge University Press, 1986. $49.50. Paperbound, $17.95.

ORREN, KAREN and STEPHEN SKOWRONEK, eds. *Studies in American Political Development.* Vol. 1. Pp. viii, 302. New Haven, CT: Yale University Press, 1986. $32.50. Paperbound, $12.95.

OSKAMP, STUART, ed. *Family Processes and Problems: Social Psychological Aspects.* Pp. 324. Newbury Park, CA: Sage, 1986. Paperbound, $14.95.

PAPPAS, PAUL CONSTANTINE. *The United States and the Greek War for Independence.* Pp. xvi, 190. Boulder, CO: East European Monographs, 1986. Distributed by Columbia University Press, New York. $20.00.

PAUL, ELLEN FRANKEL et al., eds. *Marxism and Liberalism.* Pp. xii, 223. New York: Basil Blackwell, 1986. Paperbound, $14.95.

PERALTA-RAMOS, MONICA and CARLOS H. WAISMAN, eds. *From Military Rule to Liberal Democracy in Argentina.* Pp. xvi, 175. Boulder, CO: Westview, 1987. Paperbound, $23.00.

PEREZ, LOUIS A. *Cuba under the Platt Amendment, 1902-1934.* Pp. xvii, 410. Pittsburgh, PA: University of Pittsburgh Press, 1986. $33.95.

PIERSON, CHRISTOPHER. *Marxist Theory and Democratic Politics.* Pp. viii, 229. Berkeley: University of California Press, 1986. $35.00.

POLLOCK, RALPH S., ed. *Renewing the Dream: National Archives Bicentennial '87 Lectures on Contemporary Constitutional Issues.* Pp. x, 183. Lanham, MD: University Press of America, 1986. $24.50. Paperbound, $11.50.

PRELINGER, CATHERINE M. *Charity, Challenge and Change: Religious Dimensions of the Mid-Nineteenth Century Women's Movement in Germany.* Pp. 205. Westport, CT: Greenwood, 1987. No price.

RADELET, LOUIS A. *The Police and the Community.* 4th ed. Pp. xix, 586. New York: Macmillan, 1986. No price.

RAZIS, VIC. *The American Connection: The Influence of US Business on South Africa.* Pp. 246. New York: St. Martin's Press, 1986. $32.50.

REVEL, ALIAN and CHRISTOPHE RIBOUD. *American Green Power.* Pp. xiii, 225. Baltimore, MD: Johns Hopkins University Press, 1986. $30.00. Paperbound, $12.95.

RICCI, DAVID M. *The Tragedy of Political Science: Politics, Scholarship, and Democracy.* Pp. 335. New Haven, CT: Yale University Press, 1987. Paperbound, $12.95.

RICHARDSON, DAVID. *Abolition and Its Aftermath: The Historical Context.* Pp. 279. Totowa, NJ: Frank Cass, 1985. $29.50.

RICHARDSON, JOHN, Jr. *Government Information: Education and Research, 1928-1986.* Pp. 186. New York: Greenwood, 1987. No price.

RIDD, ROSEMARY and HELEN CALLAWAY, eds. *Women and Political Conflict: Portraits of Struggle in Times of Crisis.* Pp. xi, 246. New York: New York University Press, 1986. Distributed by Columbia University Press, New York. $38.00.

RIEDER, JONATHAN. *Canarsie: The Jews and Italians of Brooklyn against Liberalism.* Pp. 290. Cambridge, MA: Harvard University Press, 1985. $22.50. Paperbound, $8.95.

RIGSBY, GREGORY U. *Alexander Crummell: Pioneer in Nineteenth-Century Pan-African Thought.* Pp. 231. Westport, CT: Greenwood, 1987. $32.95.

ROBBINS, THOMAS and ROLAND ROBERTSON, eds. *Church-State Relations: Tensions and Transitions.* Pp. ix, 296. New Brunswick, NJ: Transaction Books, 1986. $29.95. Paperbound, $14.95.

ROHNER, RONALD P. *The Warmth Dimension: Foundations of Parental Acceptance-Rejection Theory.* Pp. 246. Newbury Park, CA: Sage, 1986. No price.

ROSE, RICHARD and IAN McAL-LISTER. *Voters Begin to Choose: From Closed-Class to Open Elections in Britain.* Newbury Park, CA: Sage, 1986. $40.00. Paperbound, $14.95.

ROSEN, BARRY M., ed. *Iran since the Revolution: Internal Dynamics, Regional Conflicts, and the Superpowers.* Pp. xx, 187. Boulder, CO: East European Monographs, 1985. Distributed by Columbia University Press, New York. $20.00.

ROSENBAUM, DENNIS P. *Community Crime Prevention: Does It Work?* Pp. 318. Newbury Park, CA: Sage, 1986. $29.95. Paperbound, $14.95.

SCHAPIRO, LEONARD. *Russian Studies.* Edited by Ellen Dahrendorf. Pp. 400. New York: Viking, Elisabeth Sifton Books, 1986. $24.95.

SERPELL, JAMES. *In the Company of Animals.* Pp. vii, 215. New York: Basil Blackwell, 1986. $19.95.

SHEFFER, GABRIEL, ed. *Dynamics of Dependence: U.S.-Israeli Relations.* Pp. x, 210. Boulder, CO: Westview, 1987. Paperbound, $27.50.

SHOVER, NEAL, DONALD A. CLEL-LAND, and JOHN LYNXWILER. *Enforcement or Negotiation: Constructing a Regulatory Bureaucracy.* Pp. 193. Albany: State University of New York Press, 1986. $39.50. Paperbound, $12.95.

SIVIAN, EMMANUEL. *Radical Islam: Medieval Theology and Modern Politics.* Pp. 218. New Haven, CT: Yale University Press, 1987. Paperbound, $9.95.

SMITH, R. B. *An International History of the Vietnam War: Revolution versus Containment, 1955-1961.* Pp. xiii, 301. New York: St. Martin's Press, 1987. Paperbound, $12.95.

SO, ALVIN Y. *The South China Silk District: Local Historical Transformation and World System Theory.* Pp. 206. Albany: State University of New York Press, 1986. $39.50. Paperbound, $14.95.

SPANGLER, EVE. *Lawyers for Hire: Salaried Professionals at Work.* Pp. 233. New Haven, CT: Yale University Press, 1986. $25.00.

SPATES, JAMES L. and JOHN J. MAC-IONIS. *The Sociology of Cities.* 2nd ed. Pp. xv, 514. Belmont, CA: Wadsworth, 1987. No price.

SPENCER, HERBERT. *Pioneers of Modern Typography.* Rev. ed. Pp. 160. Cambridge: MIT Press, 1985. Paperbound, $15.00.

SPITZER, ROBERT J. *The Right to Life Movement and Third Party Politics.* Pp. 154. Westport, CT: Greenwood, 1987. $29.95.

STANILAND, MARTIN. *What Is Political Economy: A Study of Social Theory and Underdevelopment.* Pp. 229. New Haven, CT: Yale University Press, 1987. Paperbound, $8.95.

STERNHELL, ZEEV. *Neither Right nor Left: Fascist Ideology in France.* Pp. xxii, 416. Berkeley: University of California Press, 1986. $45.00.

STREEK, WOLFGANG and PHILIPPE C. SCHMITTER, eds. *Private Interest Government: Beyond Market and State.* Pp. x, 278. Newbury Park, CA: Sage, 1986. $35.00. Paperbound, $14.95.

SUNDELIUS, BENGT, ed. *The Neutral Democracies and the New Cold War.* Pp. xi, 245. Boulder, CO: Westview, 1987. Paperbound, $22.00.

SZAJKOWSKI, BOGDEN. *Documents in Communist Affairs.* Pp. 340. New York: St. Martin's Press, 1987. $60.00.

TARAS, RAY. *Poland: Socialist State, Rebellious Nation.* Pp. xviii, 200. Boulder, CO: Westview, 1986. $27.50.

TOMANDL, THEODOR and KARL FUER-BOECK. *Social Partnership: The Austrian System of Industrial Relations and Social Insurance.* Pp. viii, 165. Ithaca, NY: ILR Press, 1986. $24.00.

TRABER, MICHAEL, ed. *The Myth of the Information Revolution: Social and Ethical Implications of Communication Technology.* Pp. viii, 146. Newbury Park, CA: Sage, 1986. $27.95.

TREVERTON, GREGORY F. *Making the Alliance Work: The United States and Western Europe.* Pp. x, 211. Ithaca, NY: Cornell University Press, 1985. $24.95.

TWITCHELL, JAMES B. *Forbidden Part-*

ners: *The Incest Taboo in Modern Culture.* Pp. 311. Lawrence: University Press of Kansas, 1986. $24.95.

U.S. STATE DEPARTMENT. *Foreign Relations of the United States: 1952-1954.* Vol. 6, *Western Europe and Canada,* pts. 1 and 2. Pp. xliv, 2176. Washington, DC: Government Printing Office, 1986. No price.

VELIKHOV, YEVGENI, ROALD SAGDEEV, and ANDREI KOKOSHIN, eds. *Weaponry in Space: The Dilemma of Security.* Pp. 147. Moscow: Mir, 1986. Distributed by Imported Publications, Chicago. $8.95.

VIGIL, MAURILIO E. *Hispanics in American Politics: The Search for Political Power.* Pp. 147. Lanham, MD: University Press of America, 1987. $23.50. Paperbound, $11.75.

WALLIMANN, ISIDOR and MICHAEL N. DOBKOWSKI. *Genocide and the Modern Age: Etiology and Case Studies of Mass Death.* Pp. 317. Westport, CT: Greenwood, 1987. $39.95.

WILLIAMS, DOUGLAS. *The Specialized Agencies and the United Nations: The System in Crisis.* Pp. 279. New York: St. Martin's Press, 1987. No price.

WILLIAMS, NANCY M. *The Yolngu and Their Land: A System of Land Tenure*

and the Fight for Its Recognition. Pp. 204. Stanford, CA: Stanford University Press, 1986. No price.

WOLFE, CHRISTOPHER. *Essays on Faith and Liberal Democracy.* Pp. viii, 203. Lanham, MD: University Press of America, 1987. $24.50. Paperbound, $12.75.

WRIGHT, JAMES D. and PETER H. ROSSI. *Armed and Considered Dangerous: A Survey of Felons and Their Firearms.* Pp. xvi, 247. New York: Aldine de Gruyter, 1986. Paperbound, no price.

WYLLIE, JAMES H. *European Security in the Nuclear Age.* Pp. ix, 186. New York: Basil Blackwell, 1986. $39.95. Paperbound, $14.95.

YATES, ROBERT. *The Secret Proceedings and Debates of the Convention to Form the U.S. Constitution.* Pp. 309. Birmingham, AL: Southern University Press, 1987. $37.50. Paperbound, $17.00.

ZDRAVOMYSLOV, A. G., ed. *Developments in Marxist Sociological Theory: Modern Social Problems and Theory.* Pp. 125. Newbury Park, CA: Sage, 1986. $40.00.

ZISKIND, DAVID. *Concerning Human Aspiration: Essays in Comparative Labor Law.* Pp. 169. Los Angeles: Litlaw Foundation, 1985. No price.

INDEX

Adams, John, 46
Articles of Confederation, 29
Australia, federalism in, 137-38

Bill of Rights, 30, 37
Bills of rights (state), 97
Board of Education v. *Allen*, 57
BRIFFAULT, RICHARD, Localism in State Constitutional Law, 117-27

Canada, federalism in, 137-38
Checks and balances, 45
Child-benefit theory, 57, 70
Citizenship, 25-26
Czechoslovakia, federalism in, 135, 136-37

Declaration of Independence, 29, 30
Democracy, 134-35
Dillon, John F., 113
DUCHACEK, IVO D., State Constitutional Law in Comparative Perspective, 128-39

Economic rights, 76-87
Education, right to, 56-58
EMERGING AGENDA IN STATE CONSTITUTIONAL RIGHTS LAW, THE, Stanley Mosk, 54-64
Equal treatment in the workplace, 91-92
EVOLVING STATE LEGISLATIVE AND EXECUTIVE POWER IN THE FOUNDING DECADE, Robert F. Williams, 43-53
Exclusionary zoning, and local government, 122-26

Family, protection of by local government, 126
Federalism, 10-11, 24-25, 63, 100-101, 102, 128-39
First Amendment, 94
Founders (U.S. political system), 31-32
Free speech, 62-63, 93-96
FRIEDMAN, LAWRENCE M., State Constitutions in Historical Perspective, 33-42
FRIESEN, JENNIFER, The Public Employee's Stake in State Constitutional Rights, 88-97

Gaffney v. *State Department of Education*, 70
GALIE, PETER J., State Courts and Economic Rights, 76-87
Governorship, 37, 50-51

Home, protection of by state government, 126

Independent state grounds, doctrine of, 41-42
India, federalism in, 134, 137
INTERGOVERNMENTAL RELATIONS IN STATE CONSTITUTIONAL LAW: A HISTORICAL OVERVIEW, Michael E. Libonati, 107-16

Judicial activism, 85, 100-101, 106
Judicial review, 39-42

KINCAID, JOHN, Preface, 10-11
KINCAID, JOHN, State Constitutions in the Federal System, 12-22

Legislatures, state, 37-38, 48-50, 52-53, 85, 86, 113
and constitutionality of laws, 96
LIBONATI, MICHAEL E., Intergovernmental Relations in State Constitutional Law: A Historical Overview, 107-16
Lloyd v. *Tanner*, 63
Local government, 107-16, 117-27
capacity to sue, 114-16
LOCALISM IN STATE CONSTITUTIONAL LAW, Richard Briffault, 117-27
LOCKSTEP ANALYSIS AND THE CONCEPT OF FEDERALISM, Earl M. Maltz, 98-106
LUTZ, DONALD S., The United States Constitution as an Incomplete Text, 23-32

MALTZ, EARL M., Lockstep Analysis and the Concept of Federalism, 98-106
Managerialism, 112
Mapp v. *Ohio*, 104-6
Maryland v. *Garrison*, 59
Massachusetts Constitution of 1780, 48
Meese, Edwin, III, 58
Mexico, federalism in, 135
Miller v. *California*, 62
Miranda ruling, 58-59
Miranda warnings, 61
MOSK, STANLEY, The Emerging Agenda in State Constitutional Rights Law, 54-64
Municipal corporations, 111-12

New York Constitution of 1777, 47
Nigeria, federalism in, 137

Obscenity, 62

Paine, Thomas, 45

SAGE guides to
SURVEY RESEARCH METHODS

HOW TO CONDUCT SURVEYS: A Step-by-Step Guide
by ARLENE FINK & JACQUELINE KOSECOFF

Geared for everyone who needs to learn how to do a simple survey, regardless of his or her statistical knowledge. Didactic examples, helpful practice exercises with answers and informative appendices with rules for performing technical computations make this book appropriate for both self-teaching and classroom use.
1985 120 pages $12.00 (p)

SURVEY RESEARCH BY TELEPHONE
by JAMES H. FREY

Frey provides a clear, concise picture of the advantages and limitations of doing telephone surveys. An ideal introduction for students of research methods as well as novices at telephone interviewing, it is a handy, state-of-the-art source of ideas and information for the sophisticated researcher.
1983 208 pages $27.50 (c) $12.95 (p)

SAGE UNIVERSITY PAPERS

Quantitative Applications in the Social Sciences _____ **$6.00 each**

35 INTRODUCTION TO SURVEY SAMPLING
by GRAHAM KALTON

Explains techniques essential to survey research: simple random sampling, systematic sampling, stratification, cluster and multistage sampling, sampling with probability proportional to size, two-phase sampling, replicated sampling, panel designs, and nonprobability sampling.

58 RANDOMIZED RESPONSE A Method for Sensitive Surveys
by JAMES ALAN FOX & PAUL E. TRACY

The first comprehensive introduction and practical guide to randomized response for researchers wishing to use this technique for sensitive inquiries.

53 SECONDARY ANALYSIS OF SURVEY DATA
by K. JILL KIECOLT & LAURA E. NATHAN

Presents strategies for locating survey data, provides a comprehensive guide to social science data archives, and describes several major data files. It also reviews research designs for secondary analysis and discusses techniques for managing problems.

63 SURVEY QUESTIONS Handcrafting the Standardized Questionnaire
by JEAN M. CONVERSE & STANLEY PRESSER

Provides both general guiding principles and specific advice on how to develop a survey questionnaire, emphasizing the practical implications of the experience and research of questionnaire designers.

Titles from the APPLIED SOCIAL RESEARCH METHODS series
each $8.95 (p) $17.95 (c)

TELEPHONE SURVEY METHODS Sampling, Selection, and Supervision
by PAUL J. LAVRAKAS

Covers basic details on planning and implementation at the local level—focusing on using telephone surveys to gather information from an applied, how-to approach. Concentrates on conducting the survey utilizing proven paper-and-pencil techniques.
Vol. 7 1987 160 pages

SURVEY RESEARCH METHODS
by FLOYD J. FOWLER, Jr.

Fowler's basic introduction to survey research methods covers the spectrum of data collection procedures used in social surveys.
Vol. 1 1984 160 pages

AN EMPIRICAL STUDY OF THE RELIABILITY AND STABILITY OF SURVEY RESEARCH ITEMS
edited by GEORGE W. BOHRNSTEDT, PETER P. MOHLER & WALTER MÜLLER

(A Special Issue of SOCIOLOGICAL METHODS & RESEARCH)

Focuses on efforts to evaluate the effects of *random* measurement error on survey research items. Reports on a massive and pioneering research effort undertaken as part of the German General Social Survey (which parallels the GSS undertaken in the U.S. by NORC).

Sociological Methods & Research, Vol. 15, No. 3 1987 (Winter) 180 pages $19.50 (Inst.) $9.00 (Ind.)

SAGE PUBLICATIONS
The Publishers of Professional Social Science
Newbury Park Beverly Hills London New Delhi

NEW from Sage

WOMEN, THE COURTS, AND EQUALITY

edited by **LAURA L. CRITES,** *Chaminade University of Honolulu*
& WINIFRED L. HEPPERLE, *Director of the Office of Court Services,*
Alameda County, California

Almost ten years ago Crites and Hepperle edited a book that examined the extent of judicial commitment to freeing women from a subordinate role in American society. They concluded that there was sufficient evidence to show that judges were influenced by traditional beliefs regarding the role and nature of women and that these beliefs affected their decisions regarding women.

Women, The Courts, and Equality addresses the same subject in light of developments and events of the last decade in the women's movement. Today more women are employed in a greater variety of jobs because of the equal employment opportunity and affirmative action laws that have passed. Feminist-supported legislation has improved the rights, opportunities, and treatment of women in many areas, including spouse abuse and rape victim testimony. There is also a greater awareness of how prevalent victimization and discrimination against women has been in the U.S. In spite of these gains there have also been setbacks: the defeat of the Equal Rights Amendment, the negative effect of conservatism, the abortion controversy, and reduced emphasis on enforcement of equal opportunity laws.

"In a recent study conducted by the New York Task Force on Women in the Courts it was found that women litigants, attorneys, and court employees are denied equal justice, equal treatment, and equal opportunity—the result of problems rooted in a web of prejudice, circumstance, privilege, custom, misinformation and indifference. This gender bias in our courts is unacceptable . . . this book by Laura Crites and Winifred Hepperle should enlighten the bar, the judiciary, and the general public, thus bringing the problem of gender bias in the courts that much closer to resolution."
—Chief Judge Sol Wachtler,
New York State Court of Appeals

Sage Yearbooks in Women's Policy Studies, Volume 11
1987 (Autumn) / 258 pages / $29.95 (c) / $14.95 (p)

SAGE PUBLICATIONS, INC.
2111 West Hillcrest Drive,
Newbury Park, California 91320

SAGE PUBLICATIONS, INC.
275 South Beverly Drive,
Beverly Hills, California 90212

SAGE PUBLICATIONS LTD
28 Banner Street,
London EC1Y 8QE, England

SAGE PUBLICATIONS INDIA PVT LTD
M-32 Market, Greater Kailash I,
New Delhi 110 048 India

New and Recent Books in Political and Social Science
from Greenwood Press and Praeger Publishers

THE OPEN COVENANT Social Change in Contemporary Society by **Christopher Bates Doob**
Using examples from American history, social theory, and popular culture, Doob analyzes the concept of the covenant in American society. He shows how recent issues such as environmental protection, nuclear disarmament, and sexual equality have forced Americans to become more aware of the need for communication and cooperation between the public and private sectors, thereby challenging exclusionist covenants.
1987. ISBN 0-275-92550-1. $29.95 (hardbound)   ISBN 0-275-92661-3. $10.95 (paperback)

PHOTOGRAPHING MEDICINE Images and Power in Britain and America Since 1840
by **Daniel M. Fox** and **Christopher Lawrence**
With a perspective shaped by recent work in art history and the sociology of knowledge, the authors encourage the reader to analyze photographs as complicated historical documents, taking as their example the representation of medicine in photographs taken in Britain and the United States from 1840 to the present.
April 1988. ISBN 0-313-23719-0. $36.00 est.

COMPARABLE WORTH, PAY EQUITY, AND PUBLIC POLICY Edited by **Rita Mae Kelly** and **Jane Bayes.** Prepared under the auspices of the Policy Studies Organization.
This volume of essays focuses on major issues that must be faced before a public policy promoting pay equity can become a reality. Combining the contributions of specialists from several disciplines, it offers statistical comparisons and analyses of wage inequities in various occupations, industries, and regions; case studies of comparable worth programs; and a conceptual framework for approaching the problem on a policy level.
February 1988. ISBN 0-313-26014-1. $49.95

RETHINKING THE NINETEENTH CENTURY Contradictions and Movements
Edited by **Francisco O. Ramirez**
Consisting of fourteen essays contributed by an international group of scholars, this volume examines the social formations of the nineteenth century and integrates them into a modern theoretical framework.
March 1988. ISBN 0-313-25997-6. $39.95

INTERNATIONAL HANDBOOK ON RACE AND RACE RELATIONS Edited by **Jay A. Sigler**
This new study creates a framework for research on race relations and increases our understanding of the meaning and significance of race throughout the world. Written by a group of experts with firsthand knowledge of race and race relations in the twenty nations studied, it offers a depth and scope of information that is unique in the literature of the field.
1987. ISBN 0-313-24770-6. $95.00

THE DRAGON AND THE WILD GOOSE China and India by **Jay Taylor**
"Taylor has artfully put together a series of apt and often fascinating comparisons of all major aspects of human activity in the world's two most populous countries. By juxtaposing facts about the Chinese and Indian peoples' historical, cultural, social, economic, and political life, Taylor makes them stand out more vividly. *The Dragon and the Wild Goose* is also a good read, useful as a detailed and comprehensive work of reference, and an ingenious contribution to comparative studies."
        —Stephen Hay, Associate Professor of History, University of California, Santa Barbara
1987. ISBN 0-313-25899-6. $37.95

ALBERT ELLIS Passionate Skeptic by **Daniel N. Wiener**
This fascinating study portrays Ellis as a living model of his own therapy. Wiener shows how Ellis arrived at the theories that became rational emotive therapy through his need to handle his own psychologically neglected childhood and adolescence.
April 1988. ISBN 0-275-92751-2. $35.95

THE DEVELOPMENT OF A POSTMODERN SELF A Computer-Assisted Comparative Analysis of Personal Documents by **Michael R. Wood** and **Louis A. Zurcher, Jr.**
This study explores the changes in culture and identity that will accompany the "postindustrial" revolution that some social scientists have predicted for the end of the century.
March 1988. ISBN 0-313-25458-3. $37.95

 Greenwood Press/Praeger Publishers
Divisions of Greenwood Press, Inc.
88 Post Road West, P.O. Box 5007, Westport, Conn. 06881 (203) 226-3571